THE DEFENSE
REVOLUTION

THE DEFENSE REVOLUTION

Strategy for the Brave New World

*by an Arms Controller
and an Arms Builder*

Kenneth L. Adelman
Norman R. Augustine

ICS PRESS

Institute for Contemporary Studies
San Francisco, California

The Institute for Contemporary Studies is a nonpartisan, nonprofit public policy research organization. The analyses, conclusions, and opinions expressed in ICS Press publications are those of the authors and not necessarily those of the Institute, or of its officers, directors, or others associated with, or funding, its work.

Inquiries, book orders, and catalogue requests should be addressed to ICS Press, 243 Kearny Street, San Francisco, CA 94108. (415) 981-5353. FAX (415) 986-4878. For book orders and catalogue requests call toll free within the United States except Alaska and Hawaii: (800) 326-0236.

Distributed to the trade by
National Book Network, Lanham, Maryland.

Library of Congress Cataloging-in-Publication Data

Adelman, Kenneth L.
    The defense revolution: strategy for the brave new world / by an arms controller and an arms builder, Kenneth L. Adelman, Norman R. Augustine.
        p.   cm.
    Includes index
    ISBN 1-55815-074-9 (cloth): $19.95.
    1. United States—Defenses. I. Augustine, Norman, R.   II. Title.
UA23.A524   1990   90-49904
355'.033073—dc20   CIP

CONTENTS

FOREWORD

This book is the ninth ICS publication on U.S. defense and foreign policy in the past thirteen years. The preceding eight studies, by some of the most important geostrategic thinkers of the postwar era, were instrumental in altering the course of American policy, calling for strength at a time of weakness and insisting on military reform when it became clear that our national defense was not as good as it should be.

American defense policy is about to change yet again, in the wake of astonishing global events. We are only now beginning to realize that the postwar era ended in 1989. The world has been remade—transformed—in ways that are at once exhilarating and confusing. Now, but a year after the fall of the Berlin Wall, the United States faces a brave new world of geopolitics, embodied in the Iraqi invasion of Kuwait.

The Defense Revolution is the first book to face up to this new world. The authors assay the unprecedented revolutions that are unfolding: in geopolitics, in economics, and especially in warfare technology. All three require that the United States make radical changes in the way it defends itself. The volume culminates in a series of brief "memos," addressed to major figures in the defense establishment, that distill the book's key points and recommend action.

The careful downscaling of the American military can leave us with forces better able to prevail in the still-dangerous world we will face. *The Defense Revolution* presents the blueprint.

Robert B. Hawkins, Jr., President
Institute for Contemporary Studies

*To the memory of my classics professor, Dr. Crossett,
whose teachings of values and of life live on, so strongly.
He showed his many pupils that the path to knowing
something was by questioning nearly everything.*

*To Margareta Engman Augustine,
who arrived on America's shores at age nineteen
with $50 in her pocket, a job, and unbounded hope—
and who understands better than most
this nation's greatness.*

ACKNOWLEDGMENTS

First and foremost, thanks go to Robert W. Davis, without whom this book would have meandered along and eventually been left behind in the whirlwind of world events and personal pressures. Robert was our conceptualizer, cheerleader, and editor. That the birth of his children form the bookends for this tome—the first just as we began sketching some ideas, the second as the final draft goes to print—seems fitting. Creation accompanied creation.

Special thanks to ICS's impressively able and exceedingly dedicated president, Robert B. Hawkins, Jr. When the three of us first chewed over the project in the Martin Marietta company cafeteria, Bob furnished sound advice, along with enthusiastic encouragement.

We also would like to thank Kris Southard of the ICS office in Washington, Leann Arsenault of the ICS office in San Francisco, and Laura Cooper of the Martin Marietta headquarters in Bethesda for the multitude of services in editing, re-editing, correcting, recorrecting, copying—in short, all the nitty-gritty necessary before a book can be published.

Each of the co-authors would like to thank the other. Our book marriage not only lasted, but strengthened our relationship and respect for each other. Now knowing all that's needed to co-author a book, we each realize that it didn't have to work out as nicely as it did. Two who had been only acquaintances became fast friends as we talked through our differences—perhaps offering a lesson applicable on a greater scale.

Finally, we would like to thank those who proudly wear our country's uniform and pay the price of our misjudgments.

INTRODUCTION

Writing about downsizing America's defense is a difficult and dangerous endeavor, for several reasons. First, any writing about international politics nowadays is best done in pencil—with a large eraser nearby. Events now change so swiftly, particularly in the Soviet Union, as to make any effort to capture them in written words very hazardous.

What a turnabout from the period of roughly 1964 to 1984—the justly maligned "stagnation years" of Leonid Brezhnev—when practically nothing changed in Soviet affairs, including the Soviet economy. Some octogenarians may have appeared in slightly reshuffled positions every year atop the Lenin tomb for each spring's May Day parade (a reshuffling made more of by Western Kremlinologists than it deserved), but the basic tone and tenor of that state stayed constant. Since 1984, though, events have been moving at such an increasingly accelerating pace as to risk spinning out of control, with consequences that can barely be imagined. Today we no longer have time to be astonished. The lines outside McDonald's in Moscow are now longer than the lines at Lenin's tomb.

Media commentators are usually able to adjust relatively rapidly to such changes, but the people managing Western security cannot always do so. The forces ensuring our defense today were funded and built primarily during the Ford, Carter, and Reagan administrations. Just as it takes nearly nine miles for a supertanker at sea to stop, so it takes years for American and Western policy makers to decide on and implement adjustments in our defense apparatus.

A book such as this faces the risk of instant obsolescence in today's fast-changing international arena. Much of what the authors timidly projected in the original draft of this book is now simple reality. Not too many months ago the forecast of a collapsing Soviet economy seemed fairly controversial; now even the Soviets agree. In a second draft the prediction of a united Germany in NATO by 1991, free of Soviet troops by 1994 seemed rather intemperate; now the pace of events exceeds even this. The projection that arms control would be overtaken by world events is, at least for the time being, reality. Only the brave prediction that this world will continue to be a dangerous place seems to remain controversial; the Iraqis have done their part to help make our point. Much of what we wrote has been borne out. Yet much of what we wrote, we believe, needs to be better appreciated by those in public policy who, like others, get buffeted by momentarily fashionable ideas.

Moreover, the potential benefits of projecting now what future U.S. defense needs will be outweigh the risk of being badly embarrassed. The recent changes within Warsaw Pact countries, which have constituted the prime military threat to democracies in the post–World War II era, exponentially increase the need for ideas at this time. In this regard, Karl Marx, who has been proved wrong on so many fronts, was at least right in saying that the time of greatest contradictions is the time of greatest opportunity. With national security affairs now in a state of flux, particularly in the Middle East, those concerned with the defense of the ever-expanding free world should engage in some new thinking.

Second, this writing endeavor has been difficult also in the sense that our inclination runs against the prevailing view that we have reached the Promised Land (or that it is at least within sight) and that little thinking (and even less effort) needs to be devoted to defense any longer. According to this view, the United States should simply lie back and reap the benefits of the Soviet crack-up, turn its attention entirely to legitimate and serious home affairs (neo-isolationism) or to economic threats posed by Asian worker (and killer) bees.

Many people now, at the end of this century, take such a stance, as many also did at the beginning and middle of this century. The fashionable view before the wholesale carnage of World War I and World War II—namely, that "modern conditions" made large-scale war forevermore obsolete—was addressed in 1914 by the young Winston Churchill, paraphrasing much of the thinking of the day:

> War is too foolish, too fantastic to be thought of in the twentieth century. . . . Civilization has climbed above such perils. The interdependence of nations in trade and traffic, the sense of public law, the

> Hague Convention, liberal principles . . . have rendered such night-mares impossible.

After stating this popular position, Churchill then mockingly added,

> Are you quite sure? It would be a pity to be wrong.

It *was* a pity.

But if America could be unprepared for World War I, unprepared for World War II, unprepared for Korea—all in a single century—there is little reason to believe any lessons from Iraq will be lasting.

Third, the genesis of this book has been quite challenging, if not downright peculiar: it has been written by the two of us, of whom one is known as an arms controller and the other as an arms builder. Writing any book is tortuous, even in the simplest of circumstances. Again, Churchill said it best:

> To begin with, it is a toy and an amusement. Then it becomes a mistress, then it becomes a master, then it becomes a tyrant. The last phase is that just as you are about to be reconciled to your servitude, you kill the monster and fling him to the public.

Indeed, the two authors' separate experiences have generally been divergent (though they did work together in the Pentagon in the mid-1970s), but they have chosen to regard that as a strength: different backgrounds bring different assets to the table.

One had extensive diplomatic experience as an ambassador dealing with counterparts from around the world in the United Nations between 1981 and 1983. This foreign policy assignment was followed by a more specialized role as director of the U.S. Arms Control and Disarmament Agency from early in 1983 until the close of 1987. He attended National Security Council meetings with President Reagan on defense and arms control matters, and was principal advisor to the president—and a participant—in three summits with Gorbachev (including that in Reykjavik). The author thus participated in policy making on national security both at high levels within the U.S. government and between the American and Soviet presidents.

The other author served three presidents in six jobs in the Department of Defense, including positions in the office of the secretary of defense and as under secretary of the army. He now runs one of the nation's largest industrial firms, generally specializing in defense products, as chairman and chief executive officer. He has continued to serve in an advisory capacity, when asked, in such positions as chairman of the Defense Science Board, chairman of the Defense Policy Advisory Committee on Trade, chairman of the Aeronautics Panel of the Air Force Scientific Advisory Board, and member of the Chief of Naval Operations Executive Panel.

Together, the two authors offer suggestions, culminating in a series of memos to top decision makers, on how best to ensure security in the unpredictable years ahead. Downsizing defense—from the capability of fighting "two and a half wars" a few decades back to the capability of fighting only "half a war" a few years hence—needs to be done with great care. Even more thought should go into the Bush administration downturn than went into the Reagan administration buildup—even though that buildup has paid off handsomely: the cold war has been won without firing a shot. Reducing military capability is inherently more risky than increasing it. And there will be further military tests ahead.

Where to cut should be thought through and established from the top down rather than from the bottom up. Tasking the different armed services with the chore converts into bookkeeping something that really should be a strategic exercise—an exercise this book attempts to provide, in what might be thought of as first-draft form. Ironically and fortunately, the starting point is undoubtedly the finest armed forces America has ever had in terms of quality of people, equipment, training, and morale.

Maintaining U.S. strength with less also requires better technology and superior equipment, which in turn requires major surgery on the muscle-bound Pentagon procurement process. Incredibly, this process is currently dictated by thirty thousand pages of procurement regulations and is audited by more than twenty-six thousand persons—roughly the equivalent of two army divisions. Whereas the first aircraft ever sold to the military, by the Wright brothers, was successfully contracted on a two-page document, one contractor's bid for a new plane weighed more than twelve tons. As if this were not enough, overseeing the overseers are thirty or so congressional committees with fifty-five subcommittees, which churn out an incredible 720,000 inquiries to the Pentagon every year.

Finally, narrow politics can make this dicey downsizing business even dicier. Any defense secretary must watch Congress with the eyes of a hawk and yet treat it with the finesse of a dove so as to foil the occasional congressional inclination to cut the beef and leave only the pork. Some on Capitol Hill still vote parochial rather than national on defense projects.

Managed well, the downsizing of our defense can leave the nation secure with less, given continued favorable changes in the communist world and needed realignments in NATO. Then we shall be able to echo Shakespeare's Hotspur: "Out of this nettle, danger, we pluck this flower, safety."

ONE

THE DEFENSE REVOLUTION:
The Shape of Things to Come

When Alice asked, "Would you tell me, please, which way I ought to go from here?" the Cheshire cat replied, "That depends a good deal on where you want to get to." Similarly, defense planning depends a good deal on exactly where we want to get as a nation and on the amount and type of resistance we may face getting there.

Spelling out the basis for U.S. defense planning is a formidable task, especially today. For like the Red Queen in *Alice in Wonderland,* over the past year we've been asked to believe three impossible things before breakfast each morning. Even as we finish writing this book, such untidy ironies as the following keep cropping up:

- More Russians than Americans seem to want U.S. troops to remain in Europe, judging from observations we made during a recent trip to the Soviet Union.

- An interesting difference between Hungary and the United States is that the United States still has a Communist party.

- East Germany's minister of defense once served time in jail for draft evasion.

- Mikhail Gorbachev remains the most popular leader throughout Western Europe, whereas in Eastern Europe this honor goes to President Bush.

- President Gorbachev is cheered in Washington and, on May Day, 1990, jeered in Moscow.

These incongruities were quite inexplicable in our previous understanding, and the past year's events were virtually impossible to predict. Even so, this chapter will attempt to anticipate and sketch the coming years' events that are likely to bear on our national security.

America Will Stay Heavily Involved Overseas

Despite recurrent fears about our global withdrawal, U.S. isolationism does *not* constitute a real possibility. Such a stance is simply not credible any longer, with the increasing integration of Western Europe, the economic and energy interdependency of nations, and the disintegration of the Soviet bloc, as well as the festering problems in our own hemisphere.

Even U.S. military involvement abroad no longer faces the gut-level domestic opposition it faced in the immediate post-Vietnam era. Americans widely supported the use of U.S. force in Grenada in 1983, against Libya in 1986, in the Persian Gulf in 1988, against Panamanian dictator Manuel Noriega in 1989, and against Iraqi dictator Saddam Hussein in 1990. Most Americans appreciate how military power still plays a critical role in the way the world works (Figure 1). They understand that weakness is provocative and that strength deters.

The World May Be Messier than Before

"You saw some action once, too, didn't you?" asks a younger CIA analyst of a seasoned veteran in the movie *Three Days of the Condor*. "Do you miss the action?" the younger man asks. His elder answers slowly and carefully, "It's not the action I miss. It's the clarity."

Americans will not miss "the action" of the Berlin and Cuban crises, the nuclear alerts, the Czechoslovakian, Korean, Angolan, and Afghanistan surprises, and many others. But we *will* miss the clarity. The immediate post–World War II period was a time of relative simplicity in thought, though surely not in execution.

Figure 1   Forty-five Years of Peace Since World War II

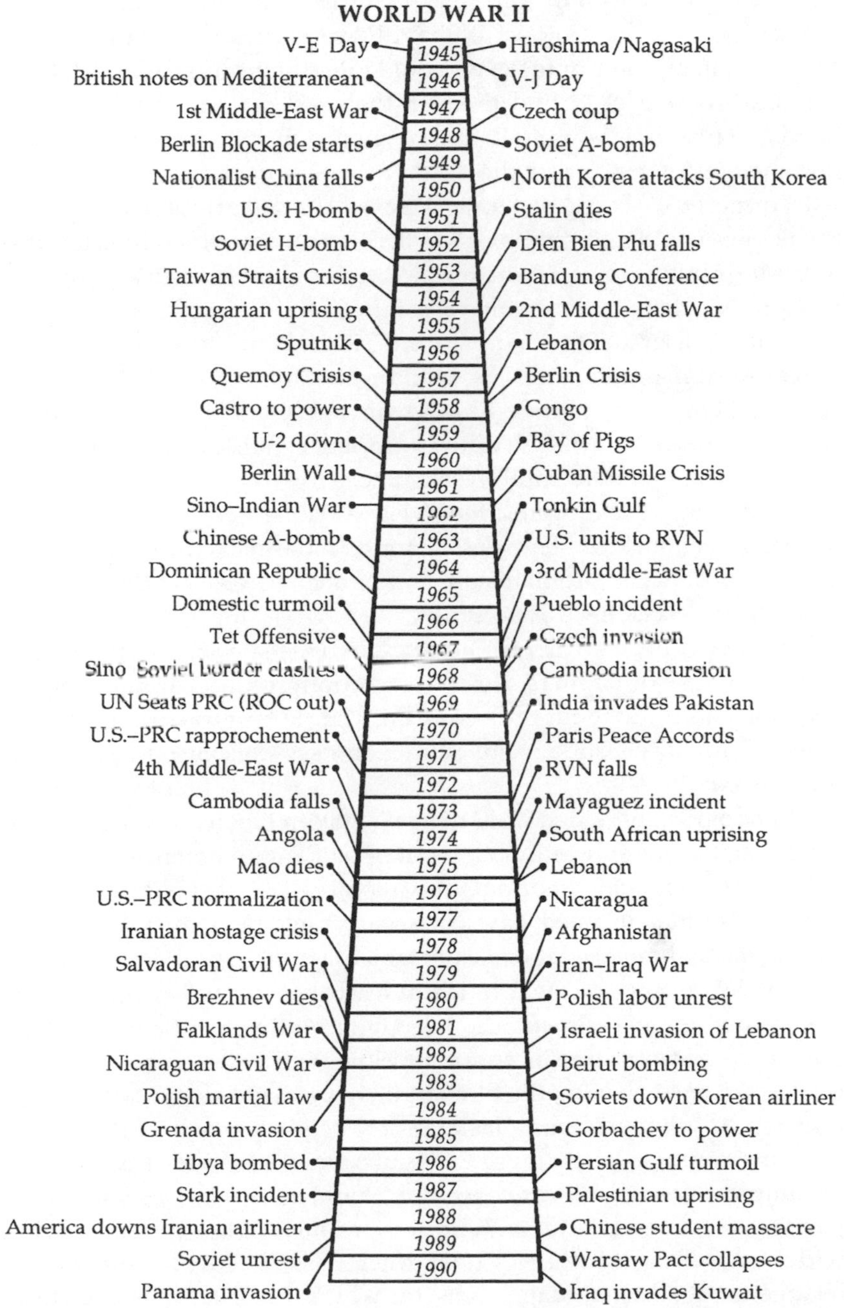

WORLD WAR II

V-E Day	1945	Hiroshima/Nagasaki
British notes on Mediterranean	1946	V-J Day
1st Middle-East War	1947	Czech coup
Berlin Blockade starts	1948	Soviet A-bomb
Nationalist China falls	1949	
	1950	North Korea attacks South Korea
U.S. H-bomb	1951	Stalin dies
Soviet H-bomb	1952	Dien Bien Phu falls
Taiwan Straits Crisis	1953	Bandung Conference
Hungarian uprising	1954	2nd Middle-East War
	1955	
Sputnik	1956	Lebanon
Quemoy Crisis	1957	Berlin Crisis
Castro to power	1958	Congo
U-2 down	1959	Bay of Pigs
Berlin Wall	1960	Cuban Missile Crisis
	1961	
Sino–Indian War	1962	Tonkin Gulf
Chinese A-bomb	1963	U.S. units to RVN
Dominican Republic	1964	3rd Middle-East War
Domestic turmoil	1965	Pueblo incident
	1966	
Tet Offensive	1967	Czech invasion
Sino-Soviet border clashes	1968	Cambodia incursion
UN Seats PRC (ROC out)	1969	India invades Pakistan
U.S.–PRC rapprochement	1970	Paris Peace Accords
4th Middle-East War	1971	RVN falls
	1972	
Cambodia falls	1973	Mayaguez incident
Angola	1974	South African uprising
Mao dies	1975	Lebanon
U.S.–PRC normalization	1976	Nicaragua
	1977	
Iranian hostage crisis	1978	Afghanistan
Salvadoran Civil War	1979	Iran–Iraq War
Brezhnev dies	1980	Polish labor unrest
Falklands War	1981	Israeli invasion of Lebanon
Nicaraguan Civil War	1982	Beirut bombing
	1983	
Polish martial law	1984	Soviets down Korean airliner
Grenada invasion	1985	Gorbachev to power
Libya bombed	1986	Persian Gulf turmoil
Stark incident	1987	Palestinian uprising
	1988	
America downs Iranian airliner	1989	Chinese student massacre
Soviet unrest	1990	Warsaw Pact collapses
Panama invasion		Iraq invades Kuwait

During the cold war, we at least knew who our enemies were, namely, the stodgy octogenarians huffing atop Lenin's tomb on May Day. Now, we may not know. Which group or individual in 1989 hanged U.S. Marine Colonel William R. Higgins serving in Lebanon? And even if, by some miracle, we could identify the ones who did it, we can scarcely expect to find them in that nest of chaos and violence. Saddam Hussein was virtually unknown to Americans one day, only to become the devil incarnate the next.

Formerly, we could presume at least a certain rationality. Although the Soviets could and did blockade Berlin, that was still a rational stab at undermining our guarantee of West Germany's security. And although they dared to sneak missiles into Cuba, that was still a rational grab for a quick fix of their strategic inferiority. Now, though, we can no longer presume rationality. The wanton shelling of Lebanon, once the "Switzerland of the Middle East," seems sheer madness. Who shells whom? For what purpose? Who is any better off for the effort? And who murders whom in South Africa, and why?

And then we could presume at least a sliver of scruples. True, the Soviets swashbuckled shamelessly and did dastardly deeds in Hungary, Czechoslovakia, Afghanistan, and hither and yon. Yet those deeds, for all their dastardliness, had limits.

Now we often can discern no morality whatsoever. The motives of vile hangings, kidnapings, threats, extortions, and what-have-you in Lebanon and throughout the rest of the Middle East lack even any pretense of morality. Saddam Hussein even uses poison gas against his own people.

Random violence in Africa, most notably in Liberia of late, goes beyond the pale not only of morality but also of any comprehensible rationality. The gangland shoot-outs in Colombia also, although based on drug-related human greed, have crossed over into random violence often lacking any fathomable rationale or result other than sheer destruction.

Finally, during cold war times, at least there was clear control. Soviet leaders, for all their sins, did keep tight control over their own people—too tight, in fact. In contrast, violent or threatening states or groups today—Lebanon, the PLO, Iran, Syria, the Medellin cartel, Liberian rebels, whoever—may lack control over members of their own state or group, especially those with guns and sophisticated weaponry.

Improving the cold war environment and mellowing the Soviet empire may in themselves actually spur more and not less turmoil worldwide. Loosening Moscow's hold over Eastern Europe allows the resurgence of ancient antagonisms, for which the Balkans have historically been infamous—particularly since the chaos there sparked both world wars. The reemergence of spats between Hungary and Romania, Bulgaria and Turkey, and Czechoslovakia and Hungary harkens back to what went on in that region for centuries before Soviet domination. And these spats are harbingers of what's to come again.

This does not mean we should be nostalgic for the cold war days. We aren't. The price of "stability" then was repression, a price never worth paying. Any individual longing for great stability might as well have sought jail, where the food, lodging, hours, and conditions are also quite stable and predictable.

Within the Soviet Union itself, however, control may now dissipate to the point of danger—not only to opposing ethnic groups but also to the world at large. Currently, ethnic groups are at each other's (or Moscow's) throat in nearly half the Soviet republics: the Armenians, the Uzbeks, the Kirghiz, and on and on. In the coming decades, the world's main ethnic strife may in fact be within the Soviet Union.

Should such instability wrack that state to the point of large-scale disorder, the chaos may spill over, in much the same way that the Kurdish and Palestinian resistance movements have led to terrorism against innocent civilians around the world. Still more frightening is the prospect of seeing nuclear or chemical weapons land in the hands of rebel Soviet groups, break-away republics, or disenchanted military units. The breakdown of Soviet command and control thus constitutes a scary scenario. For the past forty years, we have accurately presumed that a Soviet leader would keep control over the use of nuclear and chemical weapons. That *may* be true for forty years more, but we can no longer *presume* so.

As the world becomes more chaotic—one feature of freedom has always been untidiness—the United States over the long term will become less heavily engaged militarily. Our hearts and good wishes will extend farther than our military personnel and our arms. The overall American posture may begin once again to resemble that proclaimed in our early days by Secretary of State John Quincy Adams:

> Wherever the standard of freedom and independence has been or shall be unfurled, there will be America's heart, her benedictions, and her prayers. But she goes not abroad in search of monsters to destroy. She is the well-wisher to the freedom and independence of all. She is the champion and vindicator only of her own.

There will of course be exceptions, particularly in the near term, where the enemy is clear and the consequences direct. But compare this with our posture at the height of the cold war, when President John F. Kennedy told the world that we would "pay *any* price, bear *any* burden, meet *any* hardship, support *any* friend, oppose *any* foe to assure the survival and the success of liberty."

American Security Strategy Will Focus More on the Third World

Most worrisome will be threats to us from irresponsible, resentful leaders possessing ballistic missiles possibly equipped with chemical, biological, or even nuclear weapons. CIA Director William Webster has said, time and again, that before long some fifteen Third World countries will be capable of developing their own ballistic missiles. It seems that the *least* responsible countries—Iran, Iraq, Libya, and North Korea—have been among those *most* intent on acquiring such sophisticated weaponry.

Third World arsenals of relatively less sophisticated armament are alarming as well. It would be ironic, or even tragic, if Soviet (and American) efforts to disarm resulted in more Third World armament. According to defense analyst and journalist Robert Toth, more than ten thousand tanks and eighty-five hundred artillery pieces and surface-to-air missiles removed from the Soviet arsenal because of Mr. Gorbachev's unilateral cuts (announced in December 1988) have become ready for export. Given the cash-starved condition of the Soviet Union now, one could expect some or much of this and other discarded equipment to end up in developing countries. Developing countries in the Middle East have the most ready cash and the strongest desire for large arsenals. Should such a transfer happen, a much-heralded U.S.–Soviet conventional arms accord would have ended up making the world *more* dangerous by moving armaments from fairly responsible Soviet hands conceivably into irresponsible Middle Eastern hands. And even today there are large arsenals in the oil-rich areas of the world. Iraq alone has 5,500 tanks, an army of 1 million, and ballistic missiles with a range of nearly 1,000 kilometers.

Economic Power Gains in Importance; Military Power Declines

The coming times will surely feature more attention to, and competition over, economics. Trade and financial wars will replace cold wars at least for a time. The hot wars in which America is likely to become engaged will probably have strong financial roots—including energy.

Antagonism may well center on Japan. Already in February 1990, "Fear and Loathing of Japan" was the cover story of *Fortune*, a magazine not known for sensationalism. Its story reports, "Suddenly the Japanese have become the people it's okay to hate." If an American complains about any other race, others "turn away in embarrassment. Deride the Japanese," the article continues, and you hear folks "cheer and pile on with abuse of their own." Whereas once no one here had a kind word to say about the Soviets, soon it may well be the Japanese about whom no one has a kind word to say. Throughout much of the world a successor seems to have been found to the "ugly Americans."

Why? Primarily because the Japanese have *not* played by the established economic rules. Their sole and avidly pursued goal has been to build a national industrial economic base by stressing only production. The United States adopted this goal during World War II, in order to win the war, while Japan, alone among states, single-mindedly perpetuates this goal in peacetime.

Consequently, Japan avoids buying valuable products from abroad. As James Fallows points out, both Japan and Germany benefit from a big trade surplus, and both export a lot. But the Germans also import valuable products, while in general the Japanese do not. Germany's main export is cars, but its main import is also cars. Yet if Japan makes a given kind of product, it most often refuses to import it. Furthermore, unlike other multinational firms operating abroad, those owned by Japanese interests are run by Japanese citizens. Other large foreign-owned companies, like Shell Oil, are run by locals.

The intention is not to single out Japan, though others will soon do so as resentment over such practices grows. Economic difficulties with South Korea, Taiwan, European Community nations, and others will also begin to loom larger, and over the long term military security problems will not be as much in the forefront as before on the international scene.

Europe after 1992 Will Consolidate, But Not Very Quickly

The avalanche of wildly optimistic predictions on "Europe 1992" will prove excessive. The thousands of American business leaders who attended seminars on this topic should be given refunds. Although helpful, the European Economic Community's coming consolidation will not prove as revolutionary as once predicted.

West Germany, as always the area's economic engine, will surely direct its money and attention more toward absorbing East Germany than toward consolidating Western Europe. Meanwhile, other EEC members will now be more hesitant regarding rapid and thorough consolidation, in part because they are fearful of tomorrow's unexpectedly bigger, mightier Germany. And all Western European nations will feel some commitment to and involvement in economically aiding Eastern Europe.

Nonetheless, the cry "Europe '92" has already reaped real results. American and Japanese firms, worried about getting left (or shut) out, have already greatly increased their presence in Europe, an infusion that will certainly strengthen Europe's economy in the coming years.

Germany Will Be Strong, Reunified, and in NATO—with Some American Troops but No Soviet Troops and No Nuclear Weapons

To Americans, the 1989 sea change was the decline of the Soviet Union. To nearly all Europeans, it was the rise of Germany.

Nearly everyone now, however grudgingly, accepts German reunification. As Shakespeare said, "What cannot be eschewed must be embraced." To those who worry that Germany will therefore become *the* dominant power of Western Europe, we say it already is—and has been for years, without Western Europe suffering much as a result.

It is easy to exaggerate the dangers of a dominant Deutschland, as the world's brief experience with a unified Germany proved disastrous for everyone. Yet the addition of 17 million relatively poor Germans (from the East) to the 65 million relatively rich ones (in the West) will raise Germany's wealth only slightly, by perhaps 10 percent of its GNP. Moreover, we have little to fear from democratic Germans; it's the autocratic ones who unhinge the world. Liberty has been implanted in West Germany and is clearly sought in East Germany.

However deflated the previous expectations, the intertwined European Economic Community will nonetheless be a restraining force on potential German excesses. Major economic decisions, once the exclusive province of the state, are increasingly being made in Brussels by the new class of European civil servant. Besides the EEC, NATO remains an anchor of the new Germany.

Among major outside actors, the United States has the most to gain from German reunification. For one thing, a united and fairly (but not too) robust Germany will constitute a barrier to Soviet (or Russian) power on the continent. Besides, Germany's size and weight will prompt other European states to encourage U.S. activism on the continent in order to balance Germany there.

All this presumes that a unified Germany essentially resembles West Germany, as we have known it for the past forty years. A West Germany aligned with the West is clearly good for the German people, for us, and even for the Soviets, who would not really want an un-anchored neutral Germany rolling around central Europe.

Over the coming years, the presence of some American troops and removal of all Soviet troops (the latter to occur over the next three or four years) would conform to current German wishes. It conforms to Soviet wishes as well. We would not expect nor encourage the stationing of any outside (NATO) forces on territory of what had been East Germany, which is consistent with the deal Chancelor Kohl struck with Gorbachev in July 1990.

Gorbachev's December 1988 United Nations speech, announcing unilateral cuts and some withdrawals from Eastern Europe, was widely misinterpreted. Westerners, including us, failed to comprehend the true import of the speech and instead focused on the numbers and categories. The speech actually signaled a new willingness in the Kremlin to let Eastern Europe go its own way.

And since that time, the pattern has been clear; given any choice, Moscow has opted for reform within the Warsaw Pact nations and withdrawal from them. Once this signal was caught, the people across Eastern Europe echoed what Oliver Cromwell said to the British Parliament in 1659: "You have sat too long here for any good you have been doing lately. . . . Depart, I say, and let us have done with you. In the name of God—go!"

Why were the Soviets so willing to go? Primarily because they, like the British after World War II, had lost their appetite for empire. Problems at home were and are so crushing as to make problems of control abroad seem overwhelming and unnecessary. Why not cut what can be cut, they felt, and hold on tenaciously to what can be preserved, namely the USSR itself? Besides, Soviet soldiers wanted out; an old Russian saying goes, "It's nice to be a guest, but it's better to be at home."

The removal of all nuclear weapons from German soil would similarly please the Germans and delight the Soviets. Done carefully and planned fully, it would not necessarily harm Western security interests. No Western leader could desire to use any of NATO's some four thousand tactical nuclear weapons, since they could detonate only in allied Germany or a newly liberated East European state.

Should Germany stay an integrated part of the Western security and economic system, should all Soviet troops be gone, should Eastern European states succeed democratically and economically, should the countries of Western Europe grope their way closer to one another, then the United States would no doubt begin reducing its troop presence in Europe. We would perhaps revert to our posture when NATO was first formed, in the 1949–1950 period, when the United States had seventy-nine thousand American soldiers stationed in Europe. The American public is likely to become increasingly less enamored with the idea of keeping large numbers of U.S. troops in Europe to defend allies who face a decreased Soviet threat, who have standards of living matching our own, and who show a limited willingness to support America in fighting the world's tyrants. The refusal of some European allies even to permit overflights of U.S. aircraft in the attack of Libya and the hesitation to commit ground forces to Saudi Arabia following Iraq's invasion of Kuwait are but two examples of European passivity.

Regardless of precise number of U.S. troops to remain in Europe, it would nevertheless be wise for our troops to stay during a transitional phase to help ward off any Soviet temptation to use force against Western *or* Eastern European states. And our presence would help reassure Europeans, including the Soviets, against any German tendency toward revanche. Somehow, perhaps mystically, American GIs can act as temporary grounding devices to keep a highly charged situation (always the case in times of sudden transitions) from going critical.

Should all continue to go well in Europe, around the turn of the century American troops may be gone from Germany. This would be taken as a sign of success rather than retreat or expulsion. Europe's liberator and great friend, Dwight D. Eisenhower, lamented the seemingly permanent stationing of our troops there. During a National Security Council meeting soon after he became president in 1953, Eisenhower said:

> Properly speaking, the stationing of U.S. divisions in Europe had been at the outset an emergency measure not intended to last indefinitely. Unhappily, however, the European nations have been slow in building up their military forces and have now come to expect our forces to remain in Europe indefinitely.

We offer this rough timetable of European events:

1991   Decision made to remove at least land-based nuclear weapons from Germany.

1994   Last Soviet troops to leave Germany and thus all of Eastern Europe. (This will resolve the enigma of a NATO nation with Soviet troops on its soil.) U.S. troop presence to decline from more than three hundred thousand perhaps to below one hundred thousand.

2000   All remaining U.S. troops to leave Germany.

2005   NATO, as we have known it, to be deemed successful in its mission and to be restructured, perhaps as an economic forum, perhaps in other ways.

Europe Will Become a Bustling, Flexible Continent

What will Europe look like, after all this has settled down? It will most probably be little involved or concerned with the Soviet Union. It has become a cliché to say the Soviet economy is bad. One could add to that the cliché that the Soviet economy won't soon get better. Gorbachev's *glasnost* has been unable to counterbalance the increasing unavailability of goods, which all adds up to the worst possible predicament for him and his team. Given any choice, newly voting citizens anywhere in the USSR choose to "throw the rascals out." The authors even met one politician in the Soviet Union who had suffered the ignominy of running for re-election unopposed—and *losing!*

The rigid post–World War II division of Europe is gone. Although NATO and the EEC will remain, ad hoc functional groupings will also begin to pop up. One of the authors was in Hungary at the time the Berlin Wall fell in November 1989, and at that time the foreign ministers of Austria, Hungary, Italy, and Yugoslavia had assembled in Budapest to create a so-called Alps–Adria Community. This "Budapest Quartet" consists of one Eastern European member (Hungary) from the Warsaw Pact and COMECON, one Western European member (Italy) from NATO and the European Economic Community, one strictly neutral member (Austria) in the European Free Trade Association, and one founding member (Yugoslavia) of the Nonaligned Movement. Previously unthinkable, this type of ad hoc arrangement, enlarged now with Czechoslovakia's participation, will steadily become more prevalent.

America Will Go to War (If Anywhere) in the Middle East

No place else on earth contains all the ingredients for a potentially large U.S. military operation: bitter hostility between states, abundant natural resources (oil) upon which our prime allies are now dependent and we ourselves are increasingly dependent, substantial local military forces, fanatic leaders in power, and a staunch American ally whose very existence is endangered (and about whose fate many members of American society care deeply). The Persian Gulf crisis of 1990 makes all this clear.

Such an explosive situation cries out for a productive peace process, but such an initiative has proved elusive over the past decade. Security concerns have dissipated in Europe, Central America, central and southern Africa (Angola and Namibia), South Asia (Afghanistan), East

Asia (Cambodia), and elsewhere in part because of diligent diplomacy, but such diplomacy has been singularly absent from the Middle East since the Camp David Accords and the subsequent Sinai withdrawal. Moreover, Middle East diplomacy has centered around the Israeli–Arab dispute, whereas Iraq's marauding has shown that Arab–Arab disputes may be every bit as incendiary. Indeed, it seems the only thing still uniting Arabia is antagonism toward Israel. Without the Jewish state the region would perhaps be even more turbulent.

Asian Security Will Change More Slowly than European Security, But the U.S. Role Will Slowly Decline

The security situation has changed less in Asia recently than in Europe. Mellowing of the Sino–Soviet dispute, hardening of domestic policy in China, withdrawal of Vietnamese forces from Cambodia, and wider recognition of South Korea have altered security conditions in that region, but not in a revolutionary manner.

Asia's evolutionary changes could become more dramatic if a fundamental change occurs in our military base rights (or in the fate of democracy) in the Philippines, or if Kim Il Sung of North Korea finally dies and is replaced by a different type of leader, or if U.S.–South Korean relations undergo a dramatic downturn.

As current trends play out, however, Asia is generally in fine shape, with the major exception of China—and even it seems preoccupied. The so-called Nixon Doctrine of our supplying air and sea defense and the local government supplying ground forces will become the unspoken yet standard operating procedure in Asia. And as economic factors loom larger than military ones in the decades ahead, Asia will rise in international importance.

Nuclear Weapons Will Continue to Exist

When President Reagan spoke of abolishing all nuclear weapons from the face of the earth, it brought to mind that old-time prayer that goes, "Lord, let me be chaste, but not just yet."

To desire seriously a nuclear-free world would be visionary but also downright dangerous if translated into reality. Such a desire would never be shared by the Soviets, British, French, Chinese, Indians, and a few others who also possess nuclear weapons. Even if they miraculously did agree, we could never know if they complied. We could never be sure in those massive countries whether they scrapped every single nuclear weapon, some so small that they can fit in a backpack and others that can easily be placed in a car. And no responsible U.S. president would discard our last nuclear weapon on the hope that the others were doing likewise, with nothing more than hope on which to base that action.

Even if everyone agreed and in fact complied, the world would become more, and not less, dangerous: Such a development would lead to the abdication of U.S. global responsibilities, which involved furnishing a nuclear umbrella over Western Europe, Japan, and other friends and allies around the world. However leaky or improbable that umbrella may have been or appeared, our so-called extended deterrence and the existence of nuclear weapons helped keep the peace over several decades. Prime Minister Margaret Thatcher told Gorbachev in April 1989, "Both our countries know from bitter experience that conventional weapons do not deter war in Europe, whereas nuclear weapons have done so for over forty years."

Moreover—if more convincing is needed—even should the five permanent U.N. Security Council members and India destroy all their nuclear weapons, other nations would fill the void. Less responsible nations would then have more, not less, incentive to possess nuclear weapons, to become pseudo-superpowers. It is instructive to observe that the first nuclear weapons test proved successful in every known case—for us in 1945 and for the Soviets, British, French, Chinese, and Indians in subsequent years. Perhaps it is not as tough to build these terrifying weapons as scientists had once supposed.

Finally, if all these difficulties were magically overcome, the abolition of nuclear weapons would still be transitory at best. Nothing learned can become unlearned. Nothing known can be erased from human intelligence. And such countries as Iraq and Iran seem intent on exploiting that learning. Had it not been for the Israeli air strike a few years ago, Iraq may well have had nuclear weapons today.

Indeed, the first casualty in any serious war would be the ban on nuclear weapons. Scientists from both sides would scurry to the books and articles telling how to make nuclear weapons, equipped with one bit of information absent during the Manhattan Project—namely, that it *is* possible to cause a nuclear implosion.

For all practical purposes, then, nuclear weapons are here to stay. Such a realization may have influenced Winston Churchill, in his last address to the U.S. Congress, to warn: "Be careful, above all things, not to let go of the atomic weapon until you are sure, and more than sure, that other means of preserving the peace are in your hands."

Arms Control Will Focus Increasingly on Third World Rather than U.S.–Soviet Problems

Despite the virtual alphabet soup of initials representing ongoing arms control talks centering on the United States and the Soviet Union—START, NST, CFE, NTT, and CSBM—the major superpower arms reductions will come outside these talks.

Real arms reductions are under way, less the result of formal negotiations in Geneva or Vienna than of domestic financial deliberations in Washington and in Moscow. Budget cutters will do what arms controllers have generally failed to do, and their efforts will be bolstered by rapidly changing political considerations.

Indeed, the most dramatic decline in military confrontations and (eventually) of armaments has occurred over the past year as a result not of diplomats' work but of citizens' efforts across Eastern Europe and throughout the Soviet Union. The revolutions of 1989 have fundamentally changed the world and reduced its dangers.

This process is as natural as the arms control process is sometimes artificial. When nations move from being fierce enemies to strong adversaries to mere rivals, they commonly lower their armaments—not so much through arms control as through downgrading the threat. This is happening in Sino–Soviet and American–Soviet relations today, just as it has happened repeatedly throughout history—with the United States and Canada in the mid-nineteenth century, the British and the French in the early years of the present century, and China and India during the fifteen years following their 1962 conflict.

And when nations move from being totalitarian to democratic, they invariably choose both to lower their own armaments, as in virtually every nation of Eastern Europe, and to remove foreign occupation forces, as the Czechs, Hungarians, and others have done with Soviet troops on their soil.

Nevertheless, formal arms control will still have a service to perform. As the threat changes from the Soviet empire to the Third World, so the negotiations should try to address and redress problems there.

To help stop the spread of ballistic missiles, for instance, presidents Bush and Gorbachev could try to expand to all countries the Intermediate Nuclear Force (INF) Treaty ban of ballistic missiles with ranges of between 300 and 3,400 miles—the core of the accord signed by presidents Reagan and Gorbachev in December 1986. A joint U.S.–Soviet draft treaty might carry wide appeal. For unlike the Nonproliferation Treaty, the former would not be discriminatory. We would not be asking any country to give up anything we and the Soviets have not already forgone.

Prohibited would be missiles capable of carrying chemical, biological, and conventional arms as well as nuclear weapons. This would help reduce the dread of more chemical warfare and eliminate the nightmare of marrying poison gas with ballistic missiles.

Other countries might sign up because of sheer superpower sway or even simple moral suasion; it is, after all, the right thing to do. Many might buy on out of fright that otherwise their archenemies would get these dreadful weapons; arms control can contribute when neither side has a given weapon and each would rather not acquire it than end up, as usually happens, with both obtaining it.

Explicitly banned in this scheme would be existing missiles like the upgrade of the Soviet Scud B, which Iraq not only possesses but actually used in its sordid war with Iran, and missiles like the weirdly named East Winds (CSS-2) the Chinese recently sold to Saudi Arabia. Also banned would be a host of missiles now under development in Argentina, Brazil, India, Israel, Pakistan, and South Africa, and probably under development in such unpredictable countries as Iran, Libya, and North Korea.

Israel might participate if it could thereby eliminate this real threat from Iran, Iraq, Libya, and Saudi Arabia. France, even though it is increasingly pushing its nuclear deterrence force out to sea, might resist, as probably would China. But then again, France and China refused to sign the Nonproliferation Treaty, which has nonetheless been the most successful arms control agreement in history.

Such a multilateral treaty as the one suggested could in large part be verified by a ban on flight testing. Relatively high-tech systems cannot in general be *confidently* deployed if not well tested.

Parkinson's most perceptive law holds that the success of any action is measured by catastrophes that do not ensue. Here is a rare opportunity to preclude car loads of catastrophes that might otherwise ensue, at least as things around the world seem to be shaping up at this moment.

Conclusion

Before too long Saddam Hussein's "wake-up call," showing once again the continued need for a robust national defense, will be forgotten. Before too long, Americans may return to complacency and presume that dangers from the wicked world are passé.

That, we believe, would be most unfortunate. A glance at the "peace" of the past forty-five years shows that the world continues to be a dangerous place, even if the threat from the USSR has receded. The

United States may need *less* defense, but the United States still needs *capable* defense—in many ways, more capable than before. With danger most evident in the Persian Gulf, we may forget that events in the Philippines, Kashmir, the Korean peninsula, Latin America, the cauldron of Africa, and elsewhere can affect U.S. interests and citizens in ways unimaginable today. Threats remain, and we must be prepared. The defense revolution does not mean defense obsolescence.

TWO

THE GEOSTRATEGIC REVOLUTION:
Alloyed Glee

As the great American philosopher Yogi Berra put it, "The future just ain't what it used to be." Neither, it now seems, is the past. Changes in the onetime Soviet bloc are being made at such speed as to risk becoming yesterday's news before they even get into today's print.

This chapter will touch on some of the remarkable changes arising from the *glasnost* and *perestroika* movements that Mikhail Gorbachev has set in motion. First, though, let it be said that Gorbachev is one of the most impressive individuals, if not *the* most impressive, on the world stage today. As witness and participant in three Reagan-Gorbachev summits, one of the authors has seen Gorbachev in action, "up close and personal." After the very first meeting between Reagan and Gorbachev—when they spent the morning of November 21, 1985, virtually alone together in Geneva, Switzerland—Reagan remarked to those having lunch with him immediately afterward (including the same author) that Gorbachev was strikingly different from any other top Soviet leader. No matter that Mr. Reagan had never met any other top Soviet leader; he was probably right—more right than he could ever have imagined.

Gorbachev is attempting nothing less than a complete remake of Soviet society, and wherever he travels he triggers change—from Beijing to Berlin. Gorbachev continues to protest that he merely wants to rebuild socialism, not destroy it. One would be wise to take

Gorbachev's words seriously, yet realize that the *effect* of what he's done has been to dismantle what we have known as traditional Soviet-style communism. Certainly he has dismantled the old, repressive totalitarian system and sent the once rock-solid, even stolid, Soviet state careening off in a new direction.

Gorbachev has indeed made moves that have radically destabilized the Soviet Union. If America's conservatives were to have schemed how to unhinge the USSR years ago—when President Reagan was still speaking (rightly, in our opinion) of the "evil empire"—none of us could have envisioned the degree of destabilization that Mikhail Gorbachev subsequently caused.

The Triumph of Democratic Values

Much of the past four decades has been consumed with the battle of ideas: communism versus capitalism, central control versus popular control, totalitarianism versus democracy. Perhaps by no one has the Western case been made better than by Malcolm Muggeridge during the height of intellectual battles in the 1950s:

> If I accept, as millions of other Western Europeans do, that America is destined to be the mainstay of freedom in this mid- twentieth century world, it does not follow that American institutions are perfect, that Americans are invariably well behaved, or that the American way of life is flawless. It only means that in one of the most terrible conflicts in human history, I have chosen my side, as all will have to choose sooner or later.

That "most terrible conflict in human history" is over. Freedom and free enterprise have won, hands down, and the old war of ideas ends (Figure 2). In short, we have left the era when nineteenth century ideologies—unbridled nationalism and sweeping communism—deformed the twentieth century. Nazism fell in World War II, and communism is falling today.

Nonetheless, the thirst for meaning in life, the longing for something greater than self, is not fulfilled by freedom. Despite its having won the war of ideas, freedom is, strictly speaking, not a very sophisticated idea at all. For it lays no claim to be encompassing or scientific and is usually not described in emotional terms by any except those denied it, like former Soviet dissidents and current Chinese students.

Freedom's claims are indeed modest; even Winston Churchill defined democracy as "the worst form of government, except for all those

Figure 2. As the Iron Curtain fell in November 1989 the curtain was raised on a new drama on the world political stage.

other forms that have been tried from time to time." Instead of promising perfection, freedom promises opportunity. Instead of speaking in absolutes, such as "total liberation from total alienation," freedom is couched in relative terms, such as "freedom for one must be tempered by allowing freedom of others."

Above all, freedom legitimizes the individual's "pursuit of happiness" but does little to guide that search or to satisfy the natural human reach for a cause higher than individual existence.

The end of political ideology may well involve a revival of religion globally and a return to individual pursuits. The search for meaning in life, never easy, becomes tougher as political ideology fades.

Abandonment of Communist Ideology

How was this war of ideas won? By Western persistence and Soviet abandonment. Indeed, Mikhail Gorbachev's historical contribution, thus far anyway, lies not in revitalization of Soviet society, changes in its foreign policy, nor even any renewal of hope and spirit. Rather, his historic contribution consists of reducing fear as a central component of Soviet life and ending any guise or ruse of the sanctity of Marxist ideology.

His first contribution of reducing if not removing fear as a central component of Soviet life need not be labored. Russia was long distinguished by the pervasiveness of fear and by fear's triumph over thought. Indeed, in the Marquis de Custine's extraordinary work of 150 years ago, *Empire of the Czar: A Journey through Eternal Russia*, he found that "in Russia, fear replaces, that is, paralyzes, thought."

The most amazing things are now done and said in the Soviet Union simply because the doers or sayers there lack fear of punishment. When comparisons are made between Stalin and Hitler, when the once quasi-divine Lenin himself is seen as the founder not primarily of the Soviet state but of the Soviet system of terror, when Marx's writings are critically reviewed, when KGB agents must answer questions before the nascent Soviet legislature and before millions watching on call-in television shows, when Communist party politicians run for positions unopposed and lose, when Gorbachev himself is criticized hither and yon—when these and many other mind-bending developments occur in public or widely in the media—everyone can see that fear is gone, at least for now.

This freeing of thought and speech has opened the floodgates, much as Custine predicted, "Whenever the right of speech shall be restored to this muzzled people, the astonished world will hear so many disputes arise that it will believe the confusion of Babel again returned."

This notion relates to Gorbachev's second historic contribution: the end of even any veneer of Marxist ideology. The death of communism as an idea has become apparent to one and all, but neither its original appeal nor its consequences has become apparent. A word, then, on each.

How did Marxism fool so many people for so long? For nearly a century and a half, Marxism provided meaning for millions around the world by folding disparate facts into one grand theory of history. Its scientific veneer had great appeal in our rational age, particularly to intellectuals blinded by the brilliance of Marx's writing, intrigued by the complexity of his message, and positioned on the edge of society.

Communism lured the masses also—at least some of them, some of the time—because of its emotional wallop and mental simplicity. How nice to hate the rich! How easy to grasp the division of society into workers and exploiters! Communism's message was more *felt* than thought. It cried out for *action*, not reflection. For *revolution*, not compromise.

Political rulers the world over were lured by Lenin's emphasis on iron discipline. For Lenin attributed to elites the revolutionary consciousness Marx ascribed to the workers. Thus did communism become transformed into an elitist ideology, dependent for success on a disenchanted upper class rather than on an oppressed lower class. Elitists flocked to Lenin, Mao, Ho Chi Minh, and the rest. Fidel Castro, himself from a landowning family, abandoned all pretense as he formed his first cabinet without a single worker included.

So communism offered something to the masses and then to power-hungry leaders wishing, like Lenin and Stalin, to consolidate their grip over their respective societies. Some leaders around the world—those in Albania, Cuba, North Korea, Vietnam, and scattered others—still use this vehicle to cling to power. And some intellectuals around the world—including a few in American academic and religious circles, which may become the last refuges of Marxist belief—also still find the ideology attractive.

But the bloom is off. Opening what Gorbachev called "the closed pages" of his country's past has revealed such horrors as to raise questions about the legitimacy of the Soviet system itself.

Discovering, for instance, that Stalin's victims may number upward of 20 million souls finally lets the world see him in his true colors, as the greatest mass murderer in human history, probably exceeding even Hitler. No one was spared, as Stalin put even his own military under the gun. Indeed, Stalin killed more of his army and naval officers in two years (1937 and 1938) than the Germans killed in the first two years of World War II battles with the Soviets.

These cold statistics are complemented by some odd episodes, such as the one recounted by former national security advisor Zbigniew Brzezinski in his latest book, *The Grand Failure*. Imagine the scene in the Kremlin when Molotov and Kalinin attended Politburo meetings in which Stalin discussed which "comrades" were to be executed—while both of their wives suffered in concentration camps on Stalin's orders.

Publicizing such phenomenal facts helps delegitimize the entire system. What type of politics, it is increasingly asked, has for more than seventy years lived with and defended leaders who are either criminal like Stalin or inept like Brezhnev and Chernenko?

The key question today is not whether Soviet citizens still believe in the system, but whether they *ever* really did. Finding a true communist in the Soviet Union today is as hard as finding a Nazi in Germany was after World War II. The delegitimization process taking place today compares roughly to what it might be like for us as Americans to be subjected to a constant barrage of articles almost unanimously denouncing our own past leaders and belief systems conceived by John Locke, the Founding Fathers, and Abraham Lincoln.

There is nothing irreversible in economics, or even politics for that matter—as we were reminded in Tiananmen Square (Figure 3). But things *are* irreversible in psychology and in the legitimacy a regime en-

Figure 3. The Chinese convincingly demonstrated once again the reversibility of a people's attempt to attain greater freedom and achieve a market economy.

joys. Once that dissipates and then disappears, as the Shah found out, it's gone for good.

No wonder that now Marxism cries out for nothing, nothing except abandonment by most of those still having it and ridicule by those watching it pass. "It was with a sense of awe," Winston Churchill said of the Germans' granting Lenin safe passage home during World War I, "that they turned upon Russia the most grisly of all weapons. They transported Lenin in a sealed [railway car] like a plague bacillus from Switzerland into Russia." Lenin's plague has finally been contained and is now being assailed by one and all.

The consequence of this delegitimization is profound. For there cannot long be total control absent a total idea. With the death of the total-idea systems of Nazism and Fascism after the Axis defeat in World War II came the passing of totalitarianism in the host countries, West Germany and Italy. With the death of communist ideology in our times comes the passing of totalitarianism throughout the main parts of the Soviet bloc.

What caused this sudden free-fall? Eventually, truth must win out—especially in modern times, because of the tremendous effects of "liberation technology." The advent of the information revolution has spread the message of freedom and the hope of freedom more effectively than any message heretofore has been spread throughout world history. Polish leader Lech Walesa notes that satellite dishes, computers, videos, international telephone lines force pluralism and freedom onto a society. Today Stalin is impossible. Now you say, what about China? The future monuments in China will be to those who have been shot. China will come back to pluralism, democracy and freedom. They won't be able to destroy all our television sets. People can't do without telephones. Technological history can't be turned back. That's why I'm so certain about victory.

Much the same point about the impact of modern communications was made to one of the authors earlier this year by the president of Turkey. Incredibly, again, Custine forecast this a century and a half ago, when he wrote, "The political system of Russia could not survive twenty years' free communications with the west of Europe."

The Soviet Whirlpool

As mentioned earlier, stability has been shaken across the Soviet Union. The summer of 1989 brought recurrent reports in *Tass* of youth gangs wielding iron bars, hurling rocks, igniting firebombs, and firing pistols to assault "passers-by in residential areas and on city streets" and to damage "homes, stores, and administrative buildings" in the central Asian part of the USSR. Such outbreaks represent a new development in the inexorable decrepitude of the Soviet empire. *Tass* went on, "There were attempts to seize the city police station and the water supply system. There have been instances of arms being used, as well as Molotov cocktails. There have been deaths." In June 1990, some one hundred died in the Soviet Union when some group or other went on a rampage, burning homes, raping women, and killing people and then mutilating the corpses.

The roots of this spreading savagery lie in Gorbachev's two prime problems: declining economic conditions and rising ethnic resentment. "The economy is become increasingly cannibalistic, feeding on itself," said Viktor Belkin, a Soviet economist at the Academy of Sciences at the time of the summer savagery. Less flamboyant but no less truthful were the words of Prime Minister Nikolai Ryzhkov, who acknowledged that having one-fifth of adults in the USSR's central Asian region unemployed makes for real problems. Deputy Prime Minister Leonid Abalkin warned moreover that the "society will be destabilized" if the economy does not improve over the coming couple of years. "What form [the destabilization] will take is unpredictable," he added, "but it will be inevitable."

Amplifying this cascade of woes are rising ethnic tensions. Ethnic eruptions have occurred throughout the Soviet Union—more than six hundred of them in 1988, according to the CIA. "Popular disturbances" have rocked more than half the Soviet republics. Ethnicity bedevils the Soviet Union, in part because the country's republics are ethnic homelands, with the dominant Russians constituting less than half the total population and declining all the while, in relative terms.

There is no melting pot there; indeed, the greatest danger is that the pot itself may melt. Nor is there anything like, in the words of the Soviet national anthem, an "unbreakable union of free republics joined together by a Great Union." According to General Mikhail Moiseyev, Chief of the Soviet General Staff, fifty-three Soviet officers were killed in violence within the Soviet Union in 1989, including eleven "senior" officers.

Ethnic groups in the USSR have seized upon the extremely popular ecology movement to further their goals and strengthen their identities. Preservation of the land is linked with preservation of their cultures. Again, *glasnost* makes this rising pride possible. Some factors do continue to push the Soviet people together—a shared recent history, shared institutions, a common currency, and so forth—but an increasing number of factors have begun to push them apart.

The ethnic problems feed on the economic misery. As Henry S. Rowen of Stanford University and Charles Wolf, Jr., of the Rand Corporation have written in a companion book, *The Impoverished Superpower*, "The picture that emerges on the state of the economy is bleak." According to another author in that volume, Anders Åslund, "during seventy years of Soviet rule the standard of living has risen above the prerevolution level only between 1960 and 1975, and then not at a very high rate." Åslund puts the size of the Soviet economy at 30 percent of U.S. GNP per capita in the late 1980s. As Rowen and Wolf note, even this may be too high.

The bottom line leads one to pessimism regarding immediate Soviet economic prospects. Many observers, including experts in the U.S. government as well as the two of us, conclude that it is doubtful whether Gorbachev, or anyone, can indeed rejuvenate that system. He faces an economic infrastructure wildly out of kilter, with rents that have not been raised since 1928, bread prices since 1954, and meat prices since 1962. Eleven-hundred fifty of twelve hundred consumer items listed by the Soviet government are in a "shortage condition." Wacky state subsidies cause Soviet farmers to be able to feed their pigs more cheaply with bread than with grain.

Glasnost-liberated Soviet statisticians now assert that 40 percent of the entire Soviet population lives in poverty, including an appalling 79 percent of its elderly. Perhaps more graphic are the facts that per capita, more South African blacks own cars than do Soviet citizens; that the life expectancy of someone born today in the USSR is less than that of someone born today in Mexico; that so shoddy is Soviet manufacturing that the main cause of fires around that mighty country is defective home television sets.

The consumers are, of course, the hardest hit, with high inflation and low availability of ordinary products. The food lines seem perpetually to lengthen, as the most common products become scarcer. Soviet miners began a wave of strikes in 1988 demanding, among other things, a weekly supply of soap (which is certainly not the most difficult consumer good to produce). Today, an average worker's family of four can expect to live at least eight years in a single room before anything better becomes available. Now nearly a third of Soviet households lack running water, and 60 percent of Soviet hospital patients lack hot water. A Soviet economist has estimated that the time Soviet citizens spend simply standing in line is the equivalent of that spent by 35 million workers on their jobs each year.

Contrast this with the Soviets' demonstrated ability to provide modern, effective equipment to its military forces— first-rate fighter aircraft, excellent tanks, and the only deployed antisatellite systems in the world. The heavily military-oriented Soviet space program has conducted two and one-half times as many launches as the U.S. space program over the last thirty years, and continues at such a level today. The Soviets have maintained a relatively continuous manned presence in space, amassing nineteen man-years as compared with America's five man-years.

Somehow Soviet military production has been made to work better than anything in the civilian sector. This is due to a host of factors, including the compulsory creaming off of the country's very best scientists and engineers for military work; the vast amount of resources funneled into this single sector; and, ironically, the establishment of at least some competition among defense institutions and factories.

Incapable of providing even for its own people, the Soviets naturally cannot provide much to others. The gigantic USSR has fallen behind even teeny Hong Kong, as well as South Korea, Switzerland, and Taiwan, in the export of manufactured goods. During Soviet communism's entire seventy-year history, not one product "made in the Soviet Union" has competed successfully on the world civilian market.

Gorbachev knows he has big problems. He has admitted or, if anything, possibly even overstated them. And he has used dramatic exhortations: "*Perestroika* is our last chance," he said grimly a few years back, when conditions were less awful. "If we stop, it will be our death."

But he has not yet come up with big solutions for those big problems. Gorbachev's gradual escalation of free-marketry omits many essential changes, including drastic price reform, true private ownership of assets, the breakup of state-owned monopolies, and a convertible currency. His tinkering has been, in the words of U.S. Deputy National Security Advisor Robert Gates, akin to trying to make "a phased change from driving on the left-hand side of the road to the right." Or, as that great American adventurist Evel Knievel said, "trying to leap deep canyons in two bounds."

Granted, even that master of surprises, Gorbachev, may well have been surprised by his country's decrepitude. He has said as much to top party bosses, "Frankly speaking, comrades, we underestimated the full depth of the deformations and stagnation."

For certain, the Soviet government must end its phased changes and resort to dramatic ones. But this too is not without risk. The Soviet Union is surely a society in turmoil. Again, the scene there is as Custine foreshadowed: "Everything is dull, still, and regular in Russia, except in moments when the long-repressed instinct of liberty bursts forth in an explosion." Such a moment is happening now, and the explosion is on a megaton scale.

But the big question remains: Can any big bang lead the USSR into becoming a modern and free nation? Can removing despotism revive the well-being of the populace?

There are those in the West who will glibly predict where the Soviet Union is heading, but such predictions are risky, since Gorbachev and his colleagues do not themselves know where the Soviet Union is heading. To make predictions at this point would be like trying to read the mind of someone who has not made up his mind.

But there is at least one relevant observation to be made. Centuries of repression have made many Russians give up on new ideas, new ways, new notions. "The Russians are in short a resigned nation," Custine judged. "This simple description explains everything." It is not at all at odds with our own observations.

Gorbachev himself laments this cast of mind, for his prime problem is to inspire and push a reluctant, conservative, and bureaucratic society—just the opposite of most East European rulers' prime problem of containing and directing impatient peoples.

What if no system of incentives can do the trick? Indications thus far are that the Soviet people seem not to display much entrepreneurial spirit, that the oft-heralded cooperatives and other small stabs at free enterprise are themselves failing from lack of any personal striving and any great social esteem for such enterprises. There are reports of common citizens attacking and burning the property of those who have risen a bit above the economic average. Soviets with whom we have spoken lament the pervasive "dependency syndrome" that infects the land, namely, that citizens have come to expect womb-to-tomb care.

If this dependency proves to be a pattern, then one must abandon hope. Nonetheless, it is too early to make that final determination. Once again, one can do no better than to echo Custine: "It is, therefore, difficult to see how the nation will get out of the dangerous circle in which circumstances have placed it."

The Eastern European Cauldron

Empires have never died without significant reverberations, whether that empire be Roman, Turkish, Austrio–Hungarian, or British. The Soviet empire is proving to be no exception. Its death is having the most profound global consequences, most of them good for us and others who champion freedom.

Eastern Europeans under the Soviet thumb once seemed, at least on the surface, like the subjugated population portrayed by Joseph Conrad: "They hated and despised the imperial power, but most of them were ready to cringe before it. Yes, even the best were overawed by the real might under the tinsel of that greatness." This attitude clearly no longer exists among Eastern Europeans.

Gorbachev has let loose of the leash. The Brezhnev Doctrine— which had sanctioned the use of Soviet military force to make communism irreversible—has been denounced by one and all. One-time Soviet allies can now say, in the words of the Negro spiritual, "Free at last, free at last, thank God Almighty, we're free at last."

Once given this freedom, the Eastern Europeans ran with it. Over a private breakfast late in 1989, the Hungarian deputy foreign minister told one of us that the Hungarian government never even informed (let alone asked) Moscow before allowing thousands of East Germans to travel indirectly to West Germany in the summer of 1989. This decision was made solely by the Hungarians, even though it had the most profound repercussions for the future of East Germany, the one Warsaw Pact nation Moscow had long considered the most critical to keep communist and controlled. In fact, the Hungarians' go-ahead to East Germans wishing to make it around to West Germany (via Austria) unraveled the neo-Nazi regime of East Germany and led to the fall of the Berlin Wall—undoubtedly *the* dramatic event of the decade.

According to the Hungarian deputy minister, his government was faced with a mounting number of East Germans in Hungary, whom the Hungarians did not want to have to repatriate by force. So the Hungarians, contrary to a formal agreement with the East German government, decided to allow the East German emigrés to go to Austria, from where the emigrés went on to West Germany.

The Hungarian deputy minister informed the East German ambassador of this action in Budapest at around 4:00 one Friday afternoon—the East German ambassador was shocked—and then the Hungarian deputy minister told the Soviet ambassador of the action at around 5:00 that same afternoon. The Soviet ambassador was not shocked. At no point did the Hungarians debate whether to consult or even inform Moscow beforehand. That was a pivotal moment in history, as was Gorbachev's green light to the Polish Communist party chief in the summer of 1989 to accept a Solidarity majority in the new Polish coalition government. This was the first time in forty years that noncommunists (actually, anticommunists) controlled a Warsaw Pact nation's government.

The end of Soviet control over Eastern Europe, after forty years, comes as welcome relief. Yet it also lessens restraints in internal regional tensions, for which that area has been notorious. "We Americans tend to be much less aware of the dangers inherent in success," Deputy Secretary of State Lawrence S. Eagleburger said in a September 1989 address. "For all its risks and uncertainties, the cold war was characterized by a remarkably stable and predictable set of relations among the great powers." Now, according to Eagleburger, we face the "danger that changes in the East will prove too destabilizing to be sustained."

The danger should, of course, not be underestimated. Yet alongside the danger exists a great opportunity. After all, although everyone prizes stability, Americans and most others prize freedom more. Soviet domination of East European nations, although stabilizing, was also stultifying. Those countries were denied independence; their people were denied freedom; and their economies were destroyed by a profoundly unworkable system.

The Lingering Soviet Threat

The high-water mark of the Soviet empire has obviously passed and the floodwaters are now subsiding. This remarkable turnabout during the late 1980s stands in stark contrast to the Soviets' geostrategic assault of the 1970s. Between 1975 and 1980, Soviet expansionism was clearly on a roll. For Moscow then manned or planned or fanned a communist take-over of a pro-Western country every single year: in 1975 South Vietnam, in 1976 Angola, in 1977 Ethiopia, in 1978 Cambodia, and in 1979 Afghanistan and Nicaragua.

No longer on a roll, Soviet expansionism is now on a rollback. From Afghanistan to Cambodia to Angola, the Soviet war machine is backing up. Indeed, even in the onetime Soviet strategic heartland of Eastern Europe, the writing is clearly on the proverbial wall for the removal of Soviet forces across the continent. In the core of that strategic heartland, the actual wall itself is gone. Fidel Castro must feel very lonely indeed.

Yet any prudent American or other Westerner must pause for a moment and reflect. Regardless of high-sounding words from Gorbachev and some noticeable (but only incipient) changes in the Soviet military posture (more about that in a moment), there has been a marked lag in the effect of *glasnost* and *perestroika* on Soviet security spending in support of its outposts around the world and on its own arsenal.

Even under Gorbachev, Moscow has doled out more than $2 billion per year in military equipment to Vietnam, Laos, and Cambodia in recent times and some $1 billion per year in military equipment to Angola alone. As is becoming better known, the Soviets have spent between $250 million and $300 million every month, or a total of $3 billion to $3.6 billion every year, to help the Marxist regime cling to power in Afghanistan. And the Soviet Union's main outpost in our own hemisphere—Cuba—continues to reap up to $7 billion of Soviet support each year. "At a time of economic stress at home, these commitments say a great deal about Soviet priorities," according to Deputy National Security Advisor Gates.

As to Soviet military spending, Gorbachev took power after such spending had mushroomed clear out of sight. Because of mistakenly high Western estimates of the Soviets' gross national product and incorrectly low estimates of the costs of Soviet equipment, U.S. intelligence has been woefully *underestimating* Moscow's relative level of effort in the defense realm. In 1976, an assessment conducted by Secretary of Defense Donald Rumsfeld—under whom we both served in the Pentagon—nearly doubled the U.S. estimate of Soviet defense spending, from between 5 percent and 7 percent of Soviet GNP to between 11 percent and 13 percent. The estimate has been raised regularly, going from between 13 percent and 15 percent upward to between 15 percent and 17 percent. All these estimates have still been low, as Moscow must have been devoting 20 percent or more of its GNP to its military budget. Experts in the Rowen and Wolf volume *The Impoverished Superpower*, as well as some Soviet economists, say the amount may exceed 25 percent of GNP.

That staggering level of effort, even in as hobbled an industrial system as that of the Soviet Union, produced an astonishing amount of equipment. To take just one example, even during Gorbachev's first four years, the Soviet military-industrial complex cranked out enough tanks each *month* to equip one new tank division. During that time, the Soviets deployed more tanks and artillery than Britain, France, and Germany *together* possess in their entire armies. Indeed, even after the start of Gorbachev's cutbacks, the Soviets have substantially outproduced the United States in most types of modern military equipment.

Moreover, the Soviets had stationed an equally staggering number of forces in Eastern Europe, not to hold off any imagined NATO aggression but to hold down for decades the aspirations of the Warsaw Pact peoples. It must have seemed curious to the bloc's citizens that the tank traps placed by the Soviets along the Berlin Wall and elsewhere often faced the East!

As of today, the USSR has more Soviet divisions standing in East Germany than exist in the entire U.S. Army, albeit the Soviet divisions are smaller. The USSR has had more troops in one country, Czechoslovakia, than the United States has stationed all across Western Europe. Happily, these Soviet troops are now on their way out—in Czechoslovakia by the summer of 1991 and in Germany by 1994 at the latest. This reduction in forces enables Gorbachev to cut defense spending, which he announced early in 1989, by 14.2 percent overall and 19.5 percent in Soviet military hardware. Because certainly we (and probably he) do not know precisely what the Soviet military now spends, there remains room for some skepticism—at least over the precision of his statement. Nonetheless, U.S. intelligence is finding a *lowering* of Soviet defense spending for the first time in decades.

In large part, this military drawdown comes from sheer economic necessity. Yet even the economic-necessity aspect tends to be overestimated. In reality, much of the drawdown comes as the natural outgrowth of *glasnost*. Simply said, free people do not choose to spend lavish amounts on their militaries in peacetime—as the Pentagon and other Western military establishments have learned, in spades. Nor do such people care to use military force to invade or suppress others.

Much to his credit, Gorbachev has raised the attention accorded to public opinion. In the summer of 1989, he told a party conference explicitly that he would "like to dwell particularly on the political freedoms that enable a person to express his opinion on any matter. Comrades, what we are talking about is a new role of public opinion in the country."

Having carved out this strengthened role for public opinion, Gorbachev finds that the newly unmuzzled public is decidedly antimilitary. A poll conducted by a leading Soviet sociologist in *Literaturnaya gazeta* during 1989 indicated that an astonishing 71 percent of the more than two hundred thousand respondents, when asked what was the first thing the country needed to do to improve their lives, responded that the country needed to curtail military spending severely.

That survey merely reiterated what had already been made evident at the polls. In their first (at least halfway) competitive elections in more than seventy years, the spring 1989 elections, Soviet voters defeated four generals and two admirals who ran for the new legislature. A Warsaw Pact commander lost by nearly three to one to a young colonel advocating military cuts, and the commander of the Soviet navy's key northern fleet lost to a junior commander in a major naval port filled with naval personnel. Other winning candidates across the USSR campaigned for slicing the military.

What *will* happen on the military-spending score? It is safe to figure that Moscow will continue taking bites out of its military budget, with *real* reductions occurring each year for the foreseeable future. It is also safe to say that U.S. authorities, pushed hard by Congress, will cut even more from our military budget as soon as the furor over Kuwait has subsided. So it is probably safe to conclude that Soviet military spending and production, although declining, will remain higher than ours for the coming years, just as in the past. To take but one example, if the Soviets were to get rid of as many tanks as we own, they would still have nearly twice as many as we do.

A further question needs to be addressed: Will the seemingly unalterable decrepitude of the Soviet empire cause those in Moscow to become *more* aggressive? Conceivably, Marx's prediction that capitalism may lash out as it gasps its last breath may, like most of Marx's theory, now apply to the communist states. Kremlin leaders' actions may echo Henry IV's deathbed advice to his son to deflect attention from domestic woes by stirring trouble abroad: "Be it thy course to busy giddy minds with foreign quarrels."

This fear, though prevalent, is probably not a real one. It's quite improbable that Gorbachev would become like the callow Henry V, who took his dying father's counsel and led his country into battle. For one thing, Gorbachev is too sharp for such a strategy. The practical problem of where to attack—Pakistan? China? Western Europe?—arises, along with the sure realization that none of these lashings out would help much.

For another thing, there is the recent "lesson of Afghanistan"—particularly potent because, in the fall of 1989, Soviet Foreign Minister Eduard A. Shevardnadze admitted to the world that the Afghanistan invasion was illegal and immoral. It now appears that the Soviet military got burned badly from the engagement there and that most political leaders today resented the 1979 decision to invade, or at least now claim to have resented it, in the aftermath of its failure.

On this score, not only must the Soviets cry *"mea culpa"* but one of us needs to do so as well. For during the first Reagan–Gorbachev summit, in Geneva in 1985, President Reagan told his advisors that Gorbachev claimed to have first learned that Soviet troops had stormed into Afghanistan from a radio announcement. One of us, then serving as director of the U.S. Arms Control and Disarmament Agency, immediately told President Reagan that Gorbachev's claim was dubious, at best, given Gorbachev's membership then in the Politburo.

Yet Shevardnadze has publicly said that the decision to invade Afghanistan, "with such serious consequences for our country, was taken behind the backs of the party and people." It was made by a small clique around Brezhnev. That version of what happened does sound convincing now, especially after having heard the same thing in greater detail from various sources during numerous trips to Moscow.

And one last issue: Whither Gorbachev? He might well be down or out within the next few years (though he has, thus far, been spectacularly successful in keeping his balance during an amazing high-wire act). Nonetheless, his survival as a leader over the longer term does not seem a good bet.

If down, it would be because Gorbachev had been worn down. He may come to realize that, as Nicholas I once said, "I do not rule Russia; ten thousand clerks do." If ground down, Gorbachev would merely be following in the footsteps of a long line of Russian leaders, including Catherine the Great and Alexander I, who entered office as ardent reformers and subsequently resigned themselves to busywork. Gorbachev without Gorbachev pushing fundamental reforms seems most likely.

If out, it would be because Gorbachev had been tossed out. In this scenario, he would resemble Nikita Khrushchev and Alexander II, who launched reforms and lost their office (the latter, his life) as a result.

Either way, following Gorbachev may come a more nuts-and-bolts type of reformer with an eye to slow and steady resolution of Soviet economic and ethnic problems. Rather than install a Stalinist or a more stolid Brezhnevian successor at the helm, the Soviet powers that be may choose one who can efficiently implement and administer the changes Gorbachev introduced. After the visionary or revolutionary comes the more competent manager, someone who can deliver the goods—after Gandhi a Nehru, for example.

Gorbachev paved the way for a freer, more civilized Soviet Union. Any post-Gorbachev leader must find the way toward a more prosperous, decentralized Soviet Union. Such a leader must solve the economic and ethnic woes that so bedevil that society. That task will not be easy. It may not even be possible.

Implications for Arms Control

At first blush, arms control seems like an idea whose time has come. With the advent of Gorbachev and the de-emphasis of military might in the Soviet Union, conditions indeed appear riper than ever for far-reaching agreements.

Yet conditions may not actually *be* as ripe as they seem. As Florence Nightingale once said, whatever else they do, hospitals should not spread disease. Similarly, whatever else arms control does, it should not cause the Soviets to have or deploy more forces than they otherwise would.

This fear is most appropriate in relation to the arms accord that now seems more promising, the Vienna talks on conventional arms control. These much-heralded negotiations could, *if they "succeed,"* legitimize a continued large Soviet troop presence in East Europe beyond the mid-1990s. For our NATO proposal now calls for Soviet and American troops to number up to 195,000 apiece in Central Europe after that time.

This result, which seemed so desirable when the Vienna talks began, now seems behind the times. In December 1989, the new foreign minister of Czechoslovakia, Jiri Dienstbier, announced at his first official news conference that his top priority was the complete removal of all Soviet troops from his country. The Soviets agreed to complete this withdrawal by mid-1991.

Previously, Hungarian leaders had publicly urged Gorbachev to remove his troops from their country. This has now been agreed to as well, with the same date—summer 1991—for all troops out. That request echoes across other East European countries, with even the Soviets agreeing to remove all troops and nuclear weapons from German soil by 1993 or 1994. This seems now to have been planned some time ago. For at the close of 1989, Deputy Foreign Minister Vladimir Petrosky became the first Soviet official to specify that Moscow has 627,000 troops abroad. He then made a stunning statement at the United Nations: "Our final goal is to have not a single Soviet soldier abroad by the year 2000."

Why would Moscow take such a stance? Because, as Charles Gati wrote in *Foreign Affairs*, the Soviets have come to recognize "the paradox of its East European empire: that the region Stalin acquired after

World War II in order to enhance Soviet security has since become a major source of insecurity."

One of us asked during a trip to Hungary in the fall of 1989, "Is Gorbachev completely tolerant?" regarding the swift changes in Eastern Europe. "No, he's completely impotent," came the response from a Hungarian official.

So whether by choice or necessity, Gorbachev may have come around to a "triage strategy"—to concentrate on what can survive and to let the rest go. This strategy would mean clinging more tightly to the unruly parts of the Soviet Union and loosening most ties to Eastern Europe. This would account for the fact that in that same fall of 1989, Moscow was quietly tolerating the thousands protesting and leaving East Germany even as Soviet troops moved into a rebellious area in Moldavia, USSR. So this feel for Gorbachev's stance may be right. It makes sense in another way, too. For Gorbachev, as for any political leader, nothing compares to holding his country together. No leader is revered in the pages of history for overseeing the breakup of his or her own country.

Hence Gorbachev's agreeing to withdraw all forces from Eastern Europe. (Ironically, the anti-Soviet government in Poland may desire some Soviet troops to remain on Polish soil as a guard against German revanchism.) No better way exists to make the recent, stunning changes in Eastern Europe irreversible than to have the Red Army leave. Once gone, outside troops are difficult to reimpose, especially given the rising role of public opinion in the Soviet Union and in the onetime host countries themselves.

What about the Warsaw Pact? The pact could be left as it is, since a hollowed-out organization evokes no great concern. The shrewdest Hungarians seem to favor a "reverse French solution," with Hungary departing from the *political* arm of the Warsaw Pact, since that politics is passé, but staying in its military arm, since neutralism can be expensive. Neutrals like Switzerland have often spent proportionally more on defense than do some NATO members.

If the United States somehow managed to help move Gorbachev to the point of discussing at the Vienna talks a complete Soviet troop withdrawal from Europe, what, it can reasonably be asked, would the United States offer in return? Ironically, some *continued* U.S. troop presence in Europe, though at a substantially lower level than at present. In these dicey days—with the pending integration of Western Europe and the speedy disintegration of the onetime Soviet Bloc in Eastern Europe, and with German reunification coming at the end of 1990—Gorbachev may not actually want reciprocal American troop withdrawals. Departure of the Americans would leave the Germans too footloose, he could figure, and the other Europeans too unsettled.

As the Soviets (and everyone else) know, there has been *no* overall symmetry in superpower military presence in Europe. Our allies fear a precipitous U.S. withdrawal; the Soviet Union's allies mostly fear a perpetual Soviet presence. Our troops have no internal role; Soviet troops have played an occupation role. Our troops do not threaten invasion; their troops have been poised for such. American officials could seek to assure the Soviets that we would not exploit their departure. After Soviet troops ended their occupation of Austria in 1955, the United States did not exploit that departure. Besides, America's aims in Europe have been for freedom and, secondarily, for stability. Gorbachev's aims in Europe seem to be approaching these.

The overarching point is that events within the onetime Soviet Bloc, especially in Eastern Europe, are dynamic. The terms of an arms control agreement by nature are (and must be) static. It seems peculiar for U.S. arms control policy at the Vienna talks to aim at the legitimization of some 195,000 Soviet troops in countries that increasingly do not want *any* troops at all—especially when even the Soviets themselves may not want such a large troop presence, or *any* such presence.

Our stance in the Vienna talks illustrates the point that U.S. arms proposals sometimes lack a convincing geostrategic rationale. Thirty years ago, U.S. national strategy was looking for a place for arms control. Now it appears that arms control seeks a place for U.S. national strategy.

Regarding the broad array of other negotiations—on strategic arms (START), the complete elimination of chemical weapons, and nuclear testing—prospects may unfortunately look brighter than they actually are. As detailed in other writings,[*] severe problems of verification and of stability arise.

It is not at all clear, for example, how we could count with any degree of accuracy the number of cruise missiles or mobile missiles roaming around the Soviet Union, which is eleven time zones wide. After all, U.S. intelligence did not spot the Krasnoyarsk radar, which Foreign Minister Shevardnadze publicly said is "equal in size to the Egyptian pyramids," for three or four years after the radar's construction began. This was a big oversight, as that radar complex is as large as several football fields and has one structure twenty-seven stories tall. Neither mobile, remote, nor hidden, it is located on the only railroad line within a huge distance and adjacent to a sizable Soviet missile field.

---

[*] Kenneth L. Adelman, *The Great Universal Embrace* (New York: Simon & Schuster, 1989).

Problems of strategic stability are just as baffling. The START proposal the Reagan administration offered late in office, which has been largely unchanged, would now have a questionable outcome *even if* the Soviets did nothing to change it. In fact, President Bush's National Security Advisor Brent Scowcroft, the president's current ambassador to the Vienna arms talks James Woolsey, and defense expert John Deutch wrote—before two of them entered government, to be sure—that this START accord could push the United States into "a new kind of triad: vulnerability, wishful thinking, and a hair trigger." Not reassuring words, but surely a competent assessment by competent authorities.

Finally comes the problem of complexity and wasted time. The clarion call for arms control often causes top officials to lunge for the capillaries instead of for the jugular of the issue and to hold endless meetings on submarine-launched cruise missile verification, perimeter monitoring, and a host of other such technical minutiae that have mesmerized those in the field for ages. It can wantonly waste top-level time of the president, of the secretaries of state and defense, and of all their key advisors to focus on issues that may not much affect the great overriding issues of war and peace.

So where to go from here? Certainly not toward a wholesale blast against arms control per se or against all conceivable agreements. A prudent and effective approach would take the field "back to basics," toward the tried and true method of arms control without formal agreements. This tack will likely work, if attempted. In today's singular environment, it may well prevail even if not explicitly attempted.

Rather than going for an agreement without real arms control—that is, without really reducing nuclear weapons or the risks of war—the United States should seek real arms control without agreements. This can be done by adopting an approach of designing flexible policies parallel to those of the Soviets. Each side would build the forces that it believes are most sensible, stable, affordable, and likely to survive attack—instead of the forces easiest for the other side to verify or the forces best to use as bargaining chips in arms talks.

Gone would be the formal, quasipublic discussions in Geneva that are too often bogged down in a sea of strategic arcania. Back would be a focus on the big picture of greater security on each side, with fewer nuclear and conventional weapons, but those that remain configured for their stability (their inappropriateness for first-strike use).

This back-to-basics approach is no new idea. It was advocated in the 1930s by Winston Churchill after he found the disarmament efforts of the 1920s conceptually bankrupt and ultimately harmful. "The elaborate process of measuring swords around the table at Geneva . . . stirs all the suspicions and anxieties of the various powers," he wrote then. Worse still, it whets participants' appetite for weapons and stirs fears "which, but for this prolonged process, perhaps would not have crossed their minds."

So rather than perpetuating this elaborate ritual, Churchill recommended "private interchanges" of the kind he suggested in March 1933: "'If you will not do this, we shall not have to do that,'" and "'If your program did not start so early, ours would begin even later.'" This less procedural, less formal way would work better, Churchill contended. "A greater advance and progress toward a diminution of expenditure on armaments might have been achieved by these methods than by the conferences and schemes of disarmament that have been put forward at Geneva."

This approach would help keep us from getting lost among the trees and would help us focus instead on the whole forest. It would also do away with the present pactomania, which leads the public to hope, or even to expect, that parchment can bring peace. As Lord Salisbury wrote in 1891, "I am quite sure we exaggerate too much the importance and the effect of treaties."

And this approach would wipe out all the peripheral adornments of arms control today: the daily temperature taking of the talks, the back-and-forth accusations over who is stonewalling, the endless volleying of the phrase "the ball's in their court" after each teeny move by either side, and the *People* magazine tidbits of who's up and who's down and who's in and who's out of the unending arms control battles in Washington. And with less formality, parallel or reciprocal U.S.–Soviet actions could be more easily modified if conditions change.

Arms control without agreements has worked in the past. For contrary to the press barrage about an "unending nuclear arms race," the United States has markedly reduced its arsenal already, quite apart from any arms accord. We have cut the total number of our nuclear weapons by 25 percent since 1967 and the total equivalent megatonnage or blast potential by a whopping 75 percent since that time.

Moreover, the United States has removed some twenty-four hundred nuclear weapons from Europe, even before the Reagan–Gorbachev INF Treaty takes full effect. The current NATO military commander, General William M. Galvin, had said that the United States could safely remove another thousand nuclear weapons from Europe even before the Wall came down. Now even more could safely be removed.

In a nutshell, real arms reductions are happening on both the American and the Soviet sides. Future reduction will probably not result so much from bilateral negotiations in Geneva or Vienna as from domestic financial deliberations in Washington and Moscow; budget cutters will do what arms controllers have largely failed to do.

Arms control without agreements would work even better were there active diplomatic discourse with the Soviets on the big military picture rather than on the details usually discussed in the formal arms talks. Gorbachev himself may have had this in mind when telling an American group in 1988, "When we speak about defense sufficiency of the armed forces, one should keep in mind that this notion is a changing one. Its contents will depend on how the West conducts itself." Gorbachev then all but proposed the following reciprocal arrangement: "Our *perestroika* will come to pass, but we expect *perestroika* from your side as well."

As Gorbachev's defense *perestroika* unfolds—and it has come haltingly so far—we can lower our arsenal accordingly. But such cuts on our side are not in doubt. What *is* in doubt is whether the United States can avoid a Pentagon plunge—cuts that are made regardless of the size and nature of Soviet cuts (and those of other likely adversaries) and regardless of America's national security objectives. That is our fear.

— THREE —

THE REVOLUTION IN WARFARE:
Brave New World

A third revolution affecting national security has been quietly taking place alongside the social and economic upheavals that are presently restructuring the post–World War II power balances among nations. This third revolution comes in the field of military technology—a change that has occurred with less fanfare than the recent political events of Eastern Europe and the Soviet Union but that, like those events, will also have a profound impact on America's long-term ability to meet its national security objectives and remain economically competitive.

Often it has been said that the war that nations prepare themselves to fight is the previous one. The danger that this maxim might fit America today is heightened by the dizzying pace of change now occurring in military-related technology. The pace is illustrated by the fact that the famous first flight of the Wright brothers could take place *inside* the large orange fuel tank that is today used to propel the space shuttle into orbit (Figure 4), or by the fact that not even five decades passed from when Robert Goddard flew his first liquid rocket in a Massachusetts cabbage patch until Neil Armstrong and Buzz Aldrin walked on the moon while Mike Collins circled above them.

In the case of modern electronics—based on the tiny semiconductor integrated circuits ("semiconductors," for short) that now permit more than four million electronic components to be placed on a chip the size of a fingernail—an entire generation of products becomes obsolete

Figure 4. Approximate flight path of Wright Brothers' famous flight overlaid on the fuel tank carried aloft by the space shuttle.

roughly every two and a half years. A nation that lags in semiconductor technology by a mere five years is thus two generations out of date.

Today a personal computer can perform in the time of a human heartbeat computations that would have taken the World War II ENIAC computer 192 years, even with its 18,000 vacuum tubes that filled a large room. Professor Martin Chubik of Yale University has incisively observed that computer and communications networks will be to the twenty-first century what administration and roads were to Rome. By the end of this century we will almost certainly be able to store the entire *Encyclopaedia Britannica* on a single computer chip. Even today we can easily fit the dictionary on a chip. (For those perhaps overawed by these and other scientific accomplishments of humanity, it is helpful to recall that all the chips ever manufactured have a combined storage capacity less than that of one hundred average human brains.)

The purpose of this chapter is to offer a glimpse of the technological revolution in warfare that has taken place over the past twenty-five years. Upon this revolution America's ability to meet its security objectives has been, and continues to be, extremely dependent. This revolution has permitted American military forces to compensate for substantial numerical shortcomings in manpower and matériel compared with the forces of the Soviet Union. The United States Army, for example, is only the seventh-largest army in the world in terms of manpower. The ground forces of Iraq are larger than the U.S. Army and Marines combined. Superior technology has been, in other words, our advantage—a true force multiplier.

As we look to the type of battles that American forces may be called upon to fight in the future, new and sometimes even tougher demands are being placed upon technology—and perhaps ironically so. For in some respects this technological revolution that we are and have been undergoing threatens to make us relatively *less* powerful against some of those with whom we are actually *most* likely to have to do battle— certain Third World governments and terrorists, characters like Iraq's Saddam Hussein. The fact that nuclear weapons, an American technological invention, are now in the hands of a number of nations around the world almost certainly produces a destabilizing effect and unquestionably constrains some of the freedom of action America has enjoyed in the past. These weapons could in some respects be even *more* effective as political tools in the hands of irresponsible governments—governments that would more conceivably *use* them—than in the hands of the larger, more predictable, more responsible nations. And this peculiar impact of technology has not been limited to the nuclear sphere.

What is this revolution in technology? One can perhaps best understand it in terms of the effect it has already had on warfare. Throughout history, technological innovation has from time to time made possible very decisive outcomes in battle and has even changed the course of history itself. The stirrup, for example, simple by today's technology standards, was actually an enormous breakthrough. For the first time, a knight on horseback could plant his feet and thereby control a lance with great precision, an advantage that proved decisive for the English in the Battle of Crecy in 1346. In another age, the invention of the machine gun introduced dramatic changes in warfare. In the battle of the Somme during World War I, the British, using outdated infantry tactics, advanced battalion after battalion against entrenched German machine guns and promptly lost some ten thousand of their finest troops.

The machine gun produced a stalemate among large, well-entrenched forces—until another new technological development came along, namely, the invention of the tank, which could overwhelm fixed positions. Thus the concept of the viability of heavily fortified positions, the Maginot Line principle, came to a sudden demise in World War II with the advent of the *blitzkrieg*. Modern, highly mobile tank armies were able to advance an average of 30 kilometers a day for prolonged periods during major assault operations. Similarly, the airplane was to become a substantial threat to surface ships, as was so convincingly demonstrated at Pearl Harbor and in subsequent battles throughout the Pacific. And as significant as were such innovations as the widespread use of armored forces, tactical airpower, guided missiles, and radar, the most consequential technological development of World War II was, of

course, the atomic bomb, which ultimately brought an end to that terrible conflict.

The period since World War II has continued to see revolutionary developments in the field of military technology, including nuclear weapons, ballistic missiles, nuclear-powered submarines, digital computers, lasers, spacecraft, phased-array radars, infrared detectors, jet engines, precision-guided missiles, robotics, artificial intelligence, and stealth technology—to name only a few. But despite the visibility and impact of these enormous individual breakthroughs, much of the technological revolution has actually taken place behind the scenes, through the combination of far lesser advancements.

A number of years ago, the Pentagon conducted a study called "Project Hindsight," which sought to determine retrospectively what had been the major matériel developments of the previous decade and the environments that had nurtured those developments. A principal conclusion was that most of the new systems' capabilities that had been realized came not from a single quantum technological breakthrough but rather from a large number, sometimes dozens, of more modest advancements in a variety of technologies—advancements that, when insightfully coupled together, synergistically generated major new capabilities.

Modern Nonnuclear Warfare

Twentieth century technology has altered even the very nature of warfare. In centuries past, combat was seasonal: armies fought in the summer when weather permitted movement and then bivouacked in the winter—Valley Forge being a prominent American example of the bivouac phase. With the advent of machines for transportation, combat extended throughout the entire year but by and large still ceased at night, when armies would face each other in relative stillness and seek a desperately needed rest.

Now, with technological breakthroughs in photoelectric and infrared technologies producing devices that permit modern armies to see in darkness with a clarity approaching that available in daylight, even the night has been taken away as a place to hide and rest. Imaging radars offer the capability to see through fog and clouds. Combat in the future will thus continue around the clock, limited only by the endurance of the humans involved. Indeed, if one army has an advantage over the other in its ability to see and fight at night, night then becomes the preferred time for combat.

This was in fact the case in the Panamanian invasion of December 1989, during which U.S. forces elected to assault wrapped in darkness—a darkness through which our pilots could see but the adversary could not. The basic structure of warfare has thus shifted from the kind of interaction conceptually embodied in football, where there are set-piece engagements between which combatants regroup and draw plans, to a type of competition that more nearly resembles a deadly soccer match, where the flow of battle continues virtually nonstop—in the case of today's warfare, day and night, winter and summer, rain or shine.

Looking back in time, the most striking thing about conventional (nonnuclear) warfare is just how ineffective most weapon systems have been. Throughout history, the underlying expectation when a weapon was launched was that it would not hit its target. This expectation of missing the mark has been a given from the first rock thrown by a caveman through the initial development of the modern missile (perhaps even explaining the derivation of the word "miss-ile," the pronunciation still preferred by the British). In Germany at Peenemünde during World War II, it was said by the scientists developing the V-2 rocket that their immediate goal was to make it more dangerous to be at the point of predicted impact than at the point of launch.

From the American Civil War through the conflict in Vietnam, the number of rounds of rifle fire required to produce a single enemy casualty varied from ten thousand to one hundred thousand. Similarly, it has typically taken 5 tons of air munitions or 3 tons of artillery to destroy a single tactical target (using an extremely generous definition of "target"—a truck, a tank, a bunker, and so forth). In Vietnam, the point was reached that U.S. forces were delivering the equivalent of seven Hiroshima bombs a month in terms of explosive blast—but this enormous firepower was by and large landing in a widely distributed manner over open countryside.

In the case of the strategic bombing of London, the often-wide-of-mark attacks on urban targets only served to make the British more resolute. Even during the strategic bombing of Germany, which reached its peak with the delivery of some 80,000 tons of explosives a month, each 1 percent of a city destroyed reduced output by only 2.3 city-days of production. Most industrial complexes have a great deal of capacitance, or resilience, giving them residual flexibility to restore themselves unless entirely devastated or cut off from needed supplies. It was only when Allied ground force actually rolled over the factories of Rheinland that production there finally collapsed. To be effective, strategic bombing has to address specific choke points in the supply system: ball bearings, for example, or petroleum facilities. Furthermore, it must attack time-urgent supplies. *If* one can pinpoint and destroy all the resupply trains or their tracks and switches immediately behind the front when an active battle is under way, such bombing can have a major impact. Before the 1970s and 1980s, however, even that was a big *if*.

The 1970s and 1980s saw this state of affairs begin to change rather dramatically. Two truly revolutionary, albeit in retrospect seemingly simple, tasks were about to be accomplished for the first time in the history of warfare—namely, effectively *finding* most targets and then *hitting* them. These were profound developments indeed.

With respect to finding targets, modern surveillance system capabilities imply that most major military assets, particularly those that move or that unjudiciously radiate electromagnetic energy, can be monitored and located by an opponent virtually all the time. A tank formation won't be able to hide regardless of the weather, day or night. Large capital surface ships will be relatively easy to monitor and locate. Most tactical aircraft operating in combat zones will, at least in the initial phases of a war, rarely be out of the coverage envelope of at least one air defense system. A single surveillance platform even today can monitor two million cubic miles of airspace against most airborne targets. Fixed targets of high value will be particularly threatened. Air bases, for example, offer the attention-attracting formula of large amounts of valuable assets in a package that is difficult to hide. The same is true of carrier battle groups.

Once potential targets have been located, as now is much more likely to be the case, the probability that they can actually be hit has similarly increased. We then have a situation that has never before existed in the history of warfare. In the past, the ability to hit a known target depended to a large degree upon precisely launching a weapon that would, after launch, be at the mercy of the law of gravity—as in the case of rocks, bombs, bullets, and artillery shells (Figure 5).

But through technological breakthroughs in advanced sensors and control systems—including optics, infrared, and radar—so-called smart weapons were created. These weapons were able to correct errors discovered *during* the actual flight of an explosive device and then "home" the projectile on the target. The kamikaze aircraft of World War II was a primitive and desperate attempt to accomplish this objective, tragically substituting human lives for technology. Today, even bullets can be guided, as in the case of some artillery shells that contain gyroscopes, optics, and tiny computers that amazingly survive forces equal to some ten thousand times the force of gravity during launch and then guide the projectile to hit the target. As the target maneuvers in an attempt to escape, the projectile continues to home on its deadly course.

One of the earliest uses of such weapons by U.S. military forces provides a glimpse of the potential effectiveness of smart weapons. During the conflict in Southeast Asia, the Thanh Hoa bridge in North Vietnam became the target of repeated U.S. air attacks (Figure 6). A total of 873 missions (sorties) dropping 2,000 tons of conventional bombs with a loss of eleven aircraft and aircrews to enemy air defenses failed to destroy a single span of the bridge. Upon the introduction of laser-guided bombs—bombs that home on a spot illuminated by a pilot with a laser, much as one would point a flashlight—the bridge was dropped in just

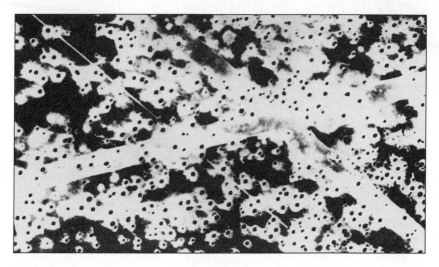

Figure 5. Runway covered with bomb craters—the old-fashioned way to close an airbase. A few of today's precision-delivered munitions can have the same net effect.

one attack involving eight aircraft, without the loss of a single aircraft or crew member.

But these first "smart" weapons were actually not really particularly smart, at least by today's standards; in human terms they probably had an IQ of about 20. In retrospect, "smart" was really a misnomer. Although the new weapons were inarguably much more capable than the original tactical guided missiles—which had depended upon an exposed operator who would remotely "fly" the weapon into the intended target, much as one would fly a radio-controlled aircraft—the new so-called smart weapons still required that the operator locate the target and thereafter continue to remind the forgetful weapon (several times a second, in fact) where the target was. The weapon's memory was so short that it had to be told repeatedly, "That is where the tank is . . . that is where the tank is. . . . " This of course made for a very vulnerable and exposed pilot, forward observer, or other operator.

The objective of the technologists thus logically became one of developing "brilliant" weapons (a phrase first coined by one of us in 1977). A brilliant weapon didn't have to be reminded where the target was. It didn't even have to have the target pointed out to it in the first place—it could find its own target. All the operator had to do was launch the weapon in the general direction of the enemy. The brilliant weapon would then depend upon its own sensor and computer to tell

Figure 6. The Thanh Hoa bridge in North Vietnam, dropped after a single strike by laser-guided bombs after repeated attacks with conventional, unguided ordnance had failed to produce significant damage.

it, "I see a tank, a tree, a bridge, and a command center." The priority list the weapon had been given told it that the command center was most important at this particular juncture in the battle. The weapon would then home on and destroy the command center, hitting within a few inches of where it was told to hit (Figure 7). In fact, it has even become possible using such weapons to prescribe whether, say, a tank should be hit on the top of the turret, on the track, on the turret ring, or on some other particularly vulnerable spot.

A peek at the future of military conflict of this sort may have been offered in the Middle East War of October 1973, during which the combat was so intense that the forces involved (from all three nations) lost about one-third of their aircraft, artillery, and tanks in just eighteen days (Figure 8).

Although not yet achieved, the trend in military technology seems clear: new global networks of sensors keeping track in real time of most targets (a few words on stealth later), and long-range, non-nuclear, very accurate weapon delivery systems embedded in that network—all tied together with digital computers. This will likely continue the trend of decreasing density of troops on the battlefield as more advanced weapons are introduced (Figure 9). Greater firepower has led to a decrease in the number of forces required to hold a given piece of land—as well as an increase in the hazard of concentrating

Figure 7. Precision-guided weaponry has introduced a new level of effective-ness on many battlefields. Shown here is a Copperhead guided projectile, fired from a cannon miles away, hitting a tank target.

Figure 8   **Equipment Losses in 1973 Middle East War (percentage of total forces)**

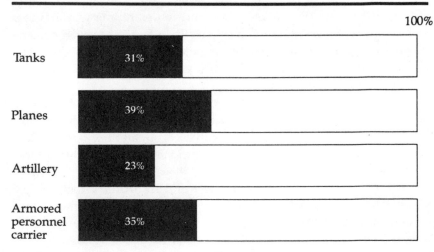

SOURCE: Aker, *Israel and the Arabs: The October 1973 War.*

NOTE: The three combatants lost major portions of their inventories in just eighteen days.

Figure 9   **Manpower Density on the Battlefield**

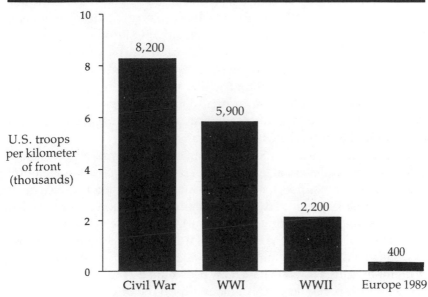

U.S. troops per kilometer of front (thousands)

- Civil War: 8,200
- WWI: 5,900
- WWII: 2,200
- Europe 1989: 400

SOURCE: Mitre Corporation.

forces. The latter is due to the coupling of nuclear and conventional warfare: the *threat* of nuclear reprisal deters the concentration of conventional forces for an assault.

In many respects, the technology of the 1970s and 1980s, which offered for the first time a reasonably high probability of finding and hitting targets, has not been particularly kind to the major world powers that created that technology. Indeed, the technology that was produced to protect us may ironically come to assault us in certain environments.

Throughout this century, conventional military confrontations have been dominated by a few capital items—namely, ships, tanks, and aircraft—that only wealthy nations could afford in significant numbers. But with the advent of this new technology, each of these capital items could be threatened by systems readily available to much less wealthy countries. Because they were relatively small and cheap, antiship, antitank, and antiaircraft missiles became available to almost all nations, either through legitimate arms sources or through clandestine avenues; the U.S. Navy was, for example, only the thirteenth navy in the world to acquire antiship missiles.

The advent of antiship missiles meant that surface ships could under certain conditions be threatened by a relatively weak enemy; the

Argentine Exocet missile attack against the British cruiser HMS *Sheffield* during the Falklands War, in which one missile killed thirty crewmen and seriously damaged the ship, illustrated the new potential vulnerability. The lightweight man-portable antitank missile, in turn, made the individual infantryman a considerable threat to the powerful tank. And the shoulder-fired antiaircraft missile substantially redressed the imbalance between the individual foot soldier and any close air support aircraft or attack helicopter that threatened him; for further proof, ask any Soviet pilot who served in Afghanistan after the *mujaheddin* received Stinger missiles from the United States.

We must, of course, remember that in combat only rarely do one-on-one set-piece battles occur, say, between tanks and antitank missiles (in the absence of air support, artillery, infantry, and the like), so that great caution must be exercised in generalizing conclusions. This is what makes the analysis of conventional warfare so difficult. Still, it seems clear that the balance of power between large capital items and those systems that would threaten them has in fact shifted—substantially.

These "anti" weapons have now been built by the thousands in the case of antiship missiles, tens of thousands in the case of shoulder-fired antiaircraft missiles, and hundreds of thousands in the case of antitank missiles. All represent major threats under many circumstances—with the latter two classes of weapons being readily carried by a single individual, thereby making them suitable weapons even for terrorists.

The hazard is enormous that shoulder-fired antiaircraft missiles— which have over the years been provided to various guerrilla forces around the world by nations on both sides of the iron curtain—could be used to interfere with aircraft commerce. Guerrillas a mile from an airport could periodically pick off commercial airliners with relative ease. Countermeasures are possible but would not be perfect. The impact on world commerce would be disconcerting, if not devastating.

On the other hand, in battles in the open desert against large forces armed with more conventional systems (tanks, artillery), the U.S. advantage in target detection (particularly at night) and in precision firepower would be overwhelming.

Modern Nuclear Deterrence

Warfare can be viewed as a spectrum extending from all-out strategic nuclear exchanges at one end to terrorism at the other. When warfare is viewed in this way, numerous ironies emerge. We are well equipped to deter the largest and most formidable and sophisticated types of con-

Figure 10   **Spectrum of Armed Conflict**

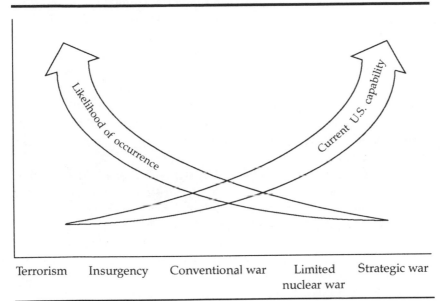

| Terrorism | Insurgency | Conventional war | Limited nuclear war | Strategic war |

flict but close to powerless to deter the most simplistic types embodied in terrorist operations. And for this very reason, it is the most simplistic types of warfare that our forces are by far most likely to confront. Correspondingly, we are least likely to be called upon to contend with the most sophisticated type of warfare, a nuclear battle, which is the kind we are best able to conduct (Figure 10).

In the intermediate portion of the spectrum are limited nuclear warfare (some would consider the term to be a *non sequitur*), all-out conventional warfare, so-called police actions, and guerrilla operations. America of course has extremely powerful nuclear forces. Our conventional forces using new technology are becoming increasingly formidable against large armies, but a single terrorist with a pipe bomb seems yet beyond the grasp of military technology. Such terrorists generally cannot impose their control over a society, but they can effectively deny that control to others—witness the situation in Lebanon.

And even though the U.S. *strategic* deterrent has obviously worked well in preventing all-out nuclear exchanges and perhaps even in discouraging the higher level of conventional conflict, it nevertheless has been only a modest deterrent on the type of guerrilla military conflict that has in fact plagued us throughout the nuclear age. With respect to our strategic deterrent, it is difficult to prove or quantify a negative—whether, for example, our robust strategic arsenal dissuaded the Soviets from being more adventurous in the Middle East in 1973 or elsewhere in other years—but certainly the strategic deterrent has contributed something to creating one of the longest periods of peace in Europe in recorded history. It unarguably affected the outcome of the Cuban missile crisis.

In short, we have an effective strategic deterrent, a moderately effective conventional deterrent, a very modest deterrent to guerrilla warfare, and an ineffective deterrent to terrorism. We can, to a considerable degree, intimidate nations such as the Soviet Union, but we find it difficult to confound nations such as North Vietnam, Iraq, and Iran and almost impossible to deter drug runners in Colombia—or, for that matter, in the District of Columbia.

Our strategic deterrent is based largely—whether we like it or not, and no matter how elegantly we package it—on mutual assured destruction. This concept of course must recognize the truism that deterrence resides in the eyes of the beholder. It is relatively unimportant what *we* think our own strategic force's capability is; what matters far more is what *our adversary* thinks. The effectiveness of this deterrent depends upon our having a rational enemy, one unwilling to precipitate enormous destruction upon itself. It also depends upon an adversary's perception of our national will to act.

As more nations acquire nuclear weapons, and especially more irresponsible nations, the assumption that the enemy is rational will be increasingly open to doubt. Such nations will not pose a traditional military threat; none could hope to defeat the United States or Soviet Union in combat. They may, however, be able to use their relatively limited stockpile of weapons to grab vital natural resources, as Iraq did in its conquest of Kuwait, or for purposes of political extortion—and, as has been noted, ironically may be able to do so with greater success than might be the case for the Soviet Union or other major power, which would be considered to be more rational. A weapon in a suitcase, in the hold of a ship, or on a passenger aircraft could in this regard be as effective as an ICBM—perhaps even more so, since the controlling party may be resentful, reckless, irrational, even suicidal.

This threat becomes even more disconcerting when one considers the technological advances that certain Third World countries have achieved with ballistic missiles and chemical weapons, and the possibility of further nuclear proliferation. Chemical weapons, the poor man's weapon of mass destruction, may yet make some people long for aspects of "the good ol'" cold war days. Unfortunately, recent combat in the Middle East between Iran and Iraq has breached much of whatever societal restraints had remained to the use of chemical weapons. And if this were not enough, at least ten nations are said to be working to produce biological weapons that, according to the head of the CIA, may "provide the broadest area coverage per pound of payload of *any* weapon system." Senator John Glenn says that a tiny bottle of biological agents could annihilate everyone in the Washington, D.C., area.

In 1963, President Kennedy warned that by 1975 there would be fifteen to twenty nuclear-armed nations. That world, fortunately, still hasn't materialized. But as more nuclear weapons do in fact come into the world, some into the hands of irresponsible nations or groups, a new set of problems is posed, not the least of which concerns the continued viability of the deterrence concept that has been largely responsible for the peace of the past forty years. Major powers in the nuclear age have gone to extraordinary lengths to avoid direct military confrontation— often making combat on the borders of such nations highly constrained as well. The concept of strategic deterrence, as the world has come to know it, has sometimes been likened to the situation faced by two (rational) adversaries locked in a small room, each holding a hand grenade.

And as important and valuable as the strategic deterrent has been, one of its by-products has seemingly been to make the world safe for low-scale conventional war. It is for this reason that the United States absolutely must continue to maintain conventional forces of a capability at least matching that of the conventional forces of any potential opponent. Any disparity in this measure simply becomes a statement of the risk the nation is, presumably, willing to accept.

In this regard, a principal lesson learned from history is that military forces must be tailored to counter the *capabilities* of potential adversaries and not merely the stated *intentions* of the current leadership of those nations. Thus, as Soviet forces withdraw from the territory of the other Warsaw Pact nations and, it is hoped, decline in absolute numbers *and* capability, it will still be necessary that the West maintain counterbalancing forces throughout the drawdown period. To do less would only increase risk and the likelihood of conflict in the unstable and strikingly unpredictable international political climate existing today. Further, there are numerous other nations possessing significant conventional military capabilities—particularly the countries of the Middle East and North Africa. Libya has nearly 2,000 main battle tanks, Syria over 4,000, Iraq over 5,000. In fact, Iraq has more tanks today than both sides combined in the North African campaign of World War II. The need for continued counterbalance on our part applies to conventional as well as nuclear weapons.

History also teaches, especially in recent years, that threats to the nation and the consequential need to deploy forces, comes from unexpected quarters. Who could have imagined that in the first twenty months of his presidency, George Bush would be deploying and using our troops in Panama, the Philippines, Saudi Arabia, and Liberia. At the time of his inauguration, few if any of these countries were on anyone's list of probable areas of U.S. military combat.

In recent years, somewhat less than 15 percent of the U.S. defense budget (although a far larger portion of the acquisition budget) has been devoted to strategic forces—a smaller percentage than most U.S. citizens would estimate. An objective for future force planners should be to increase the stability of the strategic nuclear deterrent while further drawing down its size and cost. A truly stable deterrent is one wherein the side that initiates conflict understands that it will emerge in a relatively less advantageous situation than before the exchange began. The whole concept of stability, continuing our metaphor, is to avoid locking ourselves into a small room where each adversary has a pistol—that is, where each has a strong motivation to be the first to shoot.

So how will our strategic systems shape up in the next decade? Clearly, the *bomber* portion of the nuclear triad (land-based missiles, bombers, and submarine-launched missiles) continues to encounter some difficulty. The principal burden is still carried by B-52s, which, it is widely known, are substantially older than the pilots that fly them—a tenuous state of affairs, even though these aircraft have undergone impressive upgrading both in armament and avionics. In recent years, the United States has had an inordinately difficult time settling upon a strategy for its strategic nuclear deterrent. A great deal of money was spent to develop the soon-canceled B-70 bomber. The B-1 was then developed, and it, too, was canceled—only to be resurrected as the B-1B, of which we bought only a relatively modest number (about a hundred), which themselves are said to have shortcomings in their avionics. The B-2 Stealth bomber, a very capable aircraft, is not yet fully developed; whether the nation will be able to afford a sufficient number is increasingly questionable. The arguments which have been raging clearly reflect the impact of "sticker shock" in an era of declining defense budgets. The B-2 now appears to be suffering the Chinese water-drop torture: to reduce total cost the quantity of aircraft to be purchased is reduced, which in turn increases the cost of each airplane, which in turn. . . . The B-2 may have been saved from total extinction by Saddam Hussein's vote—but the odds of purchasing a large quantity are long indeed.

Addressing the *land-based* ICBM force, the nation's record of strategic planning and forecasting generally makes astrology look good by comparison. During the greater part of the past two decades, these weapons have been mired in politics. One could say that American indecision has been the best counter to the U.S. strategic deterrent the Soviets could possibly have hoped to find—sort of a lend-lease Strategic Defense Initiative for their side. Substantial funds were spent in the United States to develop the MX/Peacekeeper missile, principally to overcome problems with the vulnerability of the earlier generation of fixed Minuteman silos to a first strike by Soviet missiles. The solution was to develop a bigger, more capable, more valuable missile—and put it in those very same silos. It seemed to be a reasonable political solution to some at the time, but it made scant strategic sense once the package of which it was a part, including a mobile companion missile and arms control agreements, became enmeshed in inaction. On the other hand, paired with appropriate arms control agreements or *de facto* changes in the threat, it could yet prove logical.

After the examination of some forty alternative deployment concepts, the "snicker factor" arose, with the defense planners and politicians involved giving the impression that what was needed was not so much a system that was MIRV-proof as one that was pork-proof. The focus then turned to the deployment of a limited number of multiple-warhead Peacekeeper missiles on rail cars to provide mobility, as well as completing development of the mobile Small ICBM. Such mobile missiles are attractive in that their survivability (the ability to withstand or escape attack) increases stability—as does the fact that some carry but a single warhead. This same mobility, however, complicates the problem of monitoring arms control agreements, and it proves extremely costly, too. At the moment, both Peacekeeper and SICBM are in limbo—a state of strategic malaise—victims of paralysis through analysis.

Meanwhile, the same uncompromising sense of purpose that so alienated the old Soviet government from its citizens and that contributed to the downfall of its political system was in contrast very effective in developing a modern strategic nuclear force for the Soviet Union. During the period of U.S. indecision, the Soviets developed and deployed many new strategic systems, including the SS-16, SS-24, SS-25, SS-N-17, SS-N-20, SS-N-21, SS-N-23, and the Blackjack manned bomber.

The *submarine-launched* portion of our strategic triad continues to be viable and, although always vulnerable to a major breakthrough in antisubmarine warfare, can be projected to be a mainstay of the U.S. strategic deterrent into the next century, carrying 75 percent of our strategic nuclear payload. It possesses the enormous added political value of being out of sight. The principal concern is that the number of ballistic missile submarines constituting the entire force is relatively small (a few dozen), and that only a part of those are fully operational at any given time.

Thus, the nation is placing a lot of eggs in very few baskets. Moreover, these systems face a growing number of Soviet attack submarines and other capabilities that threaten our submarine-based nuclear missiles.

The strategic deterrent, as we have seen, is coupled to the conventional deterrent, such as the latter may be. The concern over the years in Europe has been that in a conventional war being won by larger Soviet military forces, the West could be left with but two unsatisfactory choices: either lose the rest of our deployed forces and Western Europe or escalate to nuclear weapons. Because it was very questionable whether we would actually use *U.S.–based* strategic weapons in such a case—an action that would almost assuredly escalate into a full nuclear war—forward-based nuclear forces of more limited capability were placed in Europe. The underlying question, of course, is their real deterrent impact—which depends in part on the ability to use tactical nuclear weapons without further escalating into a strategic exchange that presumably no one could win. This is a much-debated question, the answer to which presumably no one really knows—thus ironically affording part of their deterrent value.

One of the major challenges in formulating a military strategy has resulted from the large gap in effectiveness between nuclear weapons, on the one extreme, and traditional conventional weaponry, on the other. The advent of "brilliant" nonnuclear weapons will take one more step toward closing this huge gap and should help strengthen the deterrent to large-scale conventional warfare.

The bottom line is that our offensive strategic deterrent, with technologically available improvements and, it is hoped, a lesser ration of politics, can be made to be effective well into the next century. Assuming, that is, that we have a rational opponent—and there is a danger we may be running out of these.

As has been noted, the technological revolution has introduced the likelihood that a number of countries—perhaps fifteen or more by the end of this decade—may have ballistic missiles capable of carrying chemical or biological or eventually even nuclear weapons. In early 1990 CIA director William Webster told a congressional hearing that by the year 2000 at least six Third World countries would probably have missiles with ranges up to 5,500 kilometers. This circumstance makes some sort of defense against missiles more imperative. The United States and the Soviet Union, among other nations, may ultimately share a strong *common* interest in the creation of such a capability.

In April 1990, Mu'ammar Qaddafi, speaking to fellow Libyans, remarked, "Did not the Americans almost hit you yesterday when you were asleep in your homes? If they know you have a deterrent force capable of hitting the United States they would not be able to hit you. Because if we had possessed a deterrent: missiles that could reach New York, we would have hit it in the same moment. Consequently we should build this force." In Nikita Khruschev's recent memoirs he asserts that Fidel Castro wanted to use Soviet nuclear missiles in a "preemptive strike against the U.S." during the Cuban Missile Crisis.

America's nuclear defense has in recent years depended almost entirely on maintaining a strong offense. Unlike the Soviet Union—which has expended enormous sums to maintain strong air and civil defenses, a modest ballistic missile defense, and a limited antisatellite capability—America has maintained very little strategic air defense, no civil defense, no ballistic missile defense, and no antisatellite capability.

The Strategic Defense Initiative seeks to make a major departure from this posture, but our record of decisiveness in the sphere of strategic defense has been even worse, if that's conceivable, than our record of decisiveness in strategic offense. Several decades of abortive attempts to deploy such defense systems as Nike Zeus, Nike X, Sentinel, Safeguard, and now the SDI have yet to produce any lasting capability. It is noteworthy, however, that the deployment of a limited ballistic missile defense system in North Dakota was almost certainly the principal factor that led the Soviets to agree during the early 1970s to one of the first nuclear arms control accords. Further, it is significant that the skepticism and derision with which SDI –"Star Wars" to its critics—was greeted in America contrasted sharply with the profoundly serious reaction it evoked in the Kremlin.

Many Americans even today are unaware that the nation has no defense against ballistic missiles. During the Cuban crisis, later in the midst of the huge public debate over the Safeguard defense system, and more recently during the SDI controversy, a variety of public opinion surveys found that a majority of America's citizenry believed we *already had or have* an adequate defense against ballistic missiles.

In the case of antisatellite systems, each time the United States set out to test such a nonnuclear device, concern was raised that to do so would be destabilizing and would propel warfare into space. We somehow overlooked the fact that, beginning more than twenty years ago, the Soviets had been testing their own antisatellite system, with some success—and not worrying about the niceties of appearance. The tests were discontinued some years ago.

The problem with strategic defense is, first, that technically it is very difficult, and second, it is very costly. At the present time it is not practicable to defend the entire country with a high degree of certainty against a major attack. Selected "islands" within the country can surely be defended against many threats, but this solution is not very satisfactory to the people who don't live within those islands. The arithmetic of strategic warfare thus far tends to be on the side of the offense, though the flow of technology may change this equation.

Interestingly, this is exactly the opposite of the case of conventional (nonnuclear) warfare—in which, as we have seen, huge amounts of firepower have traditionally been required to produce significant effects, and the advantage does not necessarily go to the first to attack. In fact, the rule of thumb is that a *well-prepared* defending (conventional) force can stalemate an attacker three times its size. Pursuing a previous analogy, conventional warfare has been more like two adversaries locked in a small room, each armed with thousands of pins.

In the case of strategic nuclear warfare, on the other hand, a very few offensive weapons can indeed produce very decisive results. Even if a defense is 99 percent effective, if five thousand nuclear weapons rain down upon it, the fifty penetrations that will occur can still produce major devastation. One solution is to have several *independent* layers of defenses. For instance, a system comprising three layers, each capable of discerning surviving penetrators from the previous layer and each layer 90 percent effective, produces an overall defense that is 99.9 percent effective.

The ultimate solution to the strategic defense problem seems to be to neutralize the aggressor-launched nuclear weapons early in their flight. This can perhaps one day be accomplished with large numbers of mini-interceptors or possibly with directed energy beams—so-called death-rays, in the Hollywood vernacular—before the enemy can fully deploy the multitude of multiple independently targeted reentry vehicles (MIRVs) and penetration aids that can today be carried on a single booster rocket to confound defense. Further, by conducting the defensive battle near the point of the attack's origin, the defense can better protect the area of an entire nation—not just islands within it.

Perplexingly, the technological difficulty of strategic defense is enormous, and SDI clearly cannot be expected to address the problems of nuclear weapons hidden in briefcases or in the holds of cargo ships or commercial airliners. This is a considerable limitation. Nonetheless, it is likely that the proliferation of weaponry around the world will demand more and more emphasis on defensive systems in the future. Defense can in fact be a part of a strategic deterrent and, despite the arguments of its detractors, defense is in *most* (but not all) cases stabilizing. The technology of strategic defense in the United States is already far ahead of where most objective scientists even a few years ago would have projected it to be by now.

Moreover, defense is made a more viable option by the fact that the threat the United States faces may increasingly be that of relatively few nuclear weapons aboard a ballistic missile launched by an irresponsible and irrational Third World nation or group, rather than that of five thousand nuclear weapons launched by the Soviet Union in a carefully coordinated attack. Arms control agreements can make strong defense an even more reasonable way to go by further reducing worldwide the number of potentially threatening offensive objects. The continuation of our research and development of SDI should therefore be pursued. One day, it may perhaps look like the greatest bargain the citizens of our major cities ever bought. Were the Soviet Union to *suddenly* fracture, for example, the Moslem-dominated republic of Kazakhstan could over-night become a major nuclear power. Little consolation is found in the Soviet Union's history of violent revolutions. (This of course poses a major problem for the Soviet leadership today: if they place more "reli-able" troops in such areas they begin to look increasingly like an occupying army.)

The Hazard of Technological Surprise

One of the most important characteristics of technology is that future advancements are extremely difficult to forecast. One never knows when one's own laboratories or the laboratories of an adversary will produce a new development that, if not adopted, countered, or both, can produce a decisive outcome in a future confrontation. Deputy Sec-retary of Defense Don Atwood tells of a 1946 article on future military technology he read in which ballistic missiles were mentioned as a pos-sibility but dismissed because of the V-2's limited range of two hundred miles and accuracy of seven miles. Similarly, there was no mention of satellites as a possible technology having important military implica-tions. Yet fourteen years later both were a reality. Secretary Atwood poses the question: What will be the key technologies in the year 2004?

The danger, of course, is that we may lack the needed insight to recognize the implications of such advancements. The history of mili-tary technology is not particularly reassuring in this regard, being re-plete with examples of dangerously incorrect projections made by indisputably knowledgeable observers. Major General John K. Herr of the U.S. Army, for example, said in 1938, "We must not be misled to our own detriment to assume that the untried machine can displace the proved and tried horse." This statement was uttered just as the mechanized armies of Germany were preparing to roll across much of Europe. Not to be outdone, Rear Admiral Clark Woodward of the U.S. Navy assured us in 1939, just two years before Pearl Harbor, "As far as sinking a ship with a bomb is concerned, it just can't be done." The great physicist, Ernest Rutherford, claimed as late as 1930 that "the energy produced by the breaking down of the atom is a very poor kind of thing. Anyone who expects a source of power from the transformation of these atoms is talking moonshine." And the justly famous Admiral William Leahy of the U.S. Navy, in one of his less insightful moments, told President Truman in 1945, "That's the biggest fool thing we have ever done. The [atomic] bomb will never go off, and I speak as an expert in explosives." Technological underestimation is not confined to modern times. Napoleon told Robert Fulton around the year 1800, "What, sir? Would you make a ship sail against the wind and currents by lighting a bonfire under her deck? I pray you excuse me. I have no time to listen to such nonsense."

But the problem does not cease with the mere recognition of the feasibility of a given technological innovation. One must also be creatively disposed toward recognizing its potential utility or implications. The principle of radar was first discovered in the late 1920s by American atmospheric researchers working in Washington, D.C., and using electromagnetic waves to probe the ionosphere. The experiments had been beset with interference caused by aircraft taking off from nearby Bolling Air Force Base along the Potomac River. Recognizing the importance of the phenomenon, a young navy lieutenant commander wrote a technical article on the feasibility of what, if developed, would have become radar. His article, however, was classified by senior officers as being so important a military secret that it remained hidden in limbo until radar was rediscovered years later, fortunately in time for the battle of Britain in World War II. Similarly, at the very outset of America's direct involvement in that war, U.S. radar operators detected Japanese aircraft approaching Pearl Harbor early on the morning of December 7, 1941, well before any bombs began to fall, but concluded that the large number of signals displayed on their screen could only be the result of some sort of malfunction, and at the direction of their supervisors, shut down for the day (Figure 11).

Even when smart bombs became available in Vietnam, there was initially great reluctance by operational commanders to use them because of their perceived high cost. They *were* indeed costly compared to conventional bombs—approximately $15,000 each at the time, compared with about $1,000. On the other hand, when one considers the cost of acquiring aircraft, training crews, deploying aircraft, and providing all

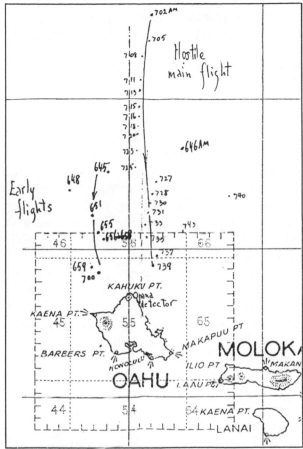

Figure 11. Track of approaching attack on Pearl Harbor made the morning of September 7, 1941— and disregarded because of the lack of confidence in the relatively new technology known as "RADAR."

SOURCE: National Archives.

the supporting elements needed in an air attack (reconnaissance, electronic warfare support, air defense suppression, tanker operations, combat air patrol, airborne command and control, search and rescue, and the like), then the cost of the ordnance that is dropped on the target becomes altogether trivial—particularly if the quality of that ordnance can have a significant positive impact on accomplishing the intended mission.

What Next?

Actually, it is not particularly difficult to project the principal items of equipment that U.S. military forces will be depending upon in the year 2000. One need only reflect upon the fact that it takes an average of eight years to develop a new weapon system and another two to ten years to acquire it in significant quantities, depending on its composition. Thus, just as American combat forces today still utilize derivatives of the Hawk missile and C-130 cargo aircraft of the 1950s, the F-4 fighter and Minuteman ICBM of the 1960s, and the F-14 and F-15 of the 1970s, U.S. forces of the year 2000 will comprise principally those items in development or procurement today: F-16s, F-18s, Tridents, Apaches, Blackhawk helicopters, and their contemporaries.

Looking *beyond* the year 2000 introduces all of the tribulations faced by General Herr, Admiral Leahy, and their fellow prognosticators. Some, although by no means all of the new technological building blocks of the as-yet undeveloped systems of the early twenty-first century, can be glimpsed today. The key technologies are likely to be optics and electronics (including artificial intelligence), with materials and stealth next, and propulsion, robotics, and power generation after that.

The key is not just to build better tanks, airplanes, and ships, but also to build altogether new capabilities that supplement or even replace tanks, airplanes, and ships. This is not easily done: it means upsetting the status quo. When Robert Goddard offered his pioneering work on rockets to the government without cost, he learned that the army's only interest in rocketry was the improvement of trench mortars, and the navy's in accelerating airplanes during takeoff.

If the 1970s witnessed the advent of military systems that actually hit their intended targets and the 1980s laid the groundwork for finding those targets, what remains is for our weapons to *survive* long enough— in the presence of a determined enemy with many of these same capabilities—for our own systems to have an effect. Much as the early space program was necessarily oriented toward the development of rockets to boost payloads into space, often at the expense of any great concern over what would be done once we got there, the decades just past have frequently witnessed the development of military systems that are extremely capable as long as they are not significantly interfered with by the enemy. Such noninterference is, of course, not a particularly enforceable assumption. That is, it presumes a cooperative enemy—and cooperative enemies are in very short supply.

The agenda for the 1990s thus focuses heavily on what has come to be called survivability: making aircraft more survivable, spacecraft more durable, ships more resilient, and indeed even making the infantryman (infantryperson?) more survivable—all in the systems concept of avoiding detection, avoiding being hit if detected, and avoiding damage if hit. A longer-term alternative may well include finding suitable substitutes for aircraft, tanks, spacecraft, ships, and in some distant day perhaps even for the ubiquitous infantryman. This later step will, ironically, be the most challenging of all.

Does all this mean that warfare will essentially become impracticable because almost everything can be found and almost everything hit? The answer is resoundingly *no*. The reason is simple: *countermeasures*. In the June 1967 war in the Middle East, the Egyptians fired four antiship missiles at the Israeli ship *Eilath*. The first three missiles hit the ship, and the fourth hit the wake where the ship had been—just before it sank. In contrast, in the subsequent Middle East war in 1973, dozens of antiship missiles were fired at Israeli ships, but not one hit its intended target, because the Israelis in the interim had developed some very effective countermeasures.

Countermeasures take many forms, ranging from the mundane to the sophisticated. Camouflage has been used since the earliest of times. Tamerlane was a master of the art in the fourteenth century. Deception also has been a fundamental element of warfare. A classic example was the Trojan horse; another was the deception as to the landing point for the Allied invasion of Europe in World War II—a plot so successful that it kept a large number of divisions of the German Army from even being committed to the actual battle for days during the initial landing phase.

Modern technology has introduced its own category of countermeasures. The British, for example, discovered how to "bend" the radar navigation beams used by German bombers attacking Great Britain in World War II, causing bombloads to be dropped relatively harmlessly in the countryside. Today, radio signals can be sent to interfere with the innermost workings of a sophisticated guidance system. Lasers can be used to interfere with the operation of optical systems. And even computer software is susceptible to countermeasures—leading to a whole new lexicon of "trap doors," "time bombs," "viruses," and a modern-day "trojan horse."

On test ranges, where we sometimes have a too cooperative "enemy," hitting targets can be relatively easy. Tactical weapons, for example, have historically achieved a kill probability well in excess of 70 percent on test ranges—more recently, near 90 percent. In the real world, however, the probability of destroying a target is dramatically lower. Of all the tactical missiles of all different types (surface to air, surface to surface, air to surface, and air to air) fired in combat by all military forces that have used such devices—American, Soviet, North Vietnamese, Israeli, Egyptian, Syrian, Afghan, and so forth—the actual kill probability overall has been not much more than 9 percent. In other words, the degradation factor between the test world and the real world has been nearly ten. The "fog of war," as it has been known throughout history, takes its toll on the performance of both hardware and humans. We must ensure that our testing is sufficiently demanding (but at the same time not allow a search for absolute perfection to become justification for the inaction preferred by those who oppose *any* new weapon system).

Efforts of decades past to permit such items as aircraft to sustain hits and still survive are likely to have less payoff in the years ahead as defense systems become increasingly lethal. Focus will shift instead toward minimizing detection, shooting first, and avoiding being hit. Stealth is of the utmost importance. Although stealth potentially offsets many of the gains in military technology of the past two decades, its use in the foreseeable future will principally be in specialized applications for specialized systems—and even stealth is not the ultimate countermeasure in this never-ending battle. An important example of stealth, however, is the use of a limited number of such aircraft to suppress enemy air defenses and thereby permit follow-up operations by larger numbers of more traditional aircraft. Stealth is just another example, albeit an extremely important one, of the countermeasures war that is raging in the military laboratories of the world today. It is a war in which to stand still is to fall rapidly and perilously behind. Today even low-tech nations can obtain high-tech weapon from amoral arms merchants willing to sell hardware to anyone. This makes countermeasures essential—not only against the hardware of our adversaries, but also against that of our allies and even ourselves.

Parallel to the growing importance of countermeasures, a revolution in the use of robots is also likely. Just as robots are already being employed in factories throughout the industrialized world, a wide spectrum of military missions is conceivable for these devices, including the use of leave-behind antitank missile platforms that automatically acquire and engage armored threats, and remotely piloted or even autonomous mini-aircraft in large numbers. Remotely implanted homing mines, also a form of robot, could be emplaced by standoff rockets, much as sensors disguised as bushes were launched by artillery and implanted along the Ho Chi Minh trail in Vietnam to radio back information on enemy activity, sometimes even eavesdropping on voice conversations. Such "mines" could be used against aircraft by scattering them in the fields beside runways, standing ready (while using anti-sweep protection and sophisticated counting and discrimination devices for target assessment) to launch small, short-range, homing antiaircraft missiles at selected aircraft taking off from an air base. Similarly, undersea robot mines will see increasing use, as will "smart" minefields emplaced by rockets, not in front of an advancing enemy column but *right on top* of that column—a sort of "instant minefield." Such minefields could be rapidly emplaced by artillery shells containing mines, rockets, or tactical aircraft. Their effect would be the same: to leave the enemy with the choice of continuing to move through the minefield it finds itself in the middle of—or of standing still and facing follow-up firepower.

Vastly increased use of standoff weapons launched from platforms well outside the range of at least the enemy's terminal defenses is also a likely development. Ardant DuPique perceptively noted several centuries ago that "to fight from a distance is instinctive in man." That seems to be one aspect of combat that has not changed—volunteer army or not.

The information revolution will soon see its way onto the battlefield in truly pervasive fashion. With the advent of modern digital computers, displays, and communications systems, enormous quantities of data can be provided to individual combat elements. This easy access to information is not without its problems: one of the foremost will be the hazard of information saturation, posing the need to separate the important data from the remainder of the information avalanche. The increasing utilization of these modern information systems opens yet another battlefield in the countermeasures war—the potential dimension of which may have been glimpsed during the (inadvertently introduced) software error that in 1990 shut down much of AT&T for a day. It has been said that the side that will win the next war will be the one with the last antenna standing—a resounding overstatement but nonetheless an instructive message, given current trends.

At the lower—and more probable—extreme of the countermeasures warfare spectrum will be a growing need for better means of simply detecting specific individuals and contraband substances, including explosives, weaponry, and drugs. Such is the state of the art of this technology that it is hard to beat the nose of a good dog. Eventually, using very large antennas in space (antennas even miles across), it will be possible to keep track of the location of specific vehicles and packages within a few feet if special small electronic tags have been implanted in them beforehand. There will be a concomitant premium on real-time command and control systems. Communications between persons at any location on earth will become a reality through the use of wrist telephones and satellite relays some 25,000 miles above the earth; this innovation could even pose a whole new challenge to the notion of chain of command, because the president would be able to speak directly to a U.S. Marine sargeant about to enter a renegade leader's palace.

Mobility will become increasingly important, both for counterguerrilla and counterterrorist forces; so will transportability, to facilitate the deployment of rapid strike forces in more conventional warfare. It continues to be likely (and hoped) that U.S. forces will be called upon to operate at substantial distances from home, and, increasingly, to do so without the benefit of overseas bases or, frustratingly, much help from allies. This trend places a premium on light forces supported by a survivable sealift and airlift capability. It also introduces the possibility for new system concepts such as the conduct of nonnuclear strike operations in such distant places as the Persian Gulf by very large, long-range aircraft capable of operating directly from U.S. bases, with refueling. A single such aircraft could carry perhaps fifty 100-mile standoff missiles, each of which in turn would eject on the order of ten small homing sub-missiles somewhat analogous to the MIRVs (multiple independently targeted reentry vehicles) now commonplace in strategic forces. Each sub-missile would contain its own terminal guidance and could attack a tank or other appropriate tactical target. If even a small fraction of the sub-missiles eventually hit a significant target, say a tank or a bunker, a single sortie of such an aircraft could provide a major destructive capability, particularly against mechanized forces.

On the surface of the ocean, the principal uncertainty concerns the survivability of major combatant ships. In any significant overseas conflict of duration, the preponderant proportion of military supplies will necessarily be shipped by sea because of the enormous tonnages involved. This fact makes our ocean control mission of the utmost importance—precisely at a time that the threat to surface ships continues to increase. This threat may ultimately include ballistic, nonnuclear, homing missiles of even intercontinental range. Embedded in a space-based worldwide system to monitor surface ships, such a weapon could potentially attack major surface ships anywhere on the surface of the earth within tens of minutes. Such potential developments, as well as already-existing threats, argue for increased roles for submarines, including land attack against high-priority targets using undersea-launched nonnuclear stealthy standoff missiles. In missions such as surgical attacks against, say, a palace or command center, the high cost of these weapons would be relatively unimportant because of the low usage rates and the major political stakes. Requirements would instead focus on guaranteeing a high confidence of destroying the intended target, assuring that nearby targets (the local hospital or school) would not inadvertently be damaged, that no U.S. pilot would be exposed to capture, and that an effective degree of secrecy would be maintained until after the mission has been completed. But in any operation that places ships near shore, even against nations with a second-rate military, naval forces should be prepared to take losses.

U.S. ground forces have fortunately not had to operate in the absence of air superiority in the lifetime of most members of today's American military. This condition is likely to continue to prevail in all combat situations except a major confrontation with the Soviet Union—in part because of the effectiveness of the U.S. ground-based air defenses and air superiority aircraft that have been developed. This does not, however, mean that U.S. ground forces will not face air threats—especially attack helicopters. And although the United States should hope that the tank does become obsolete (Soviet tanks, for example, outnumber U.S. tanks by about three to one), advances in the ability to shoot while moving, to fight at night, to exploit exceptional agility, and to utilize advanced protective armor have substantially prolonged the lifetime of the tank. For the time being, at least, reports of the demise of the *modern* tank should therefore be considered premature.

The helicopter, which came of age in the late 1960s, can be expected to take on further importance as it continues to evolve. In some respects, the helicopter can be viewed as a vehicle that has gained agility in *three* dimensions by forgoing armor such as that used to protect a tank, the latter being limited to movement in two dimensions. Today's attack helicopters carry cannon of larger caliber than those carried by some of the tanks used early in World War II, and modern helicopters also carry a variety of highly accurate missiles. Of the limited number of such missiles fired in Panama, not a single one failed to hit its target. Air-to-air combat between helicopters such as the U.S. Apache and the Soviet-built Hind will be inevitable in any conflict involving both types of machines, companions of which are becoming increasingly available throughout the world. But the helicopter will probably gradually evolve into an altogether new type of flying platform that incorporates many of the additional advantages of fixed-wing aircraft in terms of speed, operating radius, and payload capacity. Further blurring the distinction between the two classes of aircraft will be a growing overlap of their attendant roles and missions, whether for pure transport or as weapons platforms. Dependency upon large, fixed air bases and runways will necessarily be markedly reduced in the longer term.

Finally, it remains to be discovered whether we shall see that rare but overwhelming technological breakthrough that produces the same impact, relatively speaking, as the impact produced in their day by the stirrup, the longbow, the rifle, and the atomic bomb. Only time will tell whether some new technology will produce a deterrent to the lower

strata of warfare as effective as the existing strategic-warfare deterrent—
which itself was not considered feasible less than half a century ago.

The Soviet Union, despite all the changes of the past five years, continues to represent the strongest military capability that might confront
American forces. In the words of General Colin Powell, "The Soviet
Union is the only country that can destroy the United States in thirty
minutes." Although the USSR has almost no commercial technology of
consequence, it has managed to keep its military forces very modern by
borrowing, stealing, or developing its own specialized technology. In
many cases, Soviet forces are less sophisticated than those of the West,
but they do have the technology needed to do the job—and to do it with
considerable reliability. Most observers at the 1989 Paris Air Show
would conclude that the Soviets "won" the air show— whatever military significance that "victory" may have. The twentieth century Soviet
Union—a third-rate, Third World power in the economic, cultural, and
social worlds—is unmistakably a world class power in the military
sphere. To date, *perestroika*, insofar as Soviet military equipment is concerned, has largely meant shedding of old hardware while continuing
to manufacture modern hardware.

Some military reformers believe the United States should spend its
limited financial resources on "low-tech" solutions. But this approach is
not optional. Instead, as has already been noted, Americans must become comfortable with the notion that high technology need not be syn-
onymous with high cost or even with complexity. Clearly, forces of
adequate size must be maintained, and technology must not be introduced for technology's sake. But it must also be recalled that low-tech
solutions generally imply larger peacetime forces and higher casualties
in combat.

Further, if one defines what it is that America does well as a nation,
which clearly includes developing sophisticated technology, it seems
reasonable to rely on technology to provide a military edge. High tech
is still our advantage in spite of all the recent headlines to the contrary,
and it makes sense to play to our strengths. The Soviet Union and the
smaller developed nations will quite probably continue to fall farther
behind in many key technologies, particularly as those technologies become more and more closely coupled with space systems and with the
highly competitive commercial marketplace—the latter in such areas as
electronics, optics, and advanced materials. The Soviets, for example,
are far behind in the critical area of information systems. The foundation of this revolution is the semiconductor integrated circuit, which
significantly has been called "industrial rice" in Asia and "twentieth
century crude" in the Western nations. Semiconductors permeate virtu-

ally every item of modern military equipment, and the Soviets' lag of some two generations poses a severe problem for them. Lesser nations face even greater difficulty.

Another often-heard criticism of military technology is that it has led to the creation of systems too complicated to use and maintain in a battle environment. Unfortunately, there is more than a modicum of truth to this charge. But no law in nature says that advancing technology must place ever-greater demands on its user. The fact is that sophisticated hardware and software can be used, if we wish, to *reduce* the demands on the human by incorporating user-friendly designs and "transparent technology."

Consider the case of shoulder-fired antitank weapons. An infantryman firing the World War II bazooka aimed his weapon at the target, but, as has been noted, from the time the trigger was pulled the outcome was entirely up to the laws of gravity and the evasiveness of the target. Chances were that the infantryman would miss. The first-generation antitank missile changed much of this by providing the foot soldier the opportunity to guide his projectile by radio command all the way to the target. But even this improved weapon had shortcomings, the most prominent of which was the need for the GI to keep both his missile and the target in sight as he laboriously guided the missile much as one would guide a radio-controlled model airplane—all the while being shot at himself.

The second-generation antitank missile, typified by the TOW and Dragon, solved most of the human-dexterity part of this problem by requiring only that the operator keep a set of cross hairs in a target sight centered upon the intended target; a computer and communications link would then take care of everything else. But even this new missile could not eliminate the requirement that the soldier remain exposed so as to track the target throughout the time of flight, for a period of up to some ten seconds—an eternity on the battlefield.

Third-generation systems such as the AAWS-M "fire and forget" weapon now in development require only that the operator "lock" the missile on the target (locate the target in the center of the sight) and pull the trigger; the automatic guidance does everything else, including homing the missile on the target. But the soldier still needs to find the tank or other target in the first place—a need that will be eliminated with fourth-generation antitank missiles, now in the experimental phase, particularly for indirect fire use. With these latter missiles the soldier can remain at a considerable distance from harm's way and simply launch the missile in the *general* direction of a suspected enemy—leaving up to the technology embedded in the new weapon the problem of finding, hitting, and destroying the target. This is, of course, the "brilliant" missile described earlier. Importantly, each successive generation of these systems has embodied increased technological sophistication—but each has reduced the demands on the soldier who uses them.

In the years ahead we shall need to increase considerably our efforts to counter guerrilla and terrorist operations. Technology will have a role in this arena too, but even with the enormous advances now being achieved, the bottom line is that we cannot overlook the pivotal importance of the individual human combatant. Courage, training, motivation—sometimes called intangibles—can have a very tangible impact indeed on the outcome of battle.

This point was perhaps best made in a passage from a long-forgotten book that told of an American Medal of Honor winner whose squad had been pinned down by machine gun fire. As the GI ran forward firing his rifle in a one-man attack on the enemy position, he was shot and knocked off his feet. Moving forward on hands and knees, he was struck again yet somehow managed to crawl forward to the machine gun nest, into which he dropped a hand grenade, saving his squad and turning the course of the battle.

The author concluded, "It was another great victory for American technology."

FOUR

DEFENSE ECONOMICS 101:
The Fate of Great Powers

In the twenty-first century, dollars and yen may ultimately be more important than bullets and bombs—especially as the ruble looks more like rubble and sources of oil in the Middle East look more like sources of war (Figure 12). With regard to America itself, the long-range economic outlook has been the subject of growing national concern in recent years, especially in view of the measurable decline in competitiveness of American firms in the world's commercial marketplaces. In just five years, between 1982 and 1987, the United States went from being the world's greatest creditor nation to being the world's greatest debtor. Since World War II, although not altogether surprising, America's share of the gross world product dropped dramatically. Frequently overlooked by many people is the important fact that the American economy is what in the end provides the underpinning for the nation's military capability. Also often overlooked is the likelihood that economics may become the underpinning of future military conflicts. Trade wars and oil wars readily escalate into shooting wars.

The relationship between the health of a nation's economy and its level of defense spending is complex. The amount to be spent on national defense should be based on the *objectives* the nation pursues in the international security sphere and the level of *risk*—economic, political, and military—that the nation is willing to tolerate in pursuing those objectives. (It is in this latter area that the question of affordability

Figure 12   **National Wealth, Defense Commitment, and Foreign Energy Dependence**

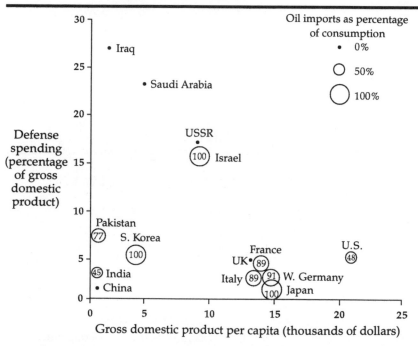

arises.) Funding for defense can be legitimately based on no other grounds: not to stimulate the economy, not to create jobs in the defense industry, not to produce technology that might have a spin-off to the commercial sector. Although defense spending can and often does produce significant concomitant benefits, these benefits do not in themselves justify defense spending. Rather, they are consequences of it.

As has been found repeatedly in the past and will be shown to be the case today, America *can* afford the defense it needs. Similarly, America should not purchase defense over and above what it needs and thereby divert funds from other areas also requiring financial resources—particularly those resources needed to generate growth in the economy itself, which is the most efficient way to ensure the strength of our long-term national defense and our standard of living.

Three economic factors play a major role in determining America's defense objectives, and the attendant risks, for the decade ahead. The first of these is the strength of the overall U.S. economy and the closely related level of the U.S. budget deficit, in that they directly affect what we believe we can afford to spend on defense. The second is potentially even more significant: the Soviet economic crisis and the impact it will ultimately

Figure 13   **Gross World Output, 1990 ($19 trillion)**

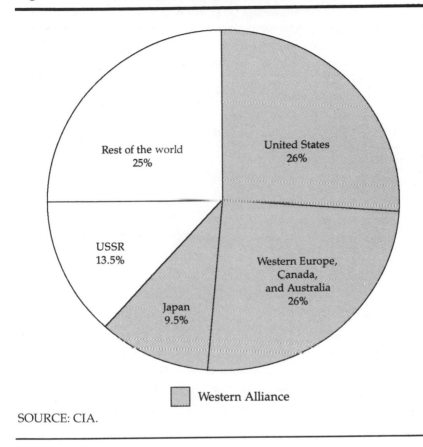

SOURCE: CIA.

have on Soviet military capability and in turn on our own need for military spending. The third is a much subtler and longer-term force, thus far largely unrecognized, that also will have a profound effect on our military strength: the extraordinary growth in the cost of providing and maintaining modern military equipment in an age of rapidly advancing (and therefore rapidly obsolescing) technology. Our nation's response to these three economic factors will determine to a considerable extent the global power of the United States in the coming decades.

To understand the strong linkage between economic health and military might, a few numbers may help place the issue in perspective. Starting at the top, the gross world product of some $19 trillion can be considered to be composed of five components (Figure 13). A little more than a quarter is produced in the United States, a little less than a quarter in Western Europe, about an eighth in Japan, about an eighth in the

Soviet Union, and the remaining quarter in all the rest of the world combined. There are but four economic power centers on earth—and two-thirds of the gross world product is produced by the Western Alliance. Japan's relative share is increasing rapidly, while that of the USSR is diminishing. This arithmetic obviously has very significant implications in terms of the Soviet Union's ability to prevail in a prolonged future conflict or to maintain technologically competitive military forces into the next century. This observation was probably not altogether lost upon Soviet military leadership, perhaps encouraging it to endorse *perestroika*—at least so far.

The U.S. Defense Burden

Just as it became clear that the United States was winning the cold war, a spate of books and articles appeared warning that America is a nation in decline. The most prominent of these, *The Rise and Fall of the Great Powers* by historian Paul Kennedy,* examines the historical relationship between military spending and economic strength. The book argues that throughout history, when great nations devote too much of their resources to warfare rather than "wealth creation," the result is "a weakening of national power in the longer term."

Kennedy goes on to suggest that America's "global overstretch"—its sizable military burden—may be responsible for the decline of our economy relative to that of other nations. Other commentators go still further. They point to the large federal budget deficits of the 1980s that coincide with the Reagan military buildup and note that the American economy, although still powerful, did not grow in the 1980s at the same rate as it did in the 1950s and 1960s. Japan and West Germany, however, experienced robust growth in the last decade, and these same commentators thus claimed that this growth was the result of the fact that our allies' military spending was (and is) a fraction of our own: Japan spends only about 1 percent of its GNP on military activities and West Germany about 4 percent; the U.S. figure approaches 6 percent. According to the "America in decline" theory, if the United States does not draw back from its "global overstretch," it will eventually be overtaken by other industrial democracies. Indeed, it was implied that if we did not dramatically reduce our military spending, we would later be *forced* to make such cuts, at much greater cost and pain. In short, the American

---

*New York: Random House, 1987.

Figure 14   **U.S. Defense as Percentage of GNP, 1901–1990**

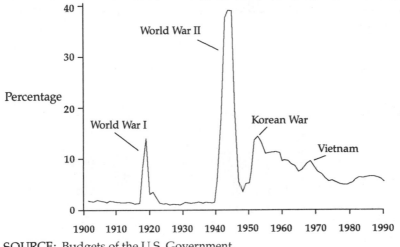

SOURCE: Budgets of the U.S. Government.

Century would soon be over, and America would follow in the footsteps of Rome and Great Britain.

Does our current level of defense spending place such a crippling burden on the U.S. economy that the nation's strength may actually be reduced? Or does this concern perhaps reflect a fear of victory—*victophobia*, to coin a new word—inasmuch as the controversy erupted at a time that world political events seem to be running in our favor?

A historical perspective is helpful in answering these questions. Today our nation spends about 5.5 percent of its gross national product on defense, a number that seems to be declining toward perhaps 4 percent (Figure 14). At the peak of the Korean War, the corresponding figure was about 14 percent, and at the height of World War II it approached 40 percent. Since World War II, defense budgets have tended to hold steady in real terms during peacetime at a level of about $250 billion per year in today's dollars (Figure 15). The exception to this is the Reagan military buildup, during which spending reached about $300 billion per year. Although it represented a substantial increase in dollar terms, this amount was a much smaller percentage of GNP and of total federal spending than during most of the post–World War II era.

Defense spending *as a fraction of federal spending* has actually declined in fairly steady fashion over the years from nearly 90 percent at the peak of the Korean War to about 23 percent just before the Reagan defense buildup. This smooth trend has been interrupted only three times since World War II—once by the Korean War, once by a comparatively modest

Figure 15   **U.S. Defense Spending, 1940–1990
(constant 1989 dollars)**

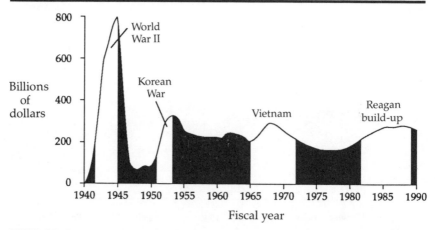

SOURCE: Department of Defense.

rise during the war in Southeast Asia, and once by the Reagan defense buildup. For the past fifteen years, annual defense outlays have remained relatively constant at between 22 percent and 28 percent of federal expenditures (Figure 16). Today's military forces are more a consequence of what was spent in the 1980s than of what is being spent today.

The evidence suggests that if the United States is economically overburdened with providing for its defense, this overburdening should have been most obvious during the years when the country was spending a much larger portion of its GNP on military activities. Murray Weidenbaum, a former chairman of the President's Council of Economic Advisers, wrote in a recent study that "both critics and supporters of defense programs have overstated their case about the impact—positive or negative—of military spending on the U.S. economy." He notes that "the major changes in the U.S. economy have been primarily the result of other factors—domestic and international, economic and political. The massive economy of the United States has not really been propelled and retarded by the relatively small share of GNP now devoted to military outlays."*

Turning to the issue of "America in decline," Weidenbaum argues that "any decline in the relative economic position of this country is really 'the rise of the rest,' a phenomenon to which the policies of the

---

*Murray Weidenbaum, *Military Spending and the Myth of Global Overstretch*, CSIS Significant Issues Series, vol. XI, no. 4 (Washington, D.C.: Center for Strategic and International Studies, 1989).

Figure 16   **U.S. Defense Spending as Percentage of Federal Spending, 1950–1990**

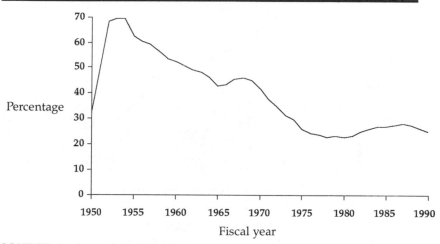

Fiscal year

SOURCE: Budgets of the U.S. Government.

United States have deliberately contributed." We won in this regard as well: the Marshall Plan in Western Europe and the MacArthur reforms in Japan succeeded spectacularly. The success of Japan and Germany left us with a smaller share of the world's economic pie but with the pie growing so much bigger that we enjoyed an "absolute rise." And the successes of these nations involves more than just economics; it has also been a victory for the democratic values in which Americans believe. Should we then care about a *"relative* decline"? It shouldn't trouble us that the Japanese and the French are living better, if we too are living better. We want them to live better, and their rising living standard helps *us* enjoy better lives. We have worked hard for a half century to make this so.

Moreover, there has in fact *been* no "relative decline" using other years of comparison besides 1945. As RAND economist Charles Wolf, Jr., demonstrates, our current share of the global pie is about where it was prewar 1938 and postwar 1965. Looking over recent times, Wolf again detects no "relative decline" since 1975—Asia grew faster but Europe slower than we since then—and he foresees none ahead. America's share of the global market should not fall from now to at least the first decade of the next century *if we pursue prudent competitive policies.*

What about the argument that military spending was responsible for the unprecedented federal budget deficits of the 1980s? In 1989, for the twentieth year in a row, the federal government spent more money

Figure 17   Composition of Federal Spending, 1950−1990

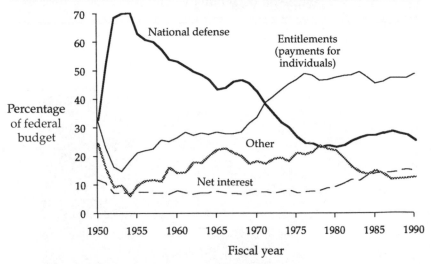

SOURCE: Historical tables, budget of the U.S. Government, FY1990 and budget of the U.S. Government, FY1991.

than it took in. That negative balance will certainly be the case in the coming years. In fact, we have not had a balanced federal budget since 1969. As a result, the national *debt* now totals 43 percent of our GNP, and fifteen cents of every dollar spent by the government is devoted to paying interest on this debt. It took the United States almost two centuries to accumulate a debt of a half trillion dollars and only fifteen years to add another $2.5 trillion.

It is convenient to think of the federal budget (which now consumes 22 percent of the U.S. GNP) as consisting of four principal elements: entitlements (money given directly to individuals based on long-term legislative commitments), defense, interest on the national debt, and everything else. Entitlements now consume roughly 50 percent of the federal budget—a growing fraction (Figure 17). Defense consumes about 25 percent, and if the president's proposed budget is executed, by the mid-1990s defense will represent the smallest fraction of annual government spending and of the GNP since just before Pearl Harbor, with the exception of 1948. Interest on the government debt now consumes about 15 percent—about two thirds of the amount spent on defense and growing as the national debt increases while defense shrinks. The rest of the government's expenditures combined total about 9 percent of the federal budget.

Figure 18   **Defense Spending as Percentage of "Discretionary"**
                    and "Nondiscretionary" Funds in Federal Budget

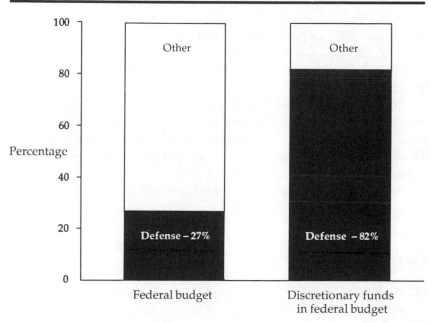

SOURCE: Department of Defense.

Defense spending, therefore, is nowhere near the nation's largest governmental expense at the federal level. Nevertheless, defense spending typically receives the most budgetary attention—in part because so much of it falls into the category of "discretionary" spending, meaning that most of the money expended on national defense requires appropriation at the discretion of the Congress each year. Nondiscretionary funds, on the other hand, such as Social Security, are appropriated *automatically* after the initial vote establishing their existence and therefore require no congressional vote in succeeding years. These nondiscretionary payments have been growing steadily. Social Security recipients now receive between four and five times what they originally paid in withholding taxes—*plus interest*. Defense spending has begun to decline in real terms, but social spending continues to climb.

Although defense appropriations constitute only a bit more than one-fourth of the federal budget, they account for a good bit more than three-fourths of the federal government's *discretionary* funds (Figure 18). This incongruity is of major significance in assessing likely support for future defense spending, since defense spending consists precisely of those funds (the discretionary funds) that are the easiest target for reductions and that therefore represent a lightning rod for deficit cutters.

In 1939, with a national debt equal to 45 percent of America's GNP (the figure today is 42 percent), it seemed there was no way that America could afford to arm itself. In the subsequent half-dozen years some 292,000 fatalities among our armed forces proved the error and the tragedy of our calculations.

In short, although the federal budget deficit is indeed cause for intense concern, the notion that defense spending is its *principal* cause is patently false. Our nation clearly has serious budgetary problems, but the evidence is that we can afford to spend on defense whatever we feel is necessary to achieve our national goals. Paul Kennedy's thesis of "global overstretch" simply does not ring true for present-day America.

The Soviet Economic Crisis

The thesis of "global overstretch" and "nation in decline" indeed more closely fits the Soviet Union. An authentic military giant, the Soviet Union has economic problems that are legendary. For many decades a third-rate economic power with a fourth-rate political system, the USSR has managed nonetheless to build a military force that in many respects exceeds that of any other nation on earth—including the United States. As mentioned, the Soviet Union may be spending up to 25 percent of its GNP on defense—a fraction close to four times that of the United States. Such a high rate is usually found only in nations at war. The *Wall Street Journal* quotes Soviet Foreign Minister Eduard A. Shevardnadze as saying "It is obvious that if we continue as before, comrades—I state this with all responsibility—to spend a quarter, a *quarter*, of our budget on military expenditure—we have ruined the country; then we simply won't be needing defense, just as we won't need an army for a ruined country and an impoverished people. There is no sense in protecting a system which has led to economic and social ruin." This poses a major dilemma for the Soviet military leadership: If the USSR is not to be a military power, it is not likely to be much of a power at all. The Soviet Union has met the enemy, and it turns out to be its own economic and social system. Victor Hugo said it over a century ago: "An invasion of armies can be resisted, but not an idea whose time has come."

The U.S. reassessment of Soviet defense spending as a portion of its GNP is largely the result of a realization that the Soviet GNP is much smaller than previously thought, perhaps even as little as one-fourth that of the United States instead of a half. Further, it is now abundantly evident that the Soviet economy has been stagnant for several years while the economies of the West have been growing. Some observers believe that the Soviet economy has failed to grow at all since the early 1970s, an accomplishment that places the USSR in the company of the Third World's most backward nations. A desire to halt this downward economic slide is the motivation for *perestroika* and, as previously noted, probably explains why the Soviet military has chosen at least for the time being to support the new movement. The military leadership of the USSR has seemingly recognized that if the Soviet economy fails to grow at the pace of other nations in the world, so, too, will the military capability it supports. Yet, as also has been discussed, *perestroika* appears to have been a failure on the same scale that *glasnost* has been a success—posing an explosive set of circumstances for Soviet military and political leadership. Soviet Prime Minister Ryzhkov has, for example, estimated that 43 million of the USSR's citizens are already living in poverty.

Today, fewer Soviet citizens per capita own cars than do blacks in South Africa; only one Soviet in eleven has a telephone (compared with two telephones per person in America). Fewer miles of paved roads exist in the USSR—a nation eleven time zones wide—than in California. According to reports, half of the potato crop and over one-fourth the grain crop rots or is lost on the way to the market. The 2 percent of Soviet agricultural land that is not farmed by the state produces 25 percent of the output. Soviet officials indicate informally that they were fortunate that the most recent winter was mild—by Soviet standards—or there would not have been sufficient fuel for heating. According to *U.S. News and World Report*, the average Soviet citizen must work two months to buy a pair of athletic shoes, one month to buy blue jeans, and half a lifetime to buy a used foreign car. A story popular in Moscow tells of a citizen striking a deal to purchase a new automobile and being advised it would be available for pick-up at 10:00 AM on June 3, 1997—to which the citizen responds, "That won't be possible. That's when the plumber is coming."

What effect will all this economic stagnation have on Soviet military spending level in the immediate future? President Gorbachev has promised a 14.2 percent cut in the Soviet defense budget (an interestingly precise projection for a nation that admits it doesn't know what its defense expenditures actually are!). For a quarter of a century Soviet defense spending as determined from actual output had steadily increased at an average of about 2.7 percent per year in real terms (with the possible exception of one year in the 1970s, when a slight decline may have occurred), but it apparently nearly leveled off in real terms in 1987 and 1988, and according to one senior Soviet official, it actually declined by 1.5 percent in 1989. Other estimates vary from 3 to 5 percent real decline during 1989. The projected 14.2 percent future reduction has been variously described as taking place over a period of two, three, or five years. It is noteworthy that U.S. defense spending already declined in real terms by 13 percent before the Soviet commitment was ever announced—another largely unnoticed fact.

Soviet Minister of Defense Dmitri Yazov has stated that Soviet defense spending in 1989 totaled 77.3 billion rubles. Further reductions to 71 billion rubles were promised in 1990, as well as an eventual overall reduction of "approximately 40 percent of our present annual defense budget." The Soviets' budget statement equates the 1990 spending figure to 114 billion U.S. dollars (or about 40 percent of U.S. defense spending—an egregiously suspect piece of arithmetic!).

These projections are certainly not quite as straightforward as one might presume. First, the Soviets themselves recently revised upward by a factor of four their twenty-five year public statements of defense spending—which has raised questions of credibility both in the West *and* in the USSR. In short, the Soviets have been cooking the books. Second, the Soviet government's announced exchange rate is virtually meaningless, differing by a factor of ten from what is available in Moscow's own official tourist hotels and by a still larger factor from the rate that can be obtained in the burgeoning black market on the streets of major Soviet cities. Third, Mr. Yazov himself points out that the 40 percent projected reduction is actually "as compared with the endorsed five-year plan"— which itself had forecast considerable growth in defense spending.

Of greater significance for budgetary comparisons is the actual purchasing power of the defense ruble, which must take into account the lower cost of military personnel in the Soviet armed forces as compared with America's all-volunteer force, the differences in equipment costs, the altogether arbitrary nature of the Soviet pricing system, and the like. A comparison of the hypothetical amount it would cost the *United States* to own the Soviet military force with the actual cost of owning the force we do possess is much more revealing. It suggests that from 1970 until 1985 the Soviets were spending significantly more for defense in absolute terms than was the United States, but since 1985 the expenditures of the two nations have been fairly comparable. Even this assessment is significant only as a starting point because, as has already been noted, both nations are now beginning to draw down their forces.

Decommissioning the Soviet military's older equipment is proceeding, but at the same time, the USSR continues to produce modern military hardware at a rate that substantially surpasses that of the West. Recently it was noted that in spite of substantial cutbacks the Soviets were still producing five thousand armored vehicles per year, compared with one thousand in the United States; Soviet production rates of fighter aircraft, submarines, surface ships, and ICBMs similarly surpass those of the United States. British defense minister Tom King, speaking to the House of Commons in early 1990, observed,

> It is a staggering thought that even now, in the fifth year of Mr. Gorbachev's time in office, the figures show that one new Soviet submarine is being launched every six weeks. Two aircraft, six tanks and one missile are produced every day. The Soviet defense minister has said that the emphasis is now on quality rather than quantity: that is certainly borne out by this year's May Day Parade in Red Square, which revealed one new main battle tank and one heavily armored infantry vehicle of very high quality. The Soviet navy recorded a record tonnage of new surface ships during 1989. These ships are larger and more powerful than their predecessors, have longer range and more accurate missiles.

It seems likely that the USSR will evolve toward a somewhat smaller, much more modern, and probably relatively larger force than our own—with the principal exception being some categories of naval forces, where the United States maintains a strong lead.

Particularly important is the withdrawal of Soviet forward deployed units in Europe, because this allows the West far more warning time of any (conventional) USSR military action. It is this increase in warning time as much as any absolute change in Soviet defense spending that affords the United States an important opportunity to reshape its military forces and to reduce U.S. spending. Moreover, given the state of modern technology, it is much less likely nowadays to encounter a large-scale total surprise of the magnitude that occurred when the Chinese moved into Korea or the Soviets into Czechoslovakia. With the loss of their East European allies the Soviets now find reality in what they must have worried about all along: the dilemma posed in *Alice in Wonderland*, "What if they gave a war and no one came?"

Among the tasks at hand is to make U.S. force reductions in a manner that does not accentuate the significance of the difference between the size of U.S. forces and the size of Soviet forces. It has been the observation of both authors in recent trips to the Soviet Union that the USSR is at the moment so intensely preoccupied with internal problems that it seems to harbor little interest in becoming embroiled in external conflicts.

This welcome state of affairs, of course, is subject to change and cannot be relied upon by U.S. long-term force planners—who must embrace the time-tested axiom that in the end it is latent military capabilities and not currently stated intentions that count. In the words of General George C. Marshall, "We have tried since the birth of our nation to promote our love of peace by a display of weakness. This course has failed us utterly." In this century alone, America found itself unprepared for World War I, after which it promptly placed itself in the same predicament for World War II, following which it cut its forces dramatically, subsequently suffering 30,000 fatalities restoring stability in Korea.

Our level of military spending *is* a matter of some discretion, but we must be prepared to live with the consequences of whatever level we elect. Unfortunately, the level that is set today establishes those consequences not for now but for the fairly distant future.

The hazards of underestimating the threats of the future are illustrated by a juxtaposition of headlines found in the August 3, 1990 edition of *Early Bird*, a collection of media articles offered by the Pentagon news clipping service. At the top of the front page the headline announced: "B-2 Bomber Survives Vote in Senate by Small Margin" and "Bush Outlines Plans to Slash the Military." Further down was a headline from the *New York Times* noting, "Invading Iraquis Seize Kuwait and its Oil. . ." (Figure 19). About the same time, the *Wall Street Journal* editorialized, "Westerners rubbed their sleepy eyes yesterday morning to the news Saddam Hussein had made his big play for the Persian Gulf's oil. His takeover of Kuwait capped a week in which the U.S. Congress has been busily gutting the President's military budget."

The same day that *Time*'s cover bore a photo of a U.S. soldier wearing a gas mask and the caption "Are We Ready for This?" the *Washington Post* ran an article that noted, "The [U.S.] Army's prototype plant for destroying [its] chemical weapons is 32 months behind schedule and will cost an additional $190 billion or more, a congressional inquiry found."

As the buildup of U.S. forces in the Persian Gulf continued, Rep. Barney Frank seemed to summarize pretty well the continuing defense budget cuts: "Iraq has not altered the course of this [budget] bill."

Techflation

A phenomenon exists in the stock market whereby various inherent "levels of resistance" are encountered as the market declines. A some-

Figure 19

CURRENT NEWS

EARLY BIRD

FRIDAY, August 3, 1990

WASHINGTON TIMES   August 3, 1990   Pg. 1

Bush outlines plans to slash the military

By Frank J. Murray
THE WASHINGTON TIMES

ASPEN, Colo. — President Bush announced yesterday his plan to restructure U.S. military forces by 1995 into a lean quick-response force, trimmed to meet the realities of the post-Cold War era but primed to meet crises like Iraq's invasion of Kuwait.

He said the strategy would hedge against reversal in Soviet intentions while targeting "terrorism, hostage-taking, renegade regimes and unpredictable rulers."

Meanwhile, the Senate, expected in some quarters earlier this week to reject Bush administration calls for Stealth bomber funding, yesterday approved such funding, with opponents suggesting that the Iraqi invasion may have saved the B-2.

"If we're going to err, let's err on the side of being prepared to respond [to military dangers]," Senate Minority Leader Robert Dole said

to brainstorm on the great international issues.

"The events of the past day underscore the vital need for a defense structure which not only preserves our security but provides the resources for supporting the legitimate self-defense needs of our friends and allies," he said soon after a press conference at which he minimized the likelihood of unilateral

BUSH...Pg. 11

WASHINGTON POST   August 3, 1990   Pg. 1

B-2 Bomber Survives Vote In Senate by Small Margin

By Helen Dewar
Washington Post Staff Writer

The Senate yesterday approved continued production of the B-2 "stealth" bomber by the smallest margin in the history of the controversial aircraft as it narrowly rejected moves by critics to kill the program or stall it for a year.

Senate approval for construction

of two more of the costly, radar-evading strategic bombers improved chances for the program's survival in conference with the House, which is expected to vote next month to build no more than the 15 planes that have been authorized by Congress.

But the loss of 11 votes since the Senate voted on the issue last year

VOTE...Pg. 11

NEW YORK TIMES   August 3, 1990   Pg. 1

INVADING IRAQIS SEIZE KUWAIT AND ITS OIL; U.S. CONDEMNS ATTACK, URGES UNITED ACTION

By R. W. APPLE Jr.
Special to The New York Times

WASHINGTON, Aug. 2 — Battle-hardened Iraqi troops stormed into the desert sheikdom of Kuwait today, seizing control of its capital city and its rich oilfields, driving its ruler into

cial markets in turmoil, Mr. Bush banned almost all imports from Iraq and froze the nation's assets in the United States Speaking at a joint news conference in Wondy Creek, Colo., the President and Prime Minister Margaret Thatcher of Britain raised the possibility of joint United Nations ac-

ease and by ambitions for regional dominance.

According to reports from witnesses in Kuwait, hundreds of people were killed or wounded as Iraqi ground forces, led by columns of tanks, surged into the desert emirate at the head of

---

what analogous concept exists as the defense budget is reduced. An enormous increase in budgetary pressure is generated over time as a nation seeks to maintain a modern defense force of any fixed size, because of a phenomenon defined here as "techflation." It turns out that a "zero real-dollar growth" defense budget is not a stationary defense budget at all, but actually entails a significant annual *decline* in force size if a balanced, modernized military is to be maintained. When the defense budget is reduced, techflation thus creates a level of resistance—a growing budgetary pressure. The consequences of techflation have not generally been explicitly recognized nor quantified; Leonard Sullivan, a former assistant secretary of defense, is in fact the only other writer known to the authors to have addressed the subject quantitatively and expressly. Nonetheless, techflation will have a profound impact on America's long-term defense capability.

The phenomenon of techflation stems from the galloping increase in *unit cost* of military hardware extended over a long period of time, an increase traceable to the advancing technology and capability each succeeding generation incorporates. If a graph is made of the cost of the hardware constituting a given category of military equipment (airplanes, for example) as that category evolved through the twentieth century, a very steady and predictable growth rate of unit cost is

Figure 20   Cost of Bomber Aircraft, 1930–1990

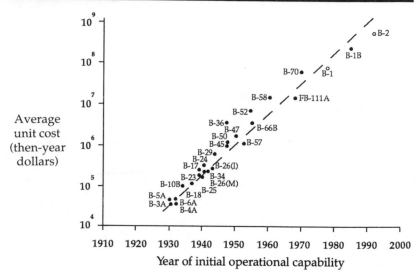

SOURCE: Norman R. Augustine.

observed (Figures 20 and 21). In the case of high-tech equipment such as aircraft, this growth rate of cost is about 15 percent per year in current dollars. For military equipment entailing lesser *overall* technology content such as tanks and ships, the inflation rate runs at about 7 percent per year. In the case of those items the military procures from the civilian sector, such as clothing, food, and fuel, the long-term cost growth rate approximates the inflation rate of the economy as a whole (about 4.5 percent per year since World War II). When allocated by proportion of the defense budget, the overall weighted long-term cost growth rate for a balanced military force (matched in size, readiness, and modernization) equals about 7.9 percent per year, or 3.4 percentage points above the rest of the economy. This difference is herein termed "techflation" and turns out to have profound consequences indeed.

The techflation rate is not truly an *inflation* rate in the customary sense of the word. Inflation usually implies that one receives less for the same amount of money or, equivalently, must pay more for the same.

Figure 21   **Cost of Tactical Aircraft, 1910–1990**

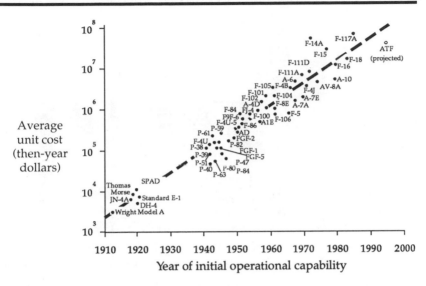

SOURCE: Norman R. Augustine.

But when someone moves from a small house to a large house, for example, the difference in costs would not ordinarily be categorized as (wasteful) inflation, nor would advancing from a generation of automobiles with stick-shift transmissions to a generation with automatic transmissions be so categorized. The same certainly holds when one progresses through the sequence of military aircraft from, say, a P-38 to an F-86 to an F-100, to an F-4 to an F-15, to an ATF. There have been enormous increases in capability of military hardware (planes, tanks, and the like) over the years, but the *unit cost* of that hardware, from generation to generation, *has accordingly increased at a rate substantially faster than the inflation rate of the economy as a whole.*

Therein lies the difficulty. Defense budget planning as conducted by the executive branch and Congress is generally measured in *constant-dollar* terms—that is, after correcting for inflation. The final Reagan defense budget, for example, was to be a 2 percent *constant-dollar* growth budget for each of the next five years based principally on the inflation

Figure 22   **Annual Rate of Change in Defense Budget Authority**
               (constant dollars)

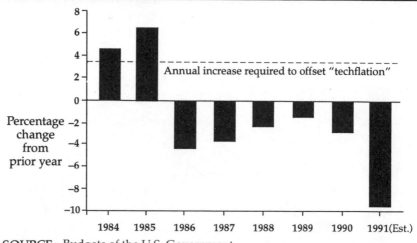

SOURCE: Budgets of the U.S. Government.

rate experienced in the civilian economy (to which government receipts are related). The initial Bush budget was zero percent constant-dollar growth the first year, followed by 1 percent the succeeding two years, and 2 percent thereafter. But it turns out that when the impact of techflation is included, a "zero constant-dollar growth" *defense* budget is not a budget that will sustain a continually modernizing force of a given size but rather is a budget that entails losing somewhere around 3.4 percent of its "buying power" each year in terms of sustainable force size. (Figure 22).

If adversary nations adopt the same degree of technology growth as the United States, they, too, may face this same techflation-induced virtual attrition. But there is no assurance that those nations will accept this. Thus, when zero constant-dollar growth or even declining U.S. defense budgets are compounded over a period of, say, five years, such as America has now experienced, the "phantom" loss becomes substantial indeed—in the present case, 18 percent *on top of* the "intended" 13 percent.

Looking to the future, further budgetary declines in real terms are probable, so it is particularly important that we be mindful of the impact of techflation on the erosion of supportability of a force of any given size. What is *truly* a stationary or status quo budget—that is, a budget holding force size constant while keeping it technologically modern and ready for combat—requires an annual *increase* of 7.9 percent (inflation plus techflation) in current dollars rather than the 4.5 percent increase (inflation only) used in official budgetary calculations.

(The latter only keeps the budget amount itself the same, in real, or constant, dollars from year to year based on the *civilian* economy's inflation index.) Thus, there is a 3.4 percent per year "hidden" erosion built into the way in which defense budgets are currently prepared.

In a so-called constant defense budget, where "zero growth" is measured in the traditional sense, there are few choices for dealing with techflation. The first and least desirable of these, but one that has on occasion been used in the past because of its political convenience, is to construct a "hollow" military force—a force that remains at a fixed size and possibly at a constant level of modernization but that declines in readiness year after year. Personnel are inadequately trained, spare parts shortages are permitted to mount, and insufficient quantities of ammunition and other expendables are stored.

Although this policy constitutes a politically comprehensible solution, the military dangers of such hollowing are quite clear. A striking example of the consequences of this policy was observed many years ago when, during a defense spending cutback, limits were placed on the fuel available to the navy for training purposes. Ships' crews soon began to conduct training exercises at relatively low speeds in order to obtain better fuel consumption and thereby operate more economically.

On one occasion during this period a destroyer flotilla that was to sail along the West Coast from San Francisco to San Diego happened to receive a supplemental fuel allotment. It was decided that the flotilla would use the fuel bonanza to train at flank speed during the transit. The navigators on board the lead ship—having become accustomed to operating at lesser speeds—found themselves operating at an altogether unfamiliar pace. The lead destroyer soon ran aground on the rocks in a heavy fog at Point Honda, near today's Vandenberg Air Force Base. Eight other ships, each trailing in sequence following the running lights of the vessel in front of it, followed at full speed onto the same rocks. Seven ships were lost altogether.

This tragedy is but one vivid example of the possible consequences—even in peacetime—of building a hollow force. Perhaps the tragedy could have been avoided if the navigators had been more adequately trained. The impact of training and selection through combat exercises is often overlooked, but it is a key role of peacetime military operations, and we give it short shrift only at our own peril.

The second solution to techflation—and the solution that seems to have been a preferred approach in the United States over the years—has been to delay replacement of obsolescing equipment, thereby permitting it to get older and older. A rough calculation shows the extent of this problem. Our defense assets today can be calculated to be worth somewhere on the order of $2.7 trillion in replacement value, excluding land, buildings, and the like. If the defense procurement budget is 28 percent of, say, a $300 billion defense budget (roughly the 1989 level), it is simply a matter of arithmetic to show that the average item in the inventory must have a life expectancy of over a quarter century. There is of course a distribution of lifetimes of various types of equipment, with aircraft averaging about thirty years, ships and tanks about thirty-five years, and electronics and missiles about twenty years. This is with today's budgets.

As we have noted before, the pilots of America's B-52 strategic bombers today fly aircraft older than themselves. There are many other such examples. The navy's A-6 may yet be flown by pilots who will be sharing that experience with their grandfathers, because this category of attack aircraft will have been in the inventory nearly fifty years, assuming that it is replaced on the (optimistic) schedule budgeted at the present time. Fifty years is, of course, a very long time for high-technology items such as aircraft, even when they have been periodically upgraded—as has in fact been the case. Not long ago, for example, 60 of the air force's 365 aging A-7 aircraft were grounded for more than four months after inspectors discovered fatigue cracks in their wings due to age. Such incidents are not isolated.

An interesting historical footnote is found in an article by a former army chief of military history, addressing the age of equipment during the early days of the U.S. Army Air Corps. By "declaring the life of all tactical aircraft to be seven years and of all training aircraft to be nine years before classification as obsolete," he noted, "the corps was following a frugal but hazardous policy. Commercial practice as indicated by insurance write-down procedures calls for obsolescence after three years. . . . Nonetheless, it is highly significant that the reported practices of the Royal Air Force in 1937 was to write off all tactical aircraft as obsolete after two years." Thus has been the pace of technology—and techflation—over the years!

The third alternative for dealing with techflation is to cut force structure in a balanced fashion and thereby reduce the amount of equipment that must be bought and maintained. This alternative is the most painful way to offset the effects of techflation in any budget environment that permits less than 3.4 percent annual *increase* in constant dollars (7.9 percent in current dollars) because it means decommissioning actual units: divisions, air wings, and battle groups—and bases, factories, and arsenals. This decommissioning is disruptive to people's lives and to politicians' election plans as well as to the country's overall military capability. This policy is particularly difficult to reverse be-

Figure 23   **Fighting Aircraft Procured by United States,**
1940–1990

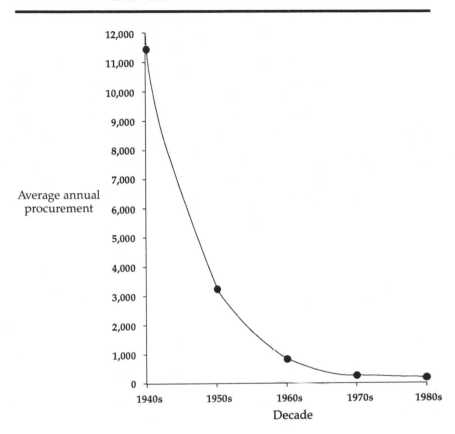

Average annual procurement

Decade

SOURCE: Norman R. Augustine.

cause of the problem of reconstituting units when supporting infrastructure has not been preserved. But it also happens, in most circumstances, to be the correct approach.

Techflation and attempts to deal with it have contributed to the dramatic decline, for example, in the number of fighter aircraft in the U.S.
inventory during recent decades (albeit each new aircraft having substantially more capability than its predecessor). At the peak of World
War II the U.S. military bought about fifty thousand (fixed-wing) aircraft per year. By the 1960s the rate had dropped to about a thousand
per year, and by the 1970s to three hundred per year (Figure 23). In the
1980s, despite the Reagan funding buildup, the number remained static

at about three hundred per year, and in the 1990s it can be expected to drop further. Ironically, such low production rates themselves drive unit costs up still higher.

But if the amount of equipment drops so precipitously over time, why hasn't the total number of personnel needed to support those systems dropped commensurately? The answer lies in large part in the additional training and maintenance demands associated with the increasing cost and complexity of each new generation of equipment. We now have about twice as many people in the air force per aircraft as we did at the end of World War II, and about double the number of sailors per ship *overall*. There are also some clear exceptions in the case of ships and aircraft designed specifically to address this problem, and one should never confuse the capability of aircraft and ships of the 1990s with those of the 1940s. Nonetheless, this has been the trend.

A series of very difficult choices is thus confronted as we are actually reducing the defense budget in constant dollars and at the same time coping with the rising costs inherent in modernized military equipment—techflation. To hollow the force would be the worst of all solutions; it is invariably better to have a smaller force with legitimate fighting capabilities than a "parade ground army." We could continue to let the force age, but we are already approaching the point of diminishing returns in this regard even *after* a major burst in defense spending. Finally, we could reduce force structure (overall size of the armed forces) and at the same time try to learn to build equipment that is less costly; this third solution provides the best course under today's circumstances, but it will require a great deal of planning and no small amount of courage and determination to implement.

In fact, whether we like it or not, we are going to be forced to learn to reduce the cost of individual items of equipment. With our past practice we have been following a mathematically incontrovertible law whereby the cost of new aircraft can be described fairly accurately simply in terms of the passage of calendar time. If the cost of, say, tactical aircraft continues to increase at the rate of a factor of four every ten years (once again, not for the identical aircraft, but for a series of ever more capable replacements), a projection of the history of the defense budget over the past century leads to the calculation that in the year 2054 (not really that far away—some readers of this book will still be alive at that time) the entire U.S. defense budget will purchase exactly one tactical aircraft (Figure 24). If this aircraft should instead be a bomber, one can determine (based on the historical interval between new generations of such aircraft) that it will be the B-4

Figure 24   **"Techflation" Compared with Inflation**

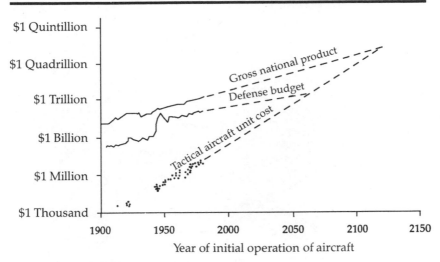

Year of initial operation of aircraft

SOURCE: Norman R. Augustine.

NOTE: Then-year dollars.

that produces this singular event and the year will be 2020—allowing pundits a wonderful opportunity for references to hindsight. This projection is noted only partially facetiously, because the trend thus far continues unchecked.

As a historical note, we shall soon have gone full circle, back to the days of Calvin Coolidge who, in a moment of pique over having to pay $25,000 for an entire squadron of eighteen aircraft, asked, "Why can't we buy just one airplane and let the aviators take turns flying it?"

This phenomenon of the increasing cost of military aircraft, incidentally, does not differ substantially from the trend in the commercial aircraft world. Data spanning the years from the Ford Tri-Motor to modern commercial jets reveal precisely the same slope of the cost growth curve—and the same record of continually improving capability. (The difference is, of course, that airline receipts have also been growing over the long term.) So do, for example, cost data on British military aircraft. And although most of this discussion has focused on aircraft (which consume 35 percent of the defense procurement budget), similar observations apply to other items of high-tech military hardware as well.

Figure 25   **Composition of U.S. Defense Budget, 1990**

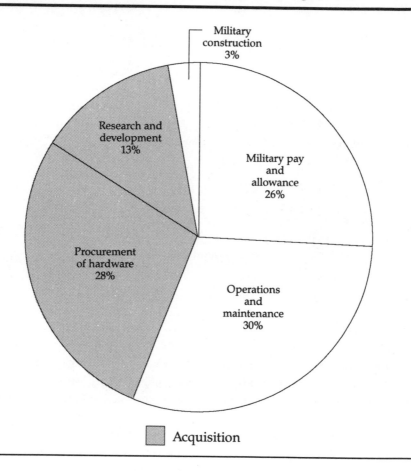

Acquisition

Maintaining a Balanced Force

A look at defense accounting is revealing, albeit somewhat arcane. The defense budget can be broken down into five basic categories (Figure 25). The first of these, *military pay and allowances*—basically the cost of uniformed manpower—consumes about 26 percent of that budget.

Operations and maintenance (O&M) runs about 30 percent and is used to purchase spare parts, train the forces, and underwrite the day-to-day functioning of the defense establishment—often equated to "readiness." *Research and development* (R&D) traditionally consumes about 13 percent of the defense budget and *procurement of hardware* about 28 percent. The latter two taken together are often referred to as the acquisition budget and determine the forces' modernization. When further combined with *military construction,* which generally comprises about 3 percent, the acquisition budget is referred to as the investment account.

The military pay and allowances category includes the pensions received by retired military personnel; the Department of Defense is virtually the only federal entity required to carry this expense within its own budget. On the other hand, the "defense" budget as traditionally reported does not include, except in special breakouts, expenditures by the Department of Energy to provide nuclear weapons for inclusion in military systems.

The R&D plus procurement budgets (the acquisition account), which underwrite the modernization of the force, consume about 41 percent of the total budget. There are typically fifty major projects in development at any one time. Of this amount of money, roughly a third is allocated to aircraft, a fifth to missiles and space, a tenth to ships, and the remaining roughly one-third to everything else. In times of changing defense budgets, the investment account (R&D plus procurement plus military construction) has traditionally seen about *twice* the swing on a percentage basis as the defense budget as a whole (Figure 26). That is, for each 1 percent change in the defense budget the investment account has typically changed by 2 percent (in the same direction, up or down). This is because of the difficulty already noted, political as well as military, of modifying the other categories, which comprise personnel levels, base structure, and the like. This trend held true once again for the major cuts proposed in 1991, which, when last seen, seemed headed for an 18 percent reduction in the investment account and 9 percent overall in real dollars (not including any adjustments to finance Middle East operations). Much as the defense budget is the happy hunting ground of federal budget cutters, the procurement account is the fertile field of Pentagon budgeteers. This poses a major problem for force modernization and industrial health. If this historical ratio persists (so far it does), and if the defense budget is cut peak to valley by 40 percent in real dollars (something that is not unlikely, given America's short memory for world events), the cut in R&D and procurement combined would be fully 80 percent. This unacceptable outcome points once again to the need for a new paradigm. (Actually, in the present environment it is likely that lesser cuts in R&D will be offset by greater cuts in procurement.)

Just as the defense budget can be viewed in terms of force structure (size), readiness (training and support), and modernization (R&D and procurement), it can also be viewed "geographically": land, sea, and air/space—that is, army, navy, and air force. This delineation may be a

Figure 26   **Growth of Total Obligational Authority for RDT&E plus Procurement versus Growth of Total Obligational Authority 1950–1991 (percentage)**

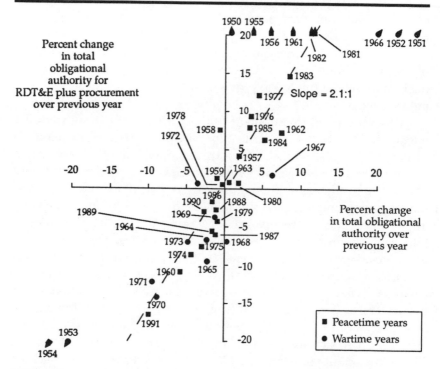

SOURCE: Norman R. Augustine, from Department of Defense data.

NOTE: In constant dollars.

bit suspect, in that the army has on occasion had more aircraft than the air force (mostly rotary wing), the navy has both ground forces (the marines) and aircraft, and the army even owns a few ships. Nonetheless, it does reflect the organization of our armed forces, which not too many years ago had the air force providing boat service to the Pentagon (from an air base across the Potomac) and the army providing air service (to the Pentagon heliport) and the navy, not to be left out, providing its own land transportation (a small motorpool).

As the threat shifts, so presumably may the proper mix among our military departments. A number of arguments, often extreme, are now being heard in this regard—some of which seem to overlook the need to maintain a carefully balanced overall military capability.

As the United States turns its primary attention away from the possibility of a major land war in Europe toward that of more limited conflicts throughout the world, the need for rapidly deployable forces becomes evident. Writing in the *Wall Street Journal*, Karen Elliott House observed that "A multi-polar world with regional aggressions unrestrained by superpower influence is going to be a more dangerous and violent age. The end of the Cold War, in short, will be the beginning of an era of Hot Wars. One need only watch the Soviets flapping in rhetorical chorus with the West over Iraq's aggression to realize that superpower amity has little effect on regional enmity."

The most rapidly deployable forces are those capable of transport with airlift and, when possible, supported with air power, including long-range air power that can rapidly be focused on locations throughout the world. The airlift capability of the United States is thus of major importance in the types of conflicts most likely to be encountered in the decade ahead. The air force has been called upon time and time again in recent years to provide air support, as in Panama and the Philippines, as well as to provide strategic airlift. Examples of the latter include the transport of 2,700 persons and 3,000 tons of supplies to Panama in a few days; 800 persons and 1,150 tons to Namibia; 1,400 persons and 610 tons after the *Stark* incident—not to mention the Saudi Arabia deployment.

But it is not possible to transport solely by air the enormous tonnages of supplies needed to support a major ground operation. Seaborne forces are essential for this purpose. America's largest transport aircraft is capable of carrying but two main battle tanks (refueling immediately after takeoff)—a minor amount in light of loss rates on the modern battlefield—and even our lightest infantry division weighs 13,000 tons, not including prodigious amounts of resupply.

Furthermore, the United States is basically a maritime power that is critically dependent upon its sea lines of supply for commercial as well as military reasons and is likely to be confronted increasingly with the lack of forward bases from which to conduct operations. Even some of our closest allies were not particularly forthcoming when the United States decided to strike back at Libya's Mu'ammar Qaddafi, denying even overflight rights to our hardpressed aviators. The navy has been called upon some fifty times in the last decade alone to participate in such diverse operations as the capture of the *Achille Lauro* hijackers, strike operations (together with the air force) against Libya, escort of tankers in the Arabian Gulf, and so forth.

But when all is said and done it is land power that often ultimately decides the issue. The army has typically suffered 75 percent of the casualties in conflicts involving U.S. forces. U.S. Admiral Harry Train, former commander in chief, Atlantic, observed, "The Falklands once again demonstrated that the ultimate outcome of a war is determined on the ground. The Royal Navy could have lost the Falklands Islands conflict at sea but could not have won it. Such is the nature of modern war." It was also the nature of ancient war. T. S. Fehrenbach noted in *Proud Legions*, "You may fly over a land forever; you may bomb it, atomize it, pulverize it, and wipe it clean of life—but if you desire to defend it, protect it, and keep it for civilization, you must do this on the ground, the way the Roman legions did, by putting your young men into the mud."

The trap of creating an unbalanced force must be studiously avoided if America is to achieve the maximum fighting power it can obtain for *whatever* amount of money it spends and for whatever set of contingencies it is desired to accommodate. And those contingencies will themselves generally involve significant uncertainties in location, time-urgency, and enemy capability. In the years ahead, flexibility will be the premium commodity.

A Dollar of a Different Color

But the accounting practices employed in defense budgeting have often led to yet another complication, and to the potential for some very bad decision making. One key practice—actually a necessary, straightforward, and common one—seems to be little noted by many who would offer advice on the formulation of defense policy. This practice consists of reporting defense budget data both in terms of *budget authority* and *outlays*. Roughly speaking, budget authority measures the approvals granted by the Congress for the government to make commitments for future defense expenditures. In contrast, outlays conform more closely to the "cash basis" of accounting widely used in commerce and measure actual money flows. Clearly it is necessary to control both—and to know the difference between the two.

Thus, when the appropriations act approves the purchase of a ship, budget authority is established for the Pentagon to sign a contract with a manufacturer for the purchase of that particular ship. The bills to be paid, however, do not become due until such time as the ship is actually built (in its entirety or in part, depending upon the specific contract terms). Several years thus may, and often do, elapse before the entire obligational authority is converted into outlays—that is, actual payments.

Historically, the government has managed budget authority as the principal control parameter in its budgeting process. The government bases its policy on the generally well-founded assumption that if it does so, it will maintain control over any ensuing bill that might eventually be presented to the Treasury for payment. But with growing concern over the near-term national debt, Gramm-Rudman-Hollings legislation was promulgated that established harsh budgetary triggers to control the deficit and was keyed not to budget authority but to *outlays*. This focus on outlays is occurring just as our near-term defense plans have begun to take on greater importance in the wake of the sudden breakup of the Warsaw Pact—a relatively unforeseeable political development that has increased the importance of our immediate defense outlays compared with our previously budgeted defense expenditures.

Reductions in defense spending therefore may not be what they seem unless it is explicitly defined which of these two flavors of money is being considered. A one-dollar cut in outlays has a much more dramatic immediate impact than does a one-dollar cut in budget authority. This is perhaps best illustrated using some data from the *Congressional Quarterly*, where a hypothetical reduction in the fiscal year 1991 defense budget is examined. Following are the items that would have to be deleted in 1991 to make an approximately $7 billion reduction in the defense budget if the standard of currency is the more traditional *budget authority:*

- kill the B-2 bomber

- buy a Trident sub every other year, instead of annually

On the other hand, this same approximate $7 billion cut takes on an entirely different character if it must be measured in terms of *outlays:*

- kill the B-2 bomber

- buy a Trident sub every other year, instead of annually

- cut the army and air force by 225,000 troops over three years

- kill the MX and Midgetman missiles

- cut SDI to $2.2 billion per year

- kill the LH helicopter

- kill the *Seawolf* submarine

- buy four Aegis destroyers per year instead of five

- kill the ATF fighter plane

- kill the C-17 cargo plane

In this particular example, a single dollar reduction in outlays really implies that $3.56 of budget authority be deleted—a difference of 256 percent. More recently, Senator Sam Nunn, addressing the same point, cited a case wherein the difference between budget authority and outlays was fully a factor of seven. Either currency of the realm can of course be used, but it is well if all the participants in the national security debate define and understand their terms of reference, because the seemingly arcane difference between the two "colors" of dollar can be the difference between an austere defense force and an unworkable one.

The Peace Dividend

The recent public debate over the defense budget seemed to focus not on what the nation's security objectives should be but rather on what we could now *not* spend on defense. A great deal of attention has been devoted to the existence of the so-called peace dividend—with long queues of would-be recipients forming in the nation's capital to share in its benefits. The difficulty of maintaining support for defense spending in peacetime was vividly demonstrated in early 1990 when senators were forced to vote explicitly on shifting $400 million from defense to treatment of crack-afflicted babies.

Exactly what the peace dividend will consist of has not yet been determined and will depend to some extent upon the outcome of matters in the Middle East (and elsewhere); some assert that it will not even exist. Others see it as a solution to all the nation's fiscal woes. Part of the difficulty of making such an assessment is that we are dealing largely with future cost avoidances—the most specious type of "saving," as was already discovered when addressing the Soviets' claims of budgetary reductions. It is difficult to assess future defense budgets even when the secretary of defense publicly states his plans. On the same day in 1989, according to former defense secretary Casper Weinberger, the Associated Press reported that Secretary Cheney would cut the defense budget by $180 billion in three years, *USA Today* said he would but the defense budget by $180 billion in five years, the *Wall Street Journal* had it as $180 billion in six years, and the *New York Times* said $180 billion in three years—beginning in 1992. In the end it is likely that Congress will prove everyone wrong—including the defense secretary.

It would be more accurate to say that the good news is that there *is* a peace dividend, but the bad news is that it has probably already been spent. And even this is only about half correct. The good news is that there will in fact *be* a peace dividend. The bad news is that it will not be nearly large enough to *dent* the major demands being created in other sectors of the federal budget, let alone governmental spending at the state and local levels.

Why this should be the case can be illustrated with a brief calculation. Assume, for example, that it had been decided to declare the peace dividend back in 1980 rather than wait for the collapse of communism at the end of the decade. At that time, it will be recalled, the Soviets had already lost their foothold in Egypt as well as in other parts of Africa, and even China was showing signs of openness and a desire to pursue an economic system more nearly approaching a market economy. Also assume, for purposes of illustration, that the dividend that was to be reaped would be used to pay for additional benefits in nondefense federal spending; each dollar actually added to the nondefense federal budget would be financed by simply reducing defense expenditures by the corresponding one dollar. The logic would be straightforward; increases in the nondefense federal budget would be paid for by decreases in the defense budget—a true peace dividend.

Unfortunately, had this policy actually been adopted, the entire defense budget would have disappeared by the time the decade was barely half over. Every single soldier, sailor, airman, and marine; every tank, airplane, and ship; every defense industrial worker and defense civil servant would have vanished from the payroll—and we still would have been unable to pay for even the *growth* in nondefense federal spending that had actually transpired during the 1980s—a decade of so-called defense emphasis (Figure 27). In fact, since the midpoint of this century, federal expenditures have exhibited an overall real growth rate of 3.5 percent per year while defense spending has averaged only about 1.0 percent real growth per year. These figures compare with a real GNP growth rate of 3.3 percent per year over the same period.

The point is not that the defense budget is an insignificant sum, but rather that other federal demands have grown to such an extent that paying for them by reducing the defense budget is like trying to offset the savings and loan deficit by asking citizens to reduce their expenditures on shoes—to adapt a piece of Russian folklore.

Nonetheless, there *will* be a peace dividend. In fact, there *has* been a peace dividend. It has actually been accruing for some five years now and already amounts to $221 billion in budget authority as compared with what it would have cost, in real (1990 dollar) terms, to have continued defense spending at the constant dollar level actually extant five years ago. The amount of savings over the past five years of declining defense budgets relative to the forecast originally made by President Reagan at the peak of defense spending is even greater: $433 billion in

Figure 27 **Defense versus Nondefense Outlays, 1945–1990**

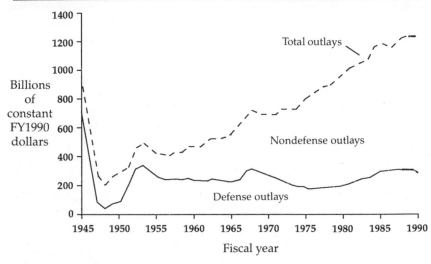

SOURCE: Budgets of the U.S. Government.

real terms. The difficulty encountered in determining the magnitude of future savings resides, of course, in deciding what projected future spending level should be used as a basis for comparison.

The budget submitted by President Bush for fiscal year 1991 and the following years, even with no cuts by Congress, would have saved $159 billion in real terms over a four-year period relative to the final Reagan budget. The same Bush budget saves $103 billion over the next four years relative to the *initial* Bush budget. Similarly, the fiscal year 1991 Bush budget represents a real savings of $254 billion over the five-year period (1991 to 1995) relative to the spending level that was actually being pursued at the peak of the Reagan defense buildup. And all this before the major additional defense budget cuts the Congress has been promulgating.

The existence of a peace dividend is real indeed. But as incredible as it may seem in view of the huge size of the figures involved, this dividend is actually insufficient to have any resounding financial impact, given today's behemoth scale of federal nondefense programs. And in themselves, discussions of a peace dividend do little toward helping the nation define its long-term security objectives in what is likely to remain a highly dangerous world.

A less asked question is who shall pay for the peace dividend—or more precisely, exactly what will be the impact of the contemplated defense budget cut, and on whom? To examine this it is instructive to place the present reductions in a historical context. For purposes of comparison, consider the reductions that have taken place in constant dollar outlays during the first three years of prior defense cutbacks.

Measured against America's GNP, the present restructuring is small, amounting to a little over a 1 percentage point drop in defense spending as a fraction of GNP, based on the average of the Senate and House budget office projections—that is, from about 5.8 to 4.3 percent of GNP. In contrast, the restructuring after World War II amounted to a 34 percentage point drop as a fraction of GNP, while the Korean and Southeast Asia wars were followed by 4 and 2 percentage point cutbacks, respectively.

Turning to overall federal spending, the impact is somewhat larger, although still not great by previous standards. The present post–Berlin Wall reduction represents about a 4 percentage point drop in defense spending as a fraction of federal spending. World War II, Korea, and Southeast Asia led to 49, 9, and 10 percent drops, respectively.

In terms of impact on the defense budget itself, we are looking at a 15 percent cutback, whereas World War II was followed by an 88 percent reduction, Korea 25 percent, and Southeast Asia 18 percent. It is probable that these numbers, each based on a three-year time span, somewhat understate the impact of the current downsizing, due to its more prolonged character. Finally, turning to one other constituency, the defense industry is undergoing a "triple-whammy." Still reeling from the procurement policies of the 1980s (fixed-price R&D, heavy up-front investment, prematurely priced production options, and so on), the defense industry is now feeling the major cutbacks in the overall defense budget *exacerbated* by the historical propensity, already discussed, to pass along a disproportionately greater share of any cuts to industry.

The Foundation of Defense

As has been noted, America's economic well-being determines to a considerable extent what we can afford to spend on national defense and therefore what risks we must take. A significantly smaller GNP would probably mean less funding for defense—no matter that our actual defense *needs* themselves are determined in large part by the spending levels and political policies embraced by other nations, and not by the level of our GNP. As a nation we may be forced to accept higher national security risks if our GNP is low than would have been the case with a stronger economy, because the smaller forces that could be afforded would presumably have less real capability and therefore would be less effective as a deterrent.

Furthermore, much of the key technology embodied in today's military hardware is no longer derived principally from government defense contracts and arsenals but now stems from the commercial world. This new and not yet fully recognized trend is particularly significant in such areas as electronics and optics, which, as has been discussed, are pivotal to modern military equipment.

The point is that the competitiveness of American firms in the nondefense arena will have an increasingly direct impact upon our ability to carry out national security objectives—in determining not only what we as a nation can afford to spend on defense but also what technology may be reliably available. In the sometimes alarming book *The Japan That Can Say No* by Akio Morita and Shintaro Ishihara (a 1989 candidate for prime minister), the authors pointedly remark that "If, for example, Japan sold [micro]chips to the Soviet Union and stopped selling them to the United States, this would upset the entire military balance."

It is disconcerting to see trends such as those reported by a *Wall Street Journal*/Nippon Research poll that Japanese below age twenty believe that in the "unlikely event your country were to go to war," the most probable opponent would be the United States. The Soviet Union and Korea were named about one-fifth and one-third less often respectively.

A National Academy of Engineering study concluded that in the case of one U.S. missile system it would take more than a year to replace all foreign parts with domestically supplied hardware. Another assessment identified sixteen components of foreign origin in one air-to-air missile and concluded that were they denied, production would be halted for up to eighteen months.

Clearly, the actions needed to assure the existence of a strong national economy and international competitiveness far transcend the responsibilities of the Department of Defense. Nonetheless, these factors' impact upon national security is of the first magnitude, and a few observations and recommendations on the subject are therefore perhaps in order.

The United States remains the world's largest economy by almost any standard—although certainly no longer the single dominant economic power, as it was in the years immediately following World War II. With 5 percent of the world's population and 6 percent of the world's land area, America today produces 26 percent of the world's goods and services—down from the approximately 50 percent of the earlier era but still a very substantial portion. As already noted, that's at least twice the GNP of the USSR, more than twice that of Japan, and more than all of the countries of Western Europe combined.

But U.S. strength in the global marketplace, a vital measure of economic health, presents a study in contrasts. We remain the world's greatest trading nation, achieving record or near-record exports each month. But imports into our prosperous economy have risen far higher and faster than exports, and U.S. market share has fallen precipitously even in high-technology sectors previously dominated by American companies. America still enjoys the highest overall economic productivity of any nation on earth; but the nation's rate of productivity *growth* is among the lowest in the industrialized countries.

Nowhere is the diminishment of our role more evident than in the vast, economically important, technology-based consumer electronics field. For instance, in the case of color television receivers, pioneered in this country, America's international market share has fallen from 90 percent in 1970 to less than 10 percent in 1987; our market share of telephones, invented in the United States, has declined from just under 100 percent to about 25 percent and is still falling; audio tape recorders, based on U.S. technology, from 40 percent to zero share of the market; VCRs, again based on U.S. technology, to zero market share; and record players, invented here and once a primary U.S. product, now also zero market share.

In 1970, there were eighteen major U.S. television manufacturers selling at home and overseas; today there is only one (hard-pressed) U.S. producer in competition with thirteen foreign companies selling into the U.S. market. In 1975, five of the top six companies in the extremely important semiconductor industry were American; within ten years four of the top six companies were Japanese (Figure 28).

In 1965, the world's top three auto manufacturers were U.S. firms, and no company from our Japanese ally was in the top ten; today two Japanese companies rank in the top four, behind General Motors and Ford, and some observers believe that before long the "Big Three" will all be non–U.S. firms.

In 1966, six of the world's largest banks were American, and no Japanese bank was in the top ten; today all ten of the world's largest banks are Japanese. The Tokyo Stock Exchange, a few years ago substantially smaller than its opposite numbers in New York and London, is now the largest exchange in the world, with stocks surpassing the value of those on the New York Stock Exchange by some 50 percent. Nomura, Japan's leading securities firm, is over twenty times larger than Merrill Lynch. By 1989 the market capitalization of Nippon Telegraph and Telephone was greater than the capitalization of IBM, AT&T, General Motors, Exxon, and General Electric *combined.* Although it has since dropped with the decline in the Japanese securities market, it still exceeds half of the combined worth of all the companies in West Germany.

Figure 28   World Semiconductor Market (six generations of dynamic random access memory)

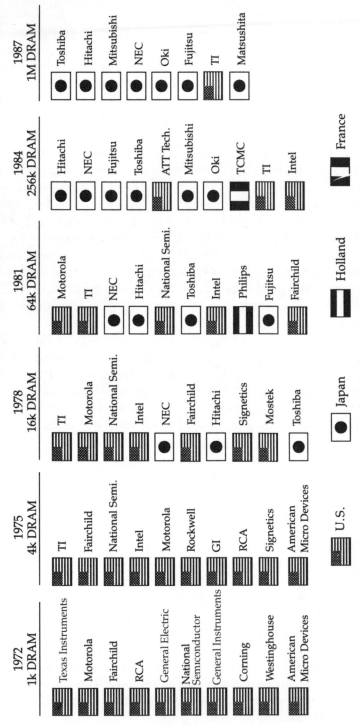

SOURCE: 1972–81 Daniel Okimoto, Stanford University; 1984–87 Dataquest Inc., San Jose, California.

Perhaps most painful of all was a recent article in *USA Today* that began, "In a surprising move, Hewlett-Packard Co., the granddaddy of Silicon Valley, is moving its personal computer headquarters to France to be run by a Frenchman, Jacques Clay. The move reflects a growing realization that Europe—not the USA or Japan—will be the world's hottest market for PC's in the 1990's. It makes sense to position yourself where the money is, says analyst Bruce Stephens of International Data Corp."

It is projected that at least one million Americans will be working for Japanese companies in the United States by the early 1990s. Overall, the percentage of Americans employed by foreign-owned companies more than doubled from the mid-1970s to the mid-1980s, with one in fourteen U.S. factory workers now working for a foreign boss.

This trend creates a particular dilemma for those charged with providing America's national security, given the growing practice whereby foreign firms are stepping in to buy "wounded" U.S. manufacturers, attracted by the latters' bargain basement prices and favorable exchange rates. Among the more recent of these is Learjet, which was bought by Integrated Resources, Inc., only to see Integrated fall into Chapter 11 and sell Learjet to a Canadian firm by the name of Bombardier. Others are the French firm Matra's acquisition of Fairchild, IBM's sale of its Rolm Telecommunications unit to a German firm, and the breakup of the once-proud Singer Company's defense sector in a hostile takeover and the subsequent dispensing of pieces to Canadian and British firms. The British firm, Plessey, has itself been the victim of a hostile takeover by a combination of British and German firms. Today, nearly one-third of the "top fifty" suppliers of electronics to the Department of Defense are foreign firms—including Marconi, Thompson CSF, Philips, Ferranti, Mitsubishi, Toshiba, and Krupp/Atlas. Arguing for relaxed domestic antitrust laws in the face of increasing foreign competition, Clyde V. Prestowitz writes, "Our policy is kind of nutty. We condone U.S. firms getting together with Mitsubishi, but not with an American company."

What are America's leading exports, say, to Japan? With a few notable exceptions (aircraft, computers, and office machine parts), our leading exports are foodstuffs and raw materials: wood, corn, meat, oilseeds, fish, and the like—not to mention jobs. Contrast this with Japan's leading exports to America: motor vehicles, television and photographic equipment, telecommunications, automatic data-processing machinery, electronic components, and radio transceivers. This trade pattern places the United States in a position similar to that of a third world developing nation trading resources for finished products. A recent survey reported in *Business Week* found that by more than a 3 to 1 margin, Americans believe the Japanese economic threat is more serious than the Soviet military threat.

There are many reasons why America has been losing market share. One of these is an initial neglect on the part of American business executives of the importance of quality—still dangerously prevalent in some instances, especially within the so-called service industries. Another is short-term oriented management. Still another is the focus on financial manipulation rather than the production of goods and services. But the *pivotal* issue today is neither quality nor focus. Rather, it is the fact that individual U.S. *firms* are being compelled to compete against foreign *nations*, with all the attendant resources those nations can muster. No individual U.S. company, regardless of its size, can by itself long compete successfully against foreign firms that are backed by major foreign governments. The latter's pockets are simply too deep. Yet this kind of competition is exactly what is taking place in a number of key, targeted industries today.

There are at least three types of "unlevel playing field" with which American firms must contend in today's international marketplace—a place where *market boundaries no longer coincide with geopolitical boundaries* and where our government can therefore no longer unilaterally impose the rules of trade.

The *first*, and most blatantly unfair, of the three occurs when a foreign government simply targets a given U.S. industry and, through predatory pricing, dumping, and other such illicit practices, sets out to destroy that industry. This, in fact, is the easiest of the three forms of unfair competition to counter. It suggests a rather straightforward, albeit sometimes unpleasant, response—namely, strong economic retaliatory sanctions imposed at the governmental level.

The second form of tilted playing field results from inherent systemic differences among the economies of various nations. Consider as but one defense-related example the highly competitive international "commercial" space launch vehicle industry, wherein the overseas sale of a single large space booster built in America can offset the import of some ten thousand Toyotas and can create some three thousand jobs for a year (the same, incidentally, is true of a 747 airliner). Unfortunately for us, this is a field in which Chinese firms sell *their* launch vehicle, the Long March, for only 20 percent to 40 percent of U.S. manufacturers' *cost*. Soviet producers are moving in the same direction. While visiting aerospace plants in China, one of us asked Chinese industrialists such questions as: "What percent of your cost is attributable to medical insurance for your retired employees? What is your cost for third-party liability insurance? What are your expenditures for environmental legal counsel?" The response was invariably one of genuine incomprehension. Such questions simply have no relevance to the Chinese (or Soviet) system of cost accounting. There is nothing necessarily nefarious involved. They just don't keep the books that way, and the organizations responsible for making these products do not have to foot the bill. But ours do, and we *require* that our industry do so.

The third form of unlevel field results from the fact that there are large numbers of very capable and motivated workers in other parts of the world who are ready to give a good day's work for a fraction of the pay Americans take for granted—including, incidentally, American managers and executives. South Korean workers generally make about 13 percent of the wages of their American counterparts, workers in Mexico often earn about 12 percent, and workers in India about 4 percent of the going rate here.

Today, in effect, we are permitting foreign nations with essentially nonmarket economies to determine the industries in which *America* is permitted to compete. Foreign nations are deciding that they want to be the ones to provide the goods from the premier high-technology industries such as semiconductors, launch vehicles, advanced materials, pharmaceuticals, high-definition television, and the largest business of the next century, the information industry. The result is that, even in technology-intensive fields of traditional U.S. leadership, America has been rapidly losing market share both at home and abroad.

Like it or not, America, with its deadly duo of budget deficit and trade imbalance, is at the threshold of some critical decisions. Either through omission or commission, these decisions will largely determine our nation's long-term viability in the evolving world market, as well as our ability to achieve our national security objectives. Although it may be possible to build a nation based upon a service economy, it most assuredly is not possible to provide for the defense of a nation by means of a service economy. The answer to this dilemma is complex and involves concerted action in at least six areas.

First, America should aggressively seek genuinely free market conditions for the world's international trade. This includes equitable, albeit not necessarily identical, access to markets. Today the marketplace is too often rigged to America's disadvantage. We should, *as a very last resort*, be prepared to wage trade wars, just as on occasion we have been willing to wage military wars.

Second, our nation must forge a comprehensive working partnership that links together the power of our government, our industrial sector including labor, and our academic community in order to "outcompete" foreign nations that are currently targeting key U.S. industries. Adversarial relationships among our different national sectors do seem to be a historical part of the American democratic tradition.

But so is cooperation to meet major national challenges. Together, we can move economic mountains. If we do not hang together, the foreign competition will surely hang us separately. It is disconcerting that we should require the chairman of Fujitsu, Takuma Yamamoto, to tell us at least in part what is wrong with America's approach to competitiveness. "The real problem," according to Yamamoto, "is that the U.S. government has no strategy to strengthen its industry's technology." As far back as 1964 the Justice Department began an antitrust investigation of one of America's premier technology firms, IBM. An antitrust suit filed in 1976 was fought for fifteen years before the assistant attorney general concluded it was "without merit." In the meantime, Japanese industry, *backed* by its government, gained control of a major segment of the world's electronics industry.

Given the realities of today's global market, we need an industry-led business-government-academia partnership, focused on encouraging technological innovation. Such a partnership does not constitute a centrally managed economy (tried throughout the communist world and shown to be an abject failure). Rather, it simply embodies a coordinated business strategy not unlike that pursued in Japan and demonstrated to be devastatingly effective—even for a nation with few natural resources. One primitive example of this approach in the United States is Sematech, an R&D consortium (belatedly) formed through the joint efforts of the semiconductor industry and the U.S. government. Another excellent example from an earlier era was the National Advisory Committee on Aviation, NACA, which laid the foundation for America's enduring position of strength in commercial aircraft manufacturing.

Third, America should move very cautiously indeed in economic dealings with nations that do not share our free enterprise traditions and our belief in the market economy, until the rules of the road have been thoroughly and equitably defined and enforcement assured. Most people learned in Economics 101 that it does not make sound business sense to try to grow oranges in Alaska or to export salmon from Florida; such enterprises would surely fail in any free-market economy given the realities of the cost and pricing structure. Certainly normal free-market risks must be accepted by participants in the marketplace. Overpriced or shoddy goods from whatever country, friend or foe, must be allowed to sink or swim in the marketplace on their own merits or lack thereof. But we should not permit other nations, by their policies of subsidization, to decide for *us* the markets in which America is to be permitted to compete. America has the good fortune of still being the world's greatest consumer nation; this position affords us considerable lever-age—leverage that we should use reluctantly and discreetly, but which we should be prepared to use vigorously when we find we are being exploited.

Fourth, a business environment must be established in America that places much greater emphasis on long-term objectives and less premium on short-term gains. The firm employing one of us announced a few years ago an extremely promising set of new research projects that it intended to pursue—with the result that the firm's stock dropped $11\frac{1}{2}$ points in just five days! Research simply takes too long to pay off for it to be compatible with the limited patience of the increasingly dominant institutional share-holders who own much of America today. As Akio Morita asserted in *The Japan That Can Say No*, "We [Japan] are focusing on business ten years in advance, while you seem to be concerned with profits ten minutes from now." In America we are strip mining our own technology.

Needed steps include the establishment of a capital gains tax rate inversely proportional to the length of time an investment is held. Re-duced rates would therefore apply for assets held for a longer period of time. The average share of stock in the United States is now held for about a year and a half, meaning that ownership of publicly held com-panies, on the average, turns over every eighteen months; making the next quarter's earning of towering concern. The situation is even worse among high-tech firms. Perhaps a graduated capital gains tax would help readjust America's economic sights to more distant horizons and at the same time encourage patient investment—which in turn leads to productivity enhancement, which in turn leads to competitiveness, which leads to job creation and improvement of our standard of living.

Hostile corporate takeovers, almost by definition, are geared to short-term, scorched-earth gains by a few individuals, and they most often divert energy, resources, and attention from productive perfor-mance. It took the company with which one of us is associated six years to recover fully from a takeover attempt which it *survived*. This particu-lar takeover led for a time to the incongruous situation in which each of the two principal combatant firms owned a majority of the other. Merg-ers and acquisitions are part of the normal system of business growth and evolution: but hostile takeovers, as ends in themselves, typically combine zero productivity enhancement with the redeeming social value of a feeding frenzy. America needs in its business sector execu-tives who are more familiar with their research laboratories and facto-ries than with their investment bankers.

Fifth, the nation must get back to the fundamentals of how busi-ness is successfully conducted—that is, to the blocking and tackling of commerce. Although American industry clearly must be assured of a more level international playing field, this alone is not sufficient. We must commit ourselves to participatory management (no one knows a particular job better than the worker performing it), unwavering emphasis on quality and renewed pride in workmanship, teamwork with suppliers, production of real wealth rather than the pointless rearranging of assets, the development of *process* technology in manufacturing, team building and employee empowerment within the work force, and insistence on absolutely ethical treatment of customers, employees, owners, and communities alike. These are the foundations of successful business; and none depends in any way on what Japan, China, Korea, the Soviet Union, or anyone else is doing.

Sixth, we must accelerate the process of streamlining our society and our economy to compete more efficiently under today's international conditions, dealing from renewed strength in the economic arena (as we have successfully been doing in the international political arena recently). This demands more nearly balanced budgets—a dubious prospect indeed, given the enormous spending pressures on Congress. (A study by James L. Payne of 1,060 witnesses at congressional hearings revealed that those favoring spending actions outnumbered those opposing them 1,014 to 7 (with 39 remaining neutral.)

Most important, we need a major effort to upgrade the nation's educational system, through longer school days and longer school years, strong incentives and higher pay for teacher excellence, higher salaries for teachers with special expertise, and energetic student focus on such core subjects as science, mathematics, history, and language.* The *Wall Street Journal* reports that the fraction of Japanese high school graduates with at least six years of English training is 100 percent; the percentage of American high school graduates with three or more years of Japanese is 0.2 percent. There are more people in China studying English than there are in the United States speaking English. It is unacceptable that American twelfth-grade students should finish next to last among youths from twelve countries or regions on mathematics tests—behind Finland, Hong Kong, and nine others. According to *U.S. News & World Report*, 22 percent of student grades in the public schools of our nation's capital in 1987 were F's. In a recent Gallup poll, 14 percent of the adult Americans surveyed couldn't find the United States on a map. Twenty-five percent couldn't find the Pacific Ocean. The average American

---

*See David T. Kearns and Denis P. Doyle, *Winning the Brain Race: A Bold Plan to Make Our Schools Competitive* (San Francisco: ICS Press, 1989).

sixth grader spends only twenty-nine minutes a school day studying science, yet finds time for three hours of television.

According to David Sheldon, former headmaster of the Middlesex School, at least one state, California, decided to get tough. It passed a law requiring that "no high school diplomas will be given to students who can't read well enough to understand labels, signs, television guides, and Social Security applications." In fairness to the students, however, it was decided that the rule should not be applied for three years and that students should be given four chances to pass the proficiency test.

Sheldon also notes that according to a 1985 survey of high school teachers in California, the most persistent school problems were alcohol and drug use, depression, suicide, pregnancy, rape, and assault. In 1945 the same survey reported the most persistent problems as talking in class, gum chewing, noise, running in the hall, cutting in line, and waste paper not making it to the wastebaskets.

Many other measures must be taken to prepare our nation for future international economic competition. For instance, we need to adopt incentives to encourage an increased personal savings rate—our current rate being only one-fifth of Japan's and one-tenth of Korea's on a relative basis—by imposing consumption taxes and other devices that raise the level of investment in national growth. David Goldman of Polyconomics, Inc., points out that the real inflation-adjusted capital gains tax on a typical fifteen-year stock investment is now 69 percent and not the widely accepted 28 percent—due to the effect of taxing inflation "gains." We should incentivize investments by industry in research and productivity, disincentivize short-term business strategies, and find means to reduce the enormous effort now being devoted to the resolution of legal disputes—such as moving more in the direction of having the losing litigant pay the legal costs of all parties. Finally, we must proceed resolutely, year after year, to control and reduce the federal budget deficit and the resultant national debt, which now approaches $3 trillion—having increased by a factor of more than three in the past decade alone.

America is richly endowed with natural resources. It has a strong, well-established process for performing research. Our institutions of higher learning enjoy worldwide renown. Nobel prizes in scientific fields received by American citizens over the past ten years total thirty-four as compared with, for example, two to Japan. In the area of innovation, Americans have been responsible for such developments as the airplane, the liquid rocket, atomic power, the transistor, and the semiconductor integrated circuit.

But in recent years, America has increasingly stood by and watched other nations beat us to the marketplace with our own technology and our own ideas. Last year the top three companies receiving U.S. patents were Japanese. Of the top ten, eight were foreign, including five Japanese. While other nations export electronics, we export ideas and jobs. We cannot long afford such an outcome.

— FIVE —

DEFENSE PROCUREMENT:
Beating Swordmakers into Plowshares

In World War I the majority of troops in the American Expeditionary Force reached Europe in British transports, fought with French and British artillery pieces, fired French-manufactured ammunition, flew Allied planes, and manned French tanks. Of the twenty-three thousand U.S. tanks on order, only seventy-six had been completed by the time of the armistice.

In contrast, many historians have argued with considerable persuasiveness that America's margin of victory in World War II was its matériel capability—not necessarily because of technological superiority, but rather because of sheer volume. Opposing forces were simply inundated with the output of the American industrial machine, the arsenal of democracy, or, as the same entity later came to be known, the military-industrial complex. As supplies piled up in Great Britain in preparation for the invasion at Normandy, it was said that a secondary purpose of the barrage balloons that dotted the skies was to keep the island from sinking under the weight of the matériel that was pouring forth from America's factories (Figure 29).

At the peak of World War II production, a new B-17 bomber rolled out of one aircraft plant in the United States every hour on the hour, twenty-four hours a day. A military aircraft was produced somewhere in America every ten minutes day and night, an artillery piece every six minutes, a tank every twenty-five minutes, and a military truck every

Figure 29. In preparation for the invasion at Normandy, supplies pile up in England—all products of the mobilized U.S. production machine.

minute. Liberty ships—substantial oceangoing vessels—were built in an average of fifty days; the record for constructing a Liberty ship— from laying the keel to sliding the ship down the gangways—was, incredibly, a little more than four days (Figure 30).

More recent years found this situation strikingly reversed, with American forces substantially outnumbered in equipment by the forces of the Soviet Union. As noted earlier, it has been U.S. policy not to seek quantitative superiority but rather to pursue aggressively the latest in military technology to generate a deterring and winning margin. Even today the Soviet Union possesses about three times the number of tanks, five times as much artillery, and half again as many tactical aircraft as the United States. There are of course exceptions, aircraft carriers being prominent among these. Such numerical imbalances favoring the Soviets have been real indeed for the past several decades, though they were somewhat redressed when other NATO and Warsaw Pact forces were included in the count. But the recent demise of the Warsaw Pact, together with the need for U.S. military forces to respond to a quite different set of national security objectives, has changed the requirements for America's military-industrial base as well as for its military forces themselves.

The means by which America's armed forces are equipped has come to be known as the defense acquisition process or, less precisely, the de-

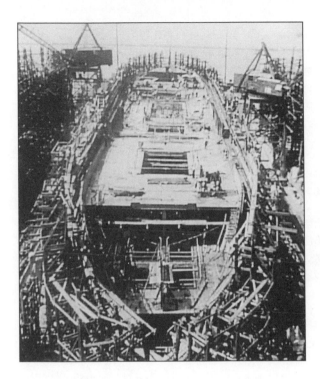

Figure 30. The large World War II ocean-going Liberty ship shown here was built—from laying the bed to sliding down the gang-ways—in a little over four days.

fense procurement process. This chapter examines why this procedure, whereby we seek to create a technological lead in laboratories and transfer that lead to the battlefield, has become so exceedingly troubled.

Technology has been the linchpin of Western military forces in recent years, and it is highly likely to continue to be of principal importance in the future as we draw down our overall defense spending and the size of our standing forces. Unfortunately, our defense acquisition system itself is, at this critical moment, approaching gridlock. Most assuredly, this near-paralysis has not occurred overnight; rather, it has been in the making for much more than a decade. The giant, complex defense acquisition process is beset by problems inherent to the system itself. The fact that the process works at all—which it does—is perhaps a testimony to the capabilities of many of the people in government who somehow manage to surmount its inherent structural obstacles and generally get the job done.

America's military hardware is still sought by virtually every nation in the world—by those who would buy it as well as those who would steal it. It is the hardware of choice throughout most of the world's military forces. But the process by which this hardware is produced does not work *nearly* as well as it should. We are therefore faced with the most egregious of situations: a process upon which we depend heavily that does not work satisfactorily.

Most Americans seem to share the belief that today's military procurement system is unacceptable, although many may well believe this for the wrong reasons. America was of course founded largely by a people seeking to escape oppression and harboring a considerable innate suspicion of all things military. This skepticism is reflected in the framing of our Constitution and endures today, exacerbated by the fact that large sums of tax money have been devoted to national defense throughout the recent peacetime years. There have of course been bursts of public support for occasional military actions (Grenada, Panama, the early days of Saudi Arabia), but most often their effect is short-lived.

During the early part of the Reagan defense buildup, newspapers carried stories almost every day about scandals in the Pentagon and in the defense industry. Editorial cartoons portrayed the defense procurement process as the robbery of America by a greedy military-industrial complex, in which defense firms were run by scoundrels and the Pentagon by selfish incompetents. One report in a major news magazine began, in not atypical fashion, "Forget the $400 hammers, the $7,000 coffee pots; forget the dreary litanies of waste, fraud, and abuse. The latest by-product of the Reagan defense buildup seems to be a new form of corruption within the military-industrial complex." Senator Proxmire told us, "If a U.S. citizen deliberately set out to sabotage U.S. military production in wartime, it would be treason. There is not much difference between that and what some U.S. corporations are allowing to happen now."

Criticism of this type has left the American public verging on the belief that the Pentagon indeed pays $400 for every hammer it buys and that most of our military hardware simply doesn't work at all. The veracity of these scandal stories aside for the moment, a more legitimate concern is that such headlines have diverted attention from the important and very real problems that *do* in fact burden the defense acquisition process and that *are* badly in need of public attention.

A burgeoning number of studies, including six since World War II by presidential commissions, have attempted to improve the acquisition process, with a few notable successes but, it is generally agreed, with far less than satisfactory results overall. One product of reform in the past few years has been the promulgation of a considerable body of new laws and regulations—more, in fact, than were generated on the subject in all the preceding quarter century (Figure 31). These "solutions" in many cases have themselves become part of the very problem they set out to resolve, as in the situation of a patient being treated si-

Figure 31   **Major Studies of Defense Procurement, 1949–1990**

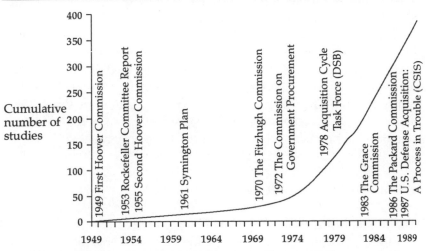

SOURCE: Committee on Armed Services, House of Representatives, "Defense Acquisition: Major U.S. Commission Reports, 1949–1988."

multaneously by a host of doctors each independently prescribing a regimen of potent experimental medications.

The dilemma, true to the spirit of the Hippocratic oath, is how to rectify the many faults of the procurement system without imposing still greater harm on the patient. Some very sage advice is offered in the following passage from a letter to a Senate committee addressing pending legislation regarding procurement contracting:

> The provisions in regard to contracts, I fear, will do little good. The legislation on this subject is already complicated, and the additional guards intended by this bill will still more embarrass officers and people in the transaction of the public business.
>
> Every additional obstacle adds to the delay and to the cost of procuring military supplies.
>
> The department needs tools to work with. Regulations, laws, customs, prescriptions as to its manner of doing business already exist in abundance.

This letter offers a great deal of sound advice regarding the problems befogging today's acquisition process. It was, however, written by M. C. Meigs, the quartermaster general of the U.S. Army—in 1864. More recently, Senator Sam Nunn, among the nation's most respected experts in national security matters, observed that many of today's procurement problems "were yesterday's procurement solutions."

The difficulty of obtaining a consensus regarding the reform task faced in the 1990s is reflected in two major newspaper stories that appeared nearly simultaneously. One blamed defense procurement problems on the *lack of competition* in the defense industry, citing the fact that the government was often stuck with a single supplier of any given item. The second article, on the other hand, blamed defense procurement problems on *excessive competition* in the defense industry created by the overuse of competitive procurement practices by the government, supposedly generating severe pressures that encourage irresponsible bidding practices and lead to shortfalls in performance.

Defense Procurement 101

What, then, *is* this process that has become the center of such a whirlwind of controversy but that hardly anyone seems able to explain—let alone fix? Clearly, defense procurement differs markedly and fundamentally from most other forms of business activity. This point was made painfully apparent in a series of articles that greeted residents of the nation's capital in the morning newspaper a few years ago. The subject of the articles would seem almost too trivial to address here in the context of the enormity of the problems confronted, except that it did occupy a part of the front page of the *Washington Post* and it does serve to illustrate why procurement conducted by the Department of Defense is not easy. The exposé revealed the seemingly ludicrously detailed eighteen-page specification for—get ready—the fruitcake the Pentagon was purchasing for its troops one Christmas. Military specification "MIL-F-1499 (Fruitcake)" contained paragraph after paragraph of descriptions of what must go into the cake, how the cake should be made, how long it should last, how it should hold together, what kinds of fruits must be found inside it, and how it should be stored, wrapped, and shipped. The article generated a veritable mountain of ridicule and abuse for the Pentagon.

But as silly as the fruitcake specification seemed, it turns out that, when one places oneself in the perspective of the government, there were some generally sound reasons that it existed—reasons that help illustrate the differences between the way the Department of Defense purchases products and the way the private sector or private individuals do.

When the CEO of a major corporation decides he or she wants fruitcake for the company's employees, the CEO picks up the telephone and tells a subordinate in the purchasing department, "Buy 40 pounds of fruitcake of good quality from a responsible supplier at the market price." That's the end of the story. The CEO can be fairly confident that the firm's employees will enjoy their Christmas fruitcake.

But when the secretary of defense decides to buy some fruitcake for the troops, the story does not end with a trip to the supermarket. In fact, it does not even begin there. If the Pentagon simply purchased the needed 250 *tons* of fruitcake from a well-stocked, responsible producer that offered a competitive price in the marketplace, complaints would pour into congressional offices and into the office of the secretary of defense and the General Accounting Office not to mention the *New York Times* and "60 Minutes." Companies (and even individuals) across the land would, not unreasonably, protest that they too were citizens, paid taxes, and could also make fine fruitcake in large quantities if given a reasonable opportunity. Recognizing this, Congress has passed laws that in effect require that anyone who wants to provide the army with fruitcake for its troops should be given a fair chance to be the selected supplier. With literally hundreds of actual fruitcake makers and perhaps thousands of would-be fruitcake makers baking away throughout the land (and abroad), the only way to be certain the fruitcake competition is fair is to stipulate precisely what the fruitcake should be like.

Furthermore, if one is to preclude the participation of those few less-than-scrupulous fruitcake makers who may lurk somewhere in the country's bakeries, and if one wants to be sure that there really *are* some cherries and a few nuts in the fruitcake our soldiers are to eat, it is probably a good idea to say exactly how many cherries and how many nuts must be included. Further, soldiers presumably do not like their fruitcake to arrive in crumbs in a paper bag, so a packaging specification seems advisable. Then there are the matters of age and shipping and storage. A Pandora's box of complications unfolds—for fruitcake and for almost everything else our military buys. Plastic whistles require sixteen pages of specifications. Olives take seventeen; hot chocolate twenty; and so on.

If one extrapolates the fruitcake predicament to nuclear-armed, intercontinental-range stealth bombers, for which there *is* no market price, then one *begins* to perceive the scope of the problem. As usual in such cases, it turns out to be much easier to dish out criticism than to dish out the fruitcake—especially if one doesn't even try to *comprehend* the problem. If, on the other hand, one cares enough about properly supplying our soldiers, sailors, aviators, and marines to seek to understand the realities of defense procurement and to offer reasonable *solutions,* one must begin with the fundamentals.

The First Fundamental of Defense Procurement is that this process should never be confused with the free enterprise system. The U.S.

defense acquisition function is not socialism. Neither can suppliers be considered to be regulated businesses in the traditional sense. But the process is certainly not *free enterprise*. The market-driven free enterprise system depends upon having many buyers for each seller and many sellers for each buyer; the competitive pressures thereby created tend to evoke responsible behavior on the part of both buyer and seller while at the same time avoiding the concentration of undue power in the hands of either. Defense procurement thereby differs at the most fundamental level from commercial business—namely, defense procurement has but a single buyer, a condition known as *monopsony*. This arrangement gives the buyer—the government, in this instance—truly enormous power. If a firm happens to be in the commercial business of manufacturing automobiles and one would-be purchaser insists upon unreasonable terms, the auto dealer simply refuses to conduct business and finds *another* buyer. But if the firm happens to build ICBMs, it accepts the terms that the U.S. government chooses to impose; there is no alternative if the company wishes to stay in the ICBM business.

This requires that the government—the sole buyer, with enormous short-term leverage—behave very responsibly and does not take undue advantage of the situation. To take advantage could indeed generate short-term benefits for the government and the taxpayer but in the long term would damage both the government and the industry by driving would-be producers from the supplier base until a strong competitive situation no longer existed.

This danger is becoming increasingly real, as reflected by the financial statements of many major government contractors, who have in recent months begun to report huge losses on specific defense projects undertaken for the government. During the past two years, ten major aerospace firms—the largest sector of the defense industrial base, with more than one million employees—have each reported losses of more than $100 million on fixed-price contracts, for a total of over $3 billion, all of which has had to be absorbed by the shareholders of those corporations. None of this was due to declining defense spending—it was due to the pathological forces at work in any monopsony—in this case taking the form of inappropriate procurement policies by the government and bidding strategies by industry. Losses of this magnitude do not seem to comport with the popular notion of a riskless industry. The *Washington Post* quotes one unnamed defense industry executive as saying, "You can make a small fortune in the defense business—if you start out with a large one."

Next, as if this circumstance of government monopsony were not sufficiently Machiavellian in its own right, there are supplier *monopolies* embedded *within* this government monopsony. Once a contracted military system is well along in production, particularly a major system, the government usually has no real alternative to the existing supplier as a source of the item. Hence, if the government wants to buy another B-1 bomber, there is probably only one place it can realistically hope to obtain it. This state of affairs now gives the *seller* extraordinary leverage—which in turn demands extraordinarily responsible behavior on the part of the latter. In the current defense industry, that too has been a trait that has not been found in great abundance. To make matters worse, this whole process is enveloped in a confounding political environment—all of which, taken together, makes the defense acquisition process something on the order of a riddle wrapped in a mystery inside an enigma (to borrow Churchill's description of the Soviet Union).

The bottom line is that the checks and balances that exist naturally in the commercial marketplace simply don't exist in the defense procurement environment and therefore must be generated by artificial means. There is a disquieting parallel here to the problem that has bedeviled the Soviet economy. Unfortunately, the legitimate objective of creating checks and balances in the defense acquisition process has over the years led to the creation of a vast medicine chest of well-intended but ineffectual remedies and preventives to assure that some specific problem that once occurred can never, ever, under any circumstances, happen again. What the patient really needs today is not yet another aspirin but something more closely approaching quadruple bypass surgery.

The matter of buying for the military is still further complicated by the fact that U.S. military acquisition is one of the largest businesses in the world, with a dollar value larger than the sales of IBM, General Electric, and Chrysler *combined,* and larger even than the individual gross national products of Switzerland, Sweden, Belgium, or Saudi Arabia. Approximately three million people are engaged in the U.S. "defense industry," depending to a degree upon the definition of "defense industry" one chooses to use.

Thus, whatever else the U.S. military-industrial complex may or may not be, it *is* complex. The Department of Defense spends about $150 billion each year in 15 million separate contract actions, or about two per second. These actions are carried out by more than 150,000 government acquisition personnel and another 300,000 supporting government personnel using 30,000 pages of regulations issued by 79 different offices. The process is overseen by 29 congressional committees with 55 subcommittees and 28,000 staff members. In one recent year, the Pentagon was required to respond to 120,000 written requests for information from Congress plus 600,000 telephone inquiries from Capitol Hill, all while supplying 1,300 witnesses who gave 1,500 hours of testimony at 450 hearings—much of it relating to the procurement process. This activity is monitored in minute detail by 26,000 auditors and assisted by the *Washington Post*. It would seem that the old axiom might apply: "When you have reached the bottom of a hole, stop digging."

Small wonder that Budget Director David Stockman once described the Pentagon as a "kind of swamp." Even if the defense acquisition process were 99.44 percent perfect, there would still be 250 horror stories to enliven each day's headlines, with several more left over for the evening news.

It is imperative that the system be made to work effectively—a goal requiring the unselfish support of government and industry alike. Today, procurement problems threaten to undermine the willingness of the public to pay for *whatever* level of defense may be appropriate to carry out the nation's legitimate security objectives. Public complaints about defense seldom concern the performance of our military in the field, and they seldom have to do with the quality of our troops—the best, incidentally, in the nation's history by almost any measure. Rather, it is plainly and simply the troubled procurement process that has been giving so many citizens such a negative general impression of all U.S. military activities.

America's defense industry bears a large part of the obligation to help fix the problems that have occurred. This industry is entrusted with very large sums of public funds. It spends these funds to produce products upon which American lives and even freedom itself may well depend. Members of the defense industry occasionally lament the high standards to which they are held; executives of companies operating in *both* the defense and commercial sectors generally agree that defense-related standards are far more stringent than the counterpart commercial standards (a view not widely held among the public). Yet these high defense standards must be viewed as altogether reasonable given the magnitude of the responsibilities entailed.

The government, too, bears considerable burden for rectifying the situation that has come to exist in defense procurement, inasmuch as the government assumes the predominant role in setting, applying, enforcing, and even interpreting the rules by which the whole process functions.

Six Myths

Misconceptions and ill-founded beliefs concerning the problems and solutions associated with defense procurement are fairly widely held today by the public and the media—and indeed by Congress, the defense industry, and the Pentagon itself.

For instance, almost all defense contractors say they believe that contract *awards* are heavily influenced by members of Congress—a notion that does not at all comport with observations made by us while serving in government for a decade (but a notion that is unfortunately perpetuated by the dubious Pentagon practice of notifying local members of Congress of the name of the winner of major contract competitions before the firms involved or the public are informed). On the other hand, many in government truly believe that contractors deliberately refuse to cut costs so as to inflate their overall business volume—a practice likewise never observed by one of us during two decades of experience in the defense industry.

Discrediting such myths is an important prerequisite to any understanding of what really is needed: a fundamental change in the system itself. Clearly, the procurement process is bedeviled by serious problems. But to accept myths, as appealing as that approach may be for some headline writers, is merely, once again, to lunge for the capillaries instead of the jugular.

Myth 1: *Huge amounts of taxpayers' money are being wasted on extravagantly overpriced toilet seats, coffee pots, hammers, diodes, pliers, and the like.*

Stories of wildly inflated prices for ordinary items first surfaced in the early years of the Reagan defense buildup when the then secretary of defense extensively publicized such incidents in an apparent effort to demonstrate that the Defense Department would be a scrupulous and tough manager of the increased funding it was seeking. Somehow the whole effort backfired. The public concluded that the department must be grossly incompetent to have paid so much money for everyday items and that the defense industry must be composed of crooks. As things turned out, it was a classic case of the government forming the firing squad into a circle.

The truth is that virtually every one of the "scandals" had another, unreported, side to it. If the whole truth had been known, the seemingly high price would often have been seen as justified.

The $640 "toilet seat," for example, was not the $10 item available at the corner hardware store. In fact, it wasn't a toilet seat at all but a complete containment structure fitting over the sanitation system aboard an aircraft. (The government paid only $9.37 for the *seat* part of the device.) After much criticism of the firm involved in the procurement (Senator William Cohen threatened that the Pentagon may have to "go in-house

'Hey! Go easy! That hammer cost the taxpayers a thousand bucks!'

Figure 32.
The infamous coffee maker, shown here by Rep. Barbara Boxer, brewed nothing but trouble for the air force.

for its outhouse"), the prime contractor for the aircraft, in an effort to escape the nuisance of having such a small item absorb inordinate management attention, sought to obtain some additional needed seats from thirty small plastics firms. All thirty firms refused even to bid on the job because of the small quantity sought, despite the trumpeted lucrativeness of the business.

The $7,000 coffee pot—also the object of much criticism—was not of the sort found in home kitchens but rather was a fairly sizable machine designed to cook large volumes of a variety of hot foods and to operate safely in flight during takeoffs, landings, turbulence, and the like (Figure 32). Commercial airlines pay about $3,000 each, for their "coffee pots"—benefiting from manufacturing cost savings of producing in *much* larger quantities.

The reports that the Pentagon was purchasing $400 hammers rightfully outraged many Americans. Most knew that a person can buy fifty hammers for that price. But the ridiculous prices cited by some in the media should have alerted more responsible reporters to the fact that there might be more to the story than was meeting the eye, even if only for the reason that if multibillion-dollar firms *were* seeking to cheat the government, they probably would not elect to do so by overpricing hammers and toilet seats.

But how *could* these extraordinary prices be legitimate? The answer was often in the accounting; as the old adage suggests, "The Devil is in the details." The support equipment the government buys from its prime contractors ranges from spare jet engines down to hand tools and other small parts, and it totals literally millions of items. When figuring the cost of contracted articles produced by their company, industry accountants often simply add together in miscellaneous collection accounts the general overhead costs such as heat, light, taxes, rent, medical care for its employees, and so forth, that apply to the government's purchases and spread these overhead costs *equally* across the large number of different government items supplied. This practice, of course, makes some of the lowest-cost items bear a disproportionate burden, while some of the higher-cost items bear a relatively lesser burden. The *total* charge to the government will be correct, but isolated items may very well appear to be overpriced—just as other items will appear to be underpriced. (One seldom hears about the latter category.) To have figured the overhead cost for each item separately and exactly and then to have allocated this cost precisely to each particular item would certainly have been possible but would have cost more in bookkeeping expenses than many of the items were worth in the first place—thereby simply adding to the supplier's aggregate administrative cost with no real value added.

Although the government has been very critical of the defense industry for this (openly disclosed) accounting practice, the principle is similar to the way the government sets some of its own prices when acting in the role of seller rather than buyer. Consider the pricing practice employed by the U.S. Postal Service.

The cost of sending a letter from an office in midtown Manhattan to another office in the same building is twenty-five cents. The cost of sending an identical letter from the firm next door in Manhattan to an affiliate in Honolulu is also twenty-five cents. Clearly, the cost to the government for providing the service to the two firms can't be the same. The firm that mailed the letter from office to office in Manhattan could perhaps rightfully claim that (in this case) the government was cheating it by requiring it to pay the full twenty-five cents, forcing it to subsidize the cost of its neighbor's Hawaiian mailing.

The alternative, of course, would be to impose a whole different schedule of charges between every conceivable pair of points of origin and destination: $0.06 per ounce, first class, between midtown Manhattan and Wall Street; $1.63 between Manhattan and Honolulu; $0.14 from Cleveland to Kalamazoo; and so on. But the expense and nuisance of this more precise postal accounting practice would probably outweigh the cost of delivering the mail in the first place. So twenty-five cents is the agreed-upon level price for *all* standard first-class letters. Overhead is sometimes spread across certain small items of procurement in a similar manner, both in the commercial world and in the military world. To hit the nail on the head, the $400 hammer is not necessarily what it appears; that inflated number may have come from the company the hammer keeps (or from other legitimate complexities to be illustrated in a moment). Unfortunately, this is not a simple story to convey in the seventeen words allowed the typical interviewee on the evening news (according to several media surveys of time allotment).

Cases do exist, of course, in which the prices of major items of military equipment *have* in fact been unconscionably high. These cases are sometimes a consequence of the very real and fundamental problems besetting the procurement process itself. It is these instances that are worthy of attention if the objective is to improve national security and save taxpayer funds and not merely to ridicule government officials and industrial firms.

To understand how legitimate but complex business practices can be made into grist for the scandal mill, it is instructive to consider the actual story of one defense contracting firm whose chairman was accused in a letter signed by the secretary of one of the military departments of cheating on spare-parts pricing. A bit of research uncovers the underlying bureaucratic red tape that produced this particular "scandal" and, more importantly, suggests what might be done to avoid similar situations in the future. This particular acquisition transaction had, significantly, taken place *before* the pricing of obscure parts had suddenly became a media *cause célèbre*.

In this particular case a military department needed several rolls of tape with the word "vent" printed on it every few inches to mark vents throughout a missile system so that mechanics could readily identify them. The government issued to the prime contractor responsible for the overall missile system a request for a price quote on the tape, indicating that *six* rolls were needed. As it happened, the contractor didn't itself make the tape; it bought the tape from another source and in so doing merely served as a procurer and deliverer on behalf of the government.

Upon receipt of the request for so small a quantity of tape, a member of the contractor's purchasing department sent a formal letter to the government suggesting that it make the purchase directly from the tape manufacturer. The missile system prime contractor's letter provided the tape company's address and the stock number that should be requested, noting that by ordering directly the government could purchase the tape for $13.45 a roll—far less than the prime contractor would have to charge after meeting all of the government's procurement regulations and serving as the government's agent.

Heeding this advice, the government purchasing official sent the procurement documents to the tape manufacturer, a small commercial firm that produces specialty tape. Here, some of the underlying problems of the acquisition process began to emerge. A single copy of the procurement document for the tape, for example, was nearly three-eighths of an inch thick. The formal specification contained mandatory requirements for compliance with a host of laws and regulations. The document referenced other indentured documents, which in turn referenced still other documents, all requiring compliance. In some procurements, as many as seven tiers of indentured specifications have been found. The tape company would have to be certified as a government supplier. It would have to employ certain accounting systems and utilize validated inspection practices. The company would have to certify that it did not buy diamond bearings from South Africa. At least 50 percent of the material in the product would have to be made in America. Equal opportunity guidelines would have to be met, documented, and substantiated.

The tape company's representative took one look at the procurement package and, in so many words, told the government, "We manufacture tape; if you want to buy tape, it's $13.45 a roll. If you want to buy bureaucracy, we can't even afford the lawyers to *read* your document, let alone comply with it." In short, the company refused to sell the tape under the government's terms. In this case the free enterprise system seemed to be working. So far.

The military department's purchasing group now faced a considerable dilemma, which it resolved by sending the original prime contractor a *second* request asking it once again to procure the tape on behalf of the government—on an expedited basis, indicating in a telephone call that there were missile sites needing the tape in order to be completed. The contractor submitted an estimate to the government indicating that it would cost $87 a roll to provide the tape while complying with the specifications that were being imposed, rather than the $13.45 charged by the original manufacturer. Still another procurement package was sent to the contractor with an informal note affixed from the government's buying officer: "Please reconsider and quote on these for us."

The contractor at this point provided the tape, calculating, documenting and including in the bill the cost of time spent estimating the price of handling the procurement, of receiving and inspecting the tape, of placing it in the required packaging, of shipping it in the prescribed fashion, and of completing all the requested documentation and certification in a manner conforming with the legal requirements of the procurement process—including the now standard internal review to be certain that no extra charges that could lead to future civil or criminal charges had inadvertently been included. The cost of all this was added to the price of the tape and clearly substantiated, with a resulting cost of $87 per roll.

It was a bit like going to the corner grocery store and ordering six apples, specially grown to your own set of conditions: raised in a certain county in the state of Washington, watered and fertilized in a prescribed manner, picked on a certain date, and delivered in a special box by a specified trucking firm on a particular date to a private home in Schenectady—all carefully documented and reviewed. Not surprisingly, these apples might cost a bit more than the ninety-five cents per pound one is accustomed to paying for apples at the corner grocery store.

Returning to the tape escapade, some months later, after spareparts scandals had become a national pastime, a government auditor unfamiliar with the whole convoluted history of the tape purchase encountered a copy of the contractor's bill and concluded that the price stood out like the proverbial fur coat on a grocery list. Shortly thereafter, the chairman of the multibillion-dollar firm that had handled the transaction for the government received a letter personally signed by the service secretary essentially accusing the firm of cheating the government in providing The Tape. In this case, cutting red tape seemed to mean splitting it lengthwise.

In virtually every one of these procurement scandals, there has been another, mitigating side to the story. These "other sides" are seldom heard—first, because they do not make very good media material; second, they are difficult to tell in seventeen words; and third, because defense contractors generally don't make a practice of biting the hand that feeds them. Such was the case in the incident just described—at least until the passing of the statute of (emotional) limitations!

Even if all of the specific incidents in the headlines *were* as bad as critics made them out to be, those particular incidents wouldn't represent even a minute fraction of the government's total defense purchases. In the infamous diode "scandal," for example, the government *almost* bought two electronic diodes that appeared to be overpriced at $110 each; no one mentioned that in the same year the government had bought 122,429 other diodes for four cents apiece. Similarly, 87,244 hammers were purchased at between $6 and $8 apiece the same year as the government nearly bought the celebrated claw hammers for $435 each. The government purchased one of the renowned $728 pliers—a procurement that garnered a great deal of attention—but the same year it purchased another thirty-five hundred pliers at $3 each.* The "error rate" in these infamous transactions, even presuming the prices *were* in fact inappropriate, was 0.002 percent—about two errors per ten thousand items for a total of $1,372.92: almost certainly less than the cost of the ink used to tell about them. Industry executives, too circumspect to note it in public, occasionally observe among themselves that the government's error rate in providing tax advice on the IRS hotline averages about 43 percent wrong answers for a total of about 15 million errors per year—according to *Money* magazine's annual test of the system. These same executives also sometimes wonder if the allocation of thousands of auditors to the toilet-seat war is the optimum use of resources when half a *trillion* dollars seems to have simply faded away in the nation's savings-and-loans crisis and the murder-a-day pace of the drug war being fought minutes from the White House continues apace.

None of this is to suggest that there are not mistakes—and, yes, tragically, even occasional cases of fraud—in the work of defense contractors. There are indeed a good deal of the former and, it now appears, some of the latter. But many of the independent reviews of government procurement, including some by such long-time critics as Senator Proxmire and the General Accounting Office, have indicated that the Defense Department overall controls costs far better than do most other government agencies (Figure 33).

The more important question is, once again, how one can avoid imposing such detailed requirements—and in particular, bureaucratic requirements that provide no value added—while still obtaining what the

---

*The famous pair of pliers were actually a special design for a unique application on jet engines and were custom made. As this book was going to print, Pratt refunded approximately $300, saying, according to the *Baltimore Sun*, "It erred by not allowing the government to buy the tool directly from the manufacturer at a lower price." An air force spokesman responded, "Because of the very small quantity and uniqueness of the tool itself, we believe the original price charged the air force was fair and reasonable."

Figure 33   Cost Growth in Major Projects

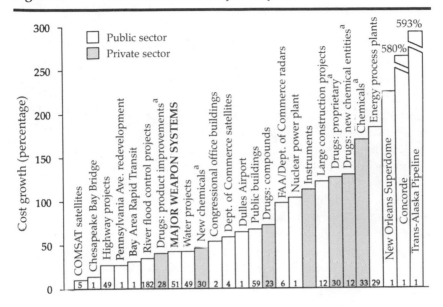

SOURCE: F. Biery, The Analytic Sciences Corporation.

NOTES: [a]Development costs only.
Adjusted for quantity and inflation. Number in each column indicates the
number of cases considered.

government needs? Fortunately, as we shall see in the next chapter, a
number of possible reforms could be instituted to improve the current
practices.

Myth 2: *Defense contractors build second-rate hardware that simply
doesn't work and in fact is often dangerous to its own user.*

"Made in America" is still viewed in most of the world to be the
most desirable seal of approval on defense products. American military
hardware has been copied abroad, even stolen, and many free-world
armies won't purchase military hardware unless it is endorsed and
used by U.S. military services, in part because U.S.–made equipment
has been through trial by fire in combat in Panama, in battle with Lib-
yan fighters over the Mediterranean, in Israeli air-to-air engagements in
the Middle East, and in a host of other confrontations. It is easy to forget, as was pointed out in the previous chapter, that unlike an automo-

bile or dishwasher, military hardware is operated in an environment wherein a determined and often very capable enemy is actively seeking to make sure that the hardware in fact does *not* work as intended.

A thorough analysis would reveal that most products of the U.S. defense acquisition process do indeed meet their critical *performance* goals; they can fly as fast as they should, can hit the target as accurately as specified, or can swim as deeply as prescribed. The major shortcoming that needs to be addressed has to do with the *reliability* with which these systems meet these goals at any given moment, and the cost and time required to obtain the systems in the first place. It is in these areas that significant deficiencies exist and improvements are required.

Despite the crescendo of criticism, America today has a main battle tank that can fight effectively in daylight and darkness, fire on the move, and regularly produce first-round hits. It has tactical aircraft that can fly at very high speed at treetop heights and deliver ordnance with pinpoint accuracy during total darkness. It has a highly agile attack helicopter with true around-the-clock capability to fight among the trees and employ firepower that in the case of the (small) number of missiles used in Panama never once failed to hit their intended target. It has created the most advanced tactical air defense umbrella in the world, a system capable of engaging from the ground or from the air large numbers of enemy aircraft simultaneously. It has submarines that are virtually immune to detection by enemy sensors and capable of accurately delivering nuclear or conventional warheads from very long standoff ranges. It has spacecraft surpassing the capabilities of those available anywhere else in the world. And all of these capabilities did not just "happen"—they were products of the Defense Department's acquisition process.

But, unfortunately, there have also been failures through the years: the Cheyenne helicopter and the MBT-70 main battle tank of years ago, the Sea Lance, the T-46 Next Generation Trainer, the Rapidly Deployable Surveillance System, the Aquilla remotely piloted vehicle, the Mobile Medium-Range Ballistic Missile, the B-70, the Roland air defense missile and the Sergeant York air defense gun, to name a few.

Nevertheless, many of the negative headlines have been overstated. In one recent case a tactical missile in development hit seven out of eight extremely difficult targets, but the sole newspaper addressing the test proclaimed it an abysmal failure. In another case a local television newscast chastised the MX missile for having half of its flight tests fall outside its specified circular error probable—overlooking the fact that the *definition* of a "circular error probable" is the radius of a circle outside which half the missiles fall! Similarly, many believe the MX to have been an abysmal failure in spite of the fact that all seventeen of its initial test

Figure 34. Photograph of aft section of a U.S. F-4 fighter after landing safely with an air-to-air missile lodged in its tail. The missile, fired from a North Vietnamese aircraft, was built in China using a Soviet design based on stolen drawings of the U.S. Sidewinder missile.

flights hit the target. And we seldom hear of the cases in which hardware performs *better* than expected, even though there have been some astonishing instances of just that. For instance, consider the American-made F-15 fighter flown by an Israeli pilot involved in a human error–produced midair collision that tore off the aircraft's entire wing—from root to tip. The plane's engine and control system were so effective that the aircraft was safely landed. Or consider the case of the F-4 fighter that provided a bonanza for intelligence analysts when it flew home from a mission over North Vietnam with an air-to-air missile "captured" in its tail (Figure 34).

It should perhaps not be surprising that American military equipment *is* often of good quality. It is supposed to be. Further, our military is by and large outfitted by many of the same people who build products that are among the best in related, highly competitive commercial sectors. These people work for well-known and respected firms such as IBM, Boeing, General Electric, Motorola, and many others. These and other firms like them have built the finest commercial jet aircraft available in the world, have placed a dozen Americans on the moon and brought them back safely, have led the world in the development of state-of-the-art mainframe computers, have dominated the commercial spacecraft industry, have built hardware that is successfully exploring the planetary system, have invented the semiconductor integrated circuit that made the modern electronics revolution possible, and so forth. Somehow it seems to defy all logic to think that these same companies that have been so effective in other marketplaces would suddenly collapse into total ineptitude when asked to produce a hammer for the Department of Defense. There must be more to the story.

Myth 3: *The military "goldplates" everything so that everything costs too much.*

Without a doubt, some military hardware does include capabilities well beyond those that are absolutely or even reasonably essential. There are, of course, pressures that tend to push the procurement process in that direction. As has been repeatedly noted herein, America has come to rely upon its technological edge as a key element in seeking superiority for its military forces. When systems are at the technological cutting edge, defining the new state of the art, they often become complex and costly not to mention risky. The problem with technological sophistication is that the last 10 percent of performance sought typically adds one-third of the cost and two-thirds of the problems, a conclusion not limited to defense products (Figure 35). On the other hand, in battle, it is sometimes that last narrow performance edge that is the difference between winning and losing, between life and death. Thus, we are dealing with a judgmental matter of the utmost consequence.

Why should we remain so precipitously perched at the edge of the state of the art? Why don't we, for example, produce large numbers of cheap tanks "like the Soviet Union"?

First of all, Soviet tanks (or aircraft, or missiles) are not cheap. By and large, the investment required to build them very closely approximates that for U.S. equipment. Second, as was previously observed, offsetting quality of hardware with quantity generally implies greater casualties in combat. Third, with the cost to the taxpayer for U.S. volunteer forces dominated by the cost of manpower (approximately 25 percent of the defense budget is for people), even if we were somehow to be *given* altogether free the nearly thirty thousand tanks that would be required to match the size of the Soviet tank force, it would take another 120,000 soldiers simply to operate those additional tanks. And this figure does not include the people needed to recruit the additional soldiers, train them, feed them, transport them, provide them with medical care, and so forth. In short, in the era of a volunteer force, it seems unlikely that America could have added the personnel needed to support a large numerical increase in hardware even if it wished to adopt such a strategy.

Figure 35   The Cost of High Performance

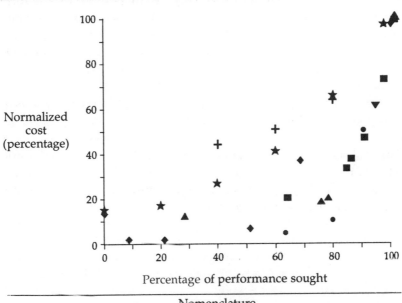

Normalized cost (percentage)

Percentage of performance sought

Nomenclature

Item	Measure of performance	Ref. value shown
◆ 35 mm optical lenses	Focal length (f5.6), mm	600 mm
● Baseball players	Batting average (vs. salary)	0.330
▲ 1960s airplanes	Mach. no. (vs. $/lb.)	Mach 3.2
▼ Inertial references[a]	Drift rate (mph)	0.1 mph
★ Diamonds	Grade (quality) ($/kt.)	$44,000/kt.
+ Machined parts	Tolerance (logarithmic) (in.)	0.00001 in.
■ Radar availability	TPQ — 36 avail. (vs. spares cost)	0.97

[a.] Source of inertial reference costs, S.J. Deitchman.

SOURCE: Norman R. Augustine, *Augustine's Laws.*

The U.S. trend toward high tech, high quality, and low quantity is not without its down side, because in some cases in combat, quantity (even though it entails greater casualties) can be very highly leveraged in terms of achieving victory. This was demonstrated in a bit more abstract sense some seventy-five years ago by the British mathematician, Frederick Lanchester, who pointed out that it is a very demanding task to offset quantity with quality. He concluded from equations he derived that the impact of quantity in combat is proportional to the second power and that quality exerts itself on the outcome only linearly—so that a factor of *four* in quality is required to compensate for a quantitative disadvantage of *two*. Although there is empirical evidence that this analysis may in fact overstate the case, there can be little argument that, all other things being equal, larger forces will generally possess an inherent advantage.

It would appear that our principal failing in the "goldplating" area has been to exploit new technology almost solely to buy more and more *performance* (speed, payload, and the like). We might be better advised to apply some of that new technology to construct systems that are simpler to maintain, easier to use, more reliable, more rapidly deployed, and far less costly. All of this can, of course, be done. A case in point is the ubiquitous semiconductor integrated circuit, which among other accomplishments dropped in price by a factor of one hundred (per unit of storage capacity) as new technology was introduced during the last decade alone.

A former Defense Department official, Bert Fowler, once noted that for some reason the galley tables in a nuclear submarine cost more than the galley tables in a conventional submarine. The same seemed to be true of a lot of other fairly peripheral items. Although stringent military-performance requirements are often essential to success in combat, mere "nice-to-haves" must be diligently rejected if we are to be able to afford the continued pursuit of high quality in the essentials. This discipline can best be achieved by setting realistic long-range budget limits and accurately forecasting the cost of each sought-after capability of a proposed system. In this manner, the decision maker will be forced to make more realistic choices between affordable quantity and the benefits of what on occasion may turn out to be only marginal attributes.

Myth 4: *The defense industry is rife with dishonesty.*

Columnist Carl Rowan told the public, "The shocking stories of greed and incompetence pour forth like a volcanic lava of sewage from Mount Pentagon." The Defense Department has itself occasionally promoted this point of view, attacking its suppliers vigorously. *Fortune* magazine said, regarding a possible hostile takeover of the Boeing Company by businessman T. Boone Pickens, "Pickens refers to some defense contractors as 'established crooks' who are 'stealing the taxpayers' money'! Pickens goes on to say that a high Defense Department official once suggested he acquire a defense contractor for patriotic reasons." Another senior Pentagon official told a congressional committee that thirty-nine of the forty-six major defense contractors who had signed a voluntary code of ethics were under criminal investigation. He didn't mention that these companies employ significantly

more than a million people (few cities of this size are without a jail) or, as was later revealed by the Pentagon's own new inspector general, that nearly three out of every four of the probes were the result of the companies' having voluntarily reported suspect activities that the firms themselves had uncovered, most involving a small number of employees. Nor did he note that, as attorney Stanley Arkin has calculated, more than three hundred thousand different federal regulations have now been criminalized.

Despite being ill-founded in many cases, these rebukes have nevertheless stung the great majority of people in the defense industry, who are in fact, as the laws of probability for large groups of citizens would seem to suggest, dedicated and decent individuals. One of us has been associated with firms that, in addition to being involved in defense contracting, have pursued such other major businesses as steel production, information systems, aluminum manufacturing, chemical processing, airline operation, car rental, aggregates mining, food processing, petroleum refining, and hotel operation; yet he has seen not a shred of evidence that the ethical standards of those associated with defense matters are in *any* way less admirable than the ethical standards of those in the myriad other fields mentioned. But this should come as no surprise.

Good, in large quantities, and bad, in small quantities, are present in people across all industries, and no industry has a monopoly on either.

What is perhaps surprising is that there seems to be so *little* impropriety, given the magnitude of the defense procurement operation and the convoluted nature of the process that distributes the funds involved. "In the defense-contracting arena, there are potential criminal ramifications at every step of the process," said Frederic M. Levy, attorney at McKenna Conner and Cuneo. Levy is further quoted in the *Washington Post* as saying that defense contractors have to worry about "conflict of interest laws when they hire employees, whether the marketing documents are illegal, whether cost estimates are accurate, whether testing is done according to government directions, and what their relationships are with government officials."

The fervor of the assault on "fraudwasteandabuse" intriguingly combines into a single concept a felony and the common human failing of being less than 100 percent efficient, lumping in for good measure such practices as *automatic* suspension of a firm upon indictment (apparently no need to wait for a fair trial), and government-sponsored anonymous "hot lines" for tipsters. All this zeal calls to mind the following passage from a book of recent years:

> They launched a mighty and irresistible struggle against corruption, waste, and bureaucracy. Boxes were set up into which anonymous informants could slip a tip against any benighted jack in office who had fallen victim. Voices were raised violently in open tribunals. One official in every twenty found himself under fire. This three-antis campaign—melted into a five-antis campaign against bribery, tax evasion, fraud, theft of state property, and divulging economic secrets—was directed against the businessmen, the industrialists, and the traders who had so far survived. Denunciations poured in.

As it happens, this is not an account from a contemporary newspaper of actions taken to monitor America's defense industry; it is an excerpt from *The Messiah and the Mandarin*—describing the activities of the Red Guard during its heyday in communist China.

One practice of the government in the mid-1980s was often to suspend or threaten suspension of firms indicted (accused) of crimes, without waiting for trials and without addressing present responsibility—the legal criteria actually specified in the law. For a large defense contractor, suspension from receiving new business from the government is the corporate equivalent of the death sentence. Similarly, the Department of Justice sought to prevent contractors from including in the cost of the products they sell the expenses of defending themselves against accusations, *even* when those accusations were proved to have been unfounded. Fortunately, these efforts have largely been stopped.

In other instances, contractor's executives have been required to waive the right to privacy of their (and their family's) personal financial records and bank accounts as a condition of doing business with the Defense Department.

General Bernard Schriever, the manager of the U.S. Air Force's highly successful project several decades ago to develop intercontinental-range ballistic missiles, recently stated, "The lack of confidence and trust between government and industry is extremely serious. There has been a complete breakdown in the arm's-length, but cooperative, relationship previously existing between the military and its contractors." Ronald Stahlschmidt of the major public accounting firm Ernst and Young observed in the *New York Times,* "Simply put, the relationship among industry, Congress, and the Department of Defense is at an all-time low. Miscommunication, mistrust, and misunderstanding are at the heart of the difficulties."

In many instances, the disputes that have occurred between government investigators and the defense industry have been the result not of dishonesty but of judgmental disagreements over the interpretation of complex regulations. As but one example of the maze of rules within which the industry must operate, consider the experience of one contractor which ran a series of newspaper advertisements to attract job applicants. Under government procurement regulations, advertisements such as these are allowable as legitimate overhead expenses that are required in the ordinary course of business to acquire a work force. Included in this particular advertisement, which was run entirely in black and white, were pictures of some trees, used to convey the attractiveness of the area in which the firm's plant was located. When the time came to repeat the ad, the printer advised the firm that on the opposite page another company would be running an advertisement in color and that if the defense contractor wished to do so, it could have the leaves in its ad printed in yellow at no extra cost. Believing this to be a reasonable way to attract further attention, the company's personnel representative readily accepted the free offer.

Months later, as a share of the expenses incurred for the second ad was being submitted to the government among the thousands of other items constituting the firm's overhead, an internal auditor on the corporation's staff noticed some fine print in a government procurement regulation that stated that advertising with color was *not* an allowable overhead expense because it was considered by the government to be *corporate* advertising with a presumed purpose of promoting the firm's stock price. Thus, the ad in black and white was an acceptable overhead item, but an otherwise *identical* ad with color was *not* a legal submittal. The ad with color went unreimbursed.

Such arcane but critically important—today even criminally important—distinctions occur by the thousands each week. According to a United Press International report, it was one such concern that caused TRW, a major defense and commercial enterprise, following a series of overhead disputes with the government, to cease Red Cross blood drives in its defense-related plants for fear government auditors would rule the incidental costs as not being permissible charges. Another contractor stopped sending out its traditional Christmas calendar because government employees, fearing the calendars would be construed as a bribe, were returning them.

Further, defense contractors are bound by a set of constantly changing rules. Of the 1,066 pages of the new Federal Acquisition Regulation (the bible that regulates government procurement of everything from toilet seats to aircraft carriers) 822 pages had been replaced within the first two years of its existence—notwithstanding its original purpose of reducing confusion.

One body of law with which defense contractors as well as all other firms operating in the United States must comply concerns the preservation of our natural environment—an important and worthy cause, but one that is supported by eleven thousand pages of federal regulations buttressed by another hundred thousand pages at the state level. Various experts in the field have made some disconcerting observations about the risks imposed on corporate America as it seeks to conform to the terms of these laws, for example:

- As a property owner you can be held responsible for actions occurring years before the establishment of hazardous laws—even if you received government approval.
  —*New Mexico Business Journal, February 1990*

- A corporation may be convicted of a crime . . . even though no single employee possessed sufficient knowledge to know that a crime was being committed.
  —*The Environmental Counselor, December 1988*

- Corporate officials are faced with the frightening prospect of criminal liability for the actions of their subordinates.
  —*Paul G. Nittoly, Esq., Stanley & Fisher,*
  P.C., RCRA and Superfund Quarterly

- It is generally true . . . that bad intent on the part of a corporate officer is not a prerequisite to his or her criminal liability.
  —*John R. Wheeler, "Corporate Law"*

- The cornerstone of criminal enforcement is the indictment of high-level responsible corporate officials.
  —*Office of Enforcement and Compliance Monitoring, USEPA*

- The white collar defendant is typically a corporate official with a business school degree or advanced technical training, and who may have had no other brush with the law than a parking ticket.
  —*BNA Toxics Law Reporter, February 18, 1987*

According to the *Los Angeles Times*, "Barry C. Groveman, a self-described environmentalist who helped develop the strike force concept while working in the Los Angeles city attorney's office, is among those who feel the pendulum has swung too far. 'We are seeing a political climate of affirmative action on the environment in which a businessman does not have civil rights.'" He went on to say, "It's offensive to people's notion of fairness that you can be put in the state penitentiary for something you knew nothing about."

A principal change in recent years affecting the evolving relationship between the government and American industry relates to the fact that in prior eras matters subject to interpretation, or even minor administrative errors, would generally have been resolved by discussion and negotiation. If, for example, the government's auditors did not entirely concur with a company's position on overhead expenses, the disputed expenses would be deleted, or, if the rules were inconclusive, the government would say, in effect, "We agree that the interpretation is somewhat vague; we will pay for 60 percent of the claimed costs, and the company will have to cover the remaining 40 percent." Such bottom-line settlements would seem to have been *de facto* recognition that some matters are not always capable of explicit determination.

In contrast, in today's procurement environment, the first a company may hear about such a disagreement is when its management notices a headline in the newspaper announcing that the government will bring criminal charges against the firm or, worse yet, when heavily armed agents suddenly appear at the contractor's plant seeking evidence from employees, as has also happened from time to time. A study published by the Logistics Management Institute began, "[The Defense Department's] relations with industry have seldom, if ever, been worse.

A wide range of issues divides the parties." Although the study was written several years ago, this circumstance unfortunately persists to a very large degree even today—in stark contrast to the situation prevailing in virtually every other nation in the world where government and industry have learned to work together.

According to Jack Coffey of Columbia Law School, "The most important criminal law development (of the moment) is the erosion of the line between the civil law and the criminal law. . . . almost any violation of an administrative rule or regulation can possibly result in a felony indictment."

One result of the existence of such an abundance of laws and regulations, containing varying degrees of vagueness compounded by a growing government tendency to presume that all actions are based upon criminal intent, has been to cause the defense industry and the government's own civil servants too often to be more concerned with "filling in the squares" of regulations rather than producing useful products. The defense industry in recent years has itself substantially increased the amount of in-house policing it pursues, employing vastly increased numbers of auditors and investigators. When a violation is found, some firms have a policy of voluntarily disclosing it to the government, despite concerns raised by legal scholars regarding the precedent of waiving personal and corporate rights.

Many companies in the defense industry are also reacting to the complexity of procurement regulations by conducting formal courses to instruct their employees not only what the rules *are* but also how these rules might be interpreted *ex post facto*. In some companies, from ten thousand to fifty thousand people have participated in courses dealing with a single new law. One prominent firm, General Electric, apparently became sufficiently concerned about the difficulty of interpreting the intent of one piece of new legislation that regulates the relationship between the Defense Department and its suppliers that GE issued to thousands of its workers a wallet-sized card—soon known among its employees as a "mini-Miranda card"—on which are printed cautionary questions its employees are advised to ask should they happen to encounter someone from the government in relation to a project in which their company is involved. (The law was later suspended by Congress.) For American firms as a whole it has been estimated that expenditures for outside legal counsel now exceed spending on research and development.

The ability of the defense industry to better serve the government's needs is often hindered by the government's unwillingness to share its broad planning data with industry. To be sure, all qualified firms should have *equal* access so as to preclude favoritism and should be required to protect the secrecy of such data. But to be denied legitimate planning information merely assures wasteful spending on irrelevant projects. The government is the only customer that asks for help and then passes a law against telling what the customer needs. It is a bit like going to a doctor and refusing to tell where it hurts.

President Eisenhower, in a seldom-quoted passage of his otherwise well-known speech drafted by political scientist Malcolm Moos, told of the development and importance of America's military and industrial capability:

> Until the last of our world conflicts, the United States had no arma-ments industry. American makers of plowshares could, with time and as required, make swords as well. But now we can no longer risk emergency improvisation of national defense; we have been com-pelled to create a permanent armaments industry of vast proportions.

But better known and probably representing a more widely held view today was Eisenhower's accompanying warning:

> We recognize the imperative need for this development. Yet we must not fail to comprehend its grave implications. Our toil, re-sources, and livelihood are all involved; so is the very structure of our society. In the councils of government we must guard against the acquisition of unwarranted influence, whether sought or un-sought, by the military-industrial complex. The potential for the di-sastrous rise of misplaced power exists and will persist.

The sad truth is that there *have* in fact been a number of cases in recent years of clear abuse by individuals and firms in the defense in-dustry as well as by a very few individuals in government. According to the deputy inspector general of the Defense Department, twenty of the largest one hundred defense contractors have been convicted or plead guilty to procurement violations—a striking contrast to the pre-ceding forty years, during which not a single major defense contractor was convicted. It is particularly noteworthy, although not widely recog-nized, that thus far none of these incidents has involved an individual in military uniform.

Although very few in number on a relative basis, these instances of outright illegal practices have had a disastrous effect on the efficiency with which the government procures goods and services from its contractors. Contractors' relationship with the government is totally different now from the relationship that exists between these same con-tractors and their commercial customers.

Today, as evidence of a growing hostility, formal protests are almost routinely filed by contractors when a major government contract is awarded. In the past, protests simply were not submitted by responsible companies except under the most egregious circumstances. One major contractor, General Dynamics, which does nearly 90 percent of its business with the government, recently took the untoward step of filing an extraordinary civil action against the government for damages the former incurred in preparing a defense to criminal charges by the government that the Department of Justice later dropped, having itself deemed the charges to be unwarranted.

Many firms in the industry can cite specific examples of what would appear to have been improper treatment received at the hands of government investigators. And almost every government investigator can cite cases of what would appear to have been improper treatment at the hands of a contractor. One of the more prominent of the former was the case of Jim Beggs (then administrator of NASA), against whom criminal charges were filed by the government relating to his prior work in the defense industry and who (after resigning his job at NASA) suffered years of harassment, only to see charges dropped with a belated apology. The government's own attorneys, it seemed, had for several years misunderstood the procurement rules. As the *Washington Post* told it, "The indictments . . . had been announced . . . at a televised news conference. But when the case was dropped, with Justice admitting its theory of prosecution was fatally flawed, the news was posted on a bulletin board in the Los Angeles Court."

Unarguably, those cases in which individuals and corporations have in fact *knowingly* and *willfully* violated government procurement regulations and laws have done a great disservice to the cause of national security. In the recent series of investigations of the defense industry, thirty-seven individuals have pleaded guilty or have been convicted of crimes ranging from illegal possession or conveying of documents to outright bribery. A survey reported by the Blue Ribbon Committee on Defense Management found that "on the average, the public believes almost *half* the defense budget is lost to waste and fraud." This incredible perception is of course erroneous but the message is shattering. And whatever the level, the answer to waste and fraud is straightforward: such cases *must* be ferreted out and dealt with energetically—according to the law. But the laws themselves must be written very clearly if for no other reason than fairness to those who must operate under their force. A few congressional staff members and employees of the Justice Department have said they favor vague laws on the grounds that they allegedly serve as a greater deterrent. This would seem to be flawed logic, indeed.

Myth 5: *Defense contractors are making exorbitant profits, getting fatter by the minute.*

One straightforward test of this Midas thesis revolves around the fact that if defense contractors had indeed been making extraordinary profits, their stock prices would surely have been soaring. The reality is that relative to the overall market, the stock of the average aerospace company has sold at a *discount* of between zero and 50 percent for all of the last quarter century, except for six brief periods totaling about three years. That is, a dollar's worth of a defense contractor's profits could be bought for as little as 50 percent of the cost of the profits of the average company on the stock exchange. Even during the period of the Reagan defense buildup, defense companies' stocks sold at a discount, which on the average steadily worsened until it reached 33 percent by the end of the period (Figure 36). During the years 1984 through 1989, only one (Boeing, largely a *commercial* aircraft manufacturer) of fifteen major defense, aerospace, and electronics contractors did not lose ground to the Standard and Poor 400 Industrials. This situation presumably reflected, at least in part, the shareholding public's perception of the risks entailed in government contracting—an assessment later found to be well justified. Today, given the added pressure of a declining defense budget, the only "defense" stocks performing strongly are those having large commercial content. Over the last twenty-five years, stock in the average aerospace company could have been purchased for an average of about 20 percent less than stock of commercial firms on the New York Stock Exchange *having comparable earnings*. Today the number is approaches 50 percent.

The *combined* market value of all the firms that constitute Standard and Poor's aerospace sector, excluding Boeing (which, again, is *heavily* commercial), is less than that of Coca-Cola. The nine largest defense prime contractors (at least 60 percent of whose sales are by definition to government) have a combined capitalization smaller than that of Walt Disney. Fruit of the Loom has nearly twice the market value of Grumman, and Toys "R" Us has a larger market capitalization than any of the U.S. aerospace/defense contractors except Boeing. So apparently somebody isn't convinced of defense companies' supposedly tremendous profitability—and this is a long-lived phenomenon not simply affiliated with the recent defense cutbacks.

Figure 36   **Aerospace Corporations in the Stock Market (excluding Boeing)**

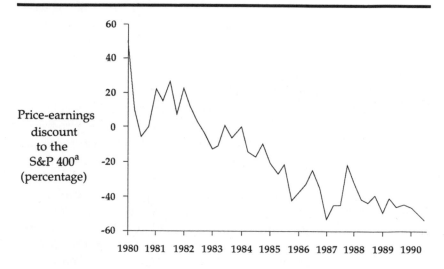

Price-earnings
discount
to the
S&P 400[a]
(percentage)

SOURCE: Standard and Poor's; selected corporate annual reports.

NOTE: [a]Excluding nonrecurring writeoffs.

Among those skeptical somebodies are a large number of Wall Street analysts. Gary Reich of Shearson Lehman Hutton has said that "it will be obvious that the wise course of action is not to make large investments in the aerospace industry." Even before the current decline in defense spending Katherine Plourde of Drexel Burnham Lambert spoke of Morton Thiokol's defense business in the following terms: "I think it's a good bet this business is gone in a couple of years. All they are getting from Aerospace is a low return on their investment and a big headache." This assessment later proved correct. In the words of Judith Comeau of Goldman Sachs, also before the current defense cutbacks, "I recommend only one aerospace stock . . . because they are getting out of the military aircraft business." Defense analyst John Simon pointedly remarks, "Boeing [has] been one of the leading defense contractors for years, and even they can't make money at it." And Jack Modzelewski of Paine Webber at one point in 1989 dismissed the entire industry with the remark, "There are currently two types of defense stocks—underperformers and those about to become underperformers."

Figure 37   **Corporate Profits: Perception and Reality**

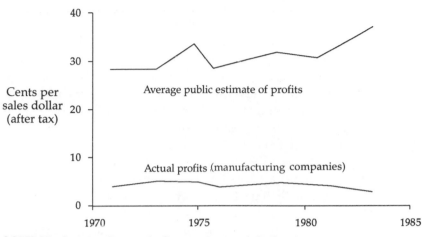

SOURCE: Opinion Research Corporation and Citibank.

The recent reduction in the threat from the Soviet Union, especially in Europe, has of course further intensified the concern investors have long held over the profitability of defense manufacturers and over those companies' vulnerability to the whims of the administration and Congress. During the thirty days surrounding the collapse of the Berlin Wall on November 9, 1989, aerospace companies' stocks fell dramatically— by an amount closely proportionate to that suffered by the stock market as a whole following the famed crash of 1929. The recent fall was, of course, wrenching for the aerospace industry. But unlike the 1929 event, the 1989 happening went largely unnoticed—except by those concerned with maintaining a solvent U.S. defense industrial base.

A poll conducted each year by a major public-opinion surveyor has consistently revealed that the American public believes the after-tax profitability of *all* U.S. industry ranges from 30 to 35 percent of sales—in contrast with the 3 to 6 percent profitability actually experienced (Figure 37). And during the five-year period from 1984 to 1988, the return on sales of firms in the aerospace industry in fact *declined* by 19 percent while it *increased* by 15 percent for the Standard and Poor 400. During that period assets required to operate defense plants grew three times faster than sales and nine times faster than net income. Not since 1984 have S&P aerospace index contractors managed to produce a net income as a percentage of assets equal to the cost of capital. During this period, debt-equity ratios for defense firms increased from 27 percent to

45 percent, which was about twice as fast as for the S&P 400 Industrials as a whole. Interest expense during this period grew from 9 percent of earnings before taxes to 22 percent—and all this occurred during a time that defense sales were growing faster than were the sales of industry as a whole. As a result, some major defense contractors now have bond ratings only one grade above the junk level. The Japanese, long interested in building an aerospace industry, could simply buy the entire U.S. aerospace industry for less than the cost of growing their own. Indeed, rumors in mid-1990 that Mitsubishi was going to buy McDonnell Douglas were apparently viewed as good news, in that it caused a rise in the share price of McDonnell Douglas, according to *USA Today*.

Why should anyone other than those employed within the defense industry *care* that times are tough for the military-industrial complex, just as times occasionally have been tough for other sectors of the economy? One reason is that a strong defense industrial base is still essential to achieve America's national security and foreign policy objectives.

Clearly, our defense industrial base in today's world environment need not be as large as it has been in the past. But neither can it be allowed to crumble or to harbor inefficiency—and there are signs that this is exactly what is happening. Unfortunately, once eroded, the base requires a long time to be reestablished, because an industry founded on technological leadership cannot instantly regain its lost superiority at the mere signing of a presidential order or upon the recording of a congressional vote. The time requirement is especially unforgiving in the matter of acquiring engineers trained in military technologies—a pipeline perhaps ten years long or even longer (more about this later).

The seriousness of the malaise afflicting the defense industrial base is now becoming painfully evident. A significant number of corporations have been putting their defense segments up for sale. Over a recent two-year period, forty-seven segments with aggregate defense sales of $13.7 billion were put on the auction block, and thirty were sold. Nearly eighty defense contractors and segments thereof are now on the block. Some are being withdrawn due to a lack of interested buyers. Ford has sold its aerospace business. Previously, Chrysler had announced the intended sale of its defense business, as had Honeywell, Gould, and Schlumberger. LTV is in Chapter 11 (although not because of its defense work); Fairchild has been sold to the French; PRC is again on the block; and BDM has in the past few years passed from private ownership to Ford and then through Loral to the Carlyle Group. McKinsey & Co. analyst Robert Paulson observes, "the battleship has not even begun to turn, and already, people are falling out."

Senator Jeff Bingaman has correctly observed, "The signs of deterioration of the defense industrial base are all around us." *Aerospace Daily* reports, "Thomas Callaghan, Jr., widely credited as the father of the NATO two-way street, predicted . . . one-third of the U.S. defense industry 'won't see it through to the year 2000.'" Even with the outbreak of hostilities in Kuwait, the stock prices of most U.S. defense contractors continued to plummet. Thus far in the defense "readjustment"—thought by many to have only begun—approximately 150,000 defense jobs have been lost. It is not unlikely that altogether several million people (military, government, civilian, and industry) will lose their jobs due to forecast defense cutbacks if "downstream" economic impacts are included. It has been estimated that in the defense industry alone a 10 percent cut in defense spending puts at least one-third of a million people on the street.

A restructuring of the industry to match today's realities will, if not conducted as a stampede, actually be healthy for the nation's defense. A few strong competitors can constitute a more effective defense sector than a large number of critically wounded firms. But for this restructuring to be realized, it is essential that freely functioning *competitive forces* be allowed to act as the principal mechanism for determining survivors—and not, as on occasion has been the case in the past, the relative political power of local congressional delegations. There is even evidence that closing unneeded military bases can in the longer term actually have a positive effect on local economies. The Defense Department's Office of Economic Adjustment found that over the last twenty-five years some 45,000 additional jobs were created by community redevelopment efforts following base closures. Defense firms as well as communities can adapt to change if that change is not too rapid. By the same token, it is difficult to adapt to being dropped off a cliff.

In assessing the future of the defense industrial base, it is important to recognize that this is not a monolithic entity. America's defense industrial base can perhaps best be viewed as an amalgam of at least four separate categories—three categories of large companies for which defense is respectively an incidental, small, or all-encompassing part of the business base and one category of small but vital companies supplying component parts.

The *first* of the components of the defense industrial base comprises the large commercial enterprises whose sales to the government are only a by-product of their other sales. The highly critical merchant semiconductor industry falls within this category, as do such industries as petroleum and steel. Most of the organizations in this category provide "commodity" products to defense buyers and the continued domestic availability of these products will depend more upon the firms' international commercial competitiveness than upon anything the Department of Defense may elect to do.

The *second* category of the defense industrial base comprises large commercial manufacturers with established defense segments or separate divisions that are nevertheless secondary to the parent company's primary operations. Ford, General Motors, IBM, AT&T, Chrysler, and more recently even Boeing (which, according to the *New York Times*, has "reported a cumulative deficit on its non-aerospace, non-government sales over the 1981–88 period"—the period of the Reagan buildup) fall into this category.

Many members of this second group have already been attempting to sell their defense segments or to phase out of the defense business and concentrate upon civilian markets—another case of having beaten our swordmakers into plowshares. These firms' defense activities generally are less profitable than their commercial efforts. And although seldom noted by analysts, very much on the mind of these companies' executives is the fact that their defense efforts consume a vastly disproportionate amount of top management attention. The impact of divestitures by firms in this category will depend largely on whether the defense segments are picked up and used by their new owners or whether the segments simply become excess capacity and ultimately are allowed to atrophy. In any event, a defense industrial base without a Ford, Chrysler, Honeywell, or IBM would clearly be a weaker base.

The *third* category comprises those large firms whose principal business involves sales to the Department of Defense, placing them squarely in the defense arena. Grumman, Northrop, Lockheed, Martin Marietta, and General Dynamics, among others, fall into this category. Of the top ten Defense Department prime contractors, four do over 85 percent of their business with the government, and six do more than 50 percent. Such firms will undoubtedly work to stay in the defense business. In fact, they have little choice, because few opportunities readily exist for them to diversify into nondefense work. Substantial excess capacity is nonetheless present in this sector of the defense industrial base and will undoubtedly lead to consolidations and mergers and a reduction in the number of participants. A few firms will probably emerge as healthy, competitive, vital entities; the others will drop by the wayside.

To understand the extent of the predicament faced by some of these companies, one must look behind their balance sheets and earning statements. In one recent quarter one major aerospace firm reported a substantial earnings gain—but inspection showed its *defense* sector taking a loss. In the same quarter another firm reported what was described in one media report as a "surprising $96 million in net income on essentially flat sales." It turned out that $67 million of the gain had come from selling its headquarters to a group of Japanese investors. Still another, in the words of *Aerospace Daily*, was helped by "a $179 million gain from accounting changes, creating net earnings of $169 million."

The often-touted option for these firms simply to convert into the civilian sector is terribly overrated. Conversion has repeatedly been attempted in previous down-cycles when defense contractors pursued the manufacture of nearly everything from canoes to coffins and buses to boats—almost totally without success.

Why should conversion be so difficult, particularly in view of the enormous technical talent employed by these firms? The answer lies in the fact that these companies lack expertise in consumer marketing and high-volume production and distribution—for openers. The fact that it is difficult for these firms to diversify into the commercial sector should be no more surprising than the fact that it might be difficult for a premier firm such as, say, Pepsi Cola to diversify into building nuclear submarines or interplanetary spacecraft. The CEO of General Dynamics recently told a Senate committee, "I believe money spent on trying to convert a tank plant, or a missile plant, or a submarine plant to commercial products would be wasted." Unfortunately, the plight of defense firms has not been helped by the fact that at the very time the government is encouraging them to create new markets the government has a law that precludes their spending the new-business money they earn from their government work on anything other than defense.

The other option for these third-category firms is to diversify through acquisitions into other *related* (high-tech, systems, and so forth) markets (perhaps oriented toward large customers). Unfortunately, many of the firms no longer have the financial assets to do so, and even if the switchover is successful, the benefits accrue principally to the shareholders and not to the current employees—who may lose their jobs anyway.

A 1966 report of the U.S. Arms Control and Disarmament Agency, then looking to another down-cycle in the defense industry, noted that "there is a discouraging history of failure in commercial diversification efforts by defense firms. There is doubt that the defense customer wants diversification of these firms. There is little indication that owners of defense firms or the financial community wish defense manufacturing to diversify. The failures of ventures by defense firms attempting to diversify into commercial markets have been cited repeatedly. Practically every major firm in the industry has one or more such failures." Murray

Weidenbaum, director of the Center for the Study of American Business, concludes, "No comprehensive study of past attempts by large defense contractors to use their capabilities beyond the aerospace market has been able to find any important examples of success."

This heavily defense-oriented third category of our defense industrial base has of course been through this wringer many times before, with fewer survivors after each cycle. "Confronted with severe financial difficulties in current programs, mounting public criticism, multiple congressional investigations, and a cutback in new development programs, the defense industry is experiencing very hard times," noted the *Harvard Business Review*—back in 1969. The consolidation within the U.S. aerospace industry, for example, is still much less than in most other countries. Since World War II the number of manufacturers of military aircraft in France has declined from eleven to two, principally through mergers and acquisitions. Similarly, in Great Britain, the number has declined from nineteen to two. In contrast, of the twenty manufacturers in the United States in business in 1945, ten are still seeking to remain in the business, or roughly one manufacturer for every forty military aircraft likely to be built each year in the next decade. Somewhere in these statistics are likely to lurk some corporate fatalities during the 1990s—just as the European aerospace industry was restructured about thirty years earlier.

Even more disconcerting is the lot of the U.S. shipbuilding industry, which has been on the verge of demise for years. Today America's merchant marine transports less than 4 percent of the nation's *own* outgoing foreign trade. During the recent Middle East buildup at least one chartered Soviet vessel was used to haul U.S. military supplies to the Persian Gulf.

Unfortunately, the defense industry has not done a lot to prepare itself for this downturn. Although it is now five years into a period of declining defense budget authority, it failed to adequately recognize that actual spending *outlays* (see Chapter Four) only began to drop in 1990 because of lags in the spending pipeline. There was a tendency to say "This isn't so bad"—and only now is the budget-cutting wave beginning to crash down upon the industry.

Turning to the *fourth* and final category of firms constituting the U.S. defense industrial base, this group consists of the lower-tier, smaller manufacturers who supply indispensable component parts such as fasteners, seals, ball bearings, optics, pumps, forgings, specialty castings, and so forth. This is the category about which we should be most concerned, not the major defense contractors, who as it happens are receiving a disproportionate share of attention and concern thus far. When times get tough the government's own laboratories tend to keep for themselves a lion's share of the money normally passed on to major

Figure 38   **Manufacturing Establishments Supplying U.S.
Department of Defense**

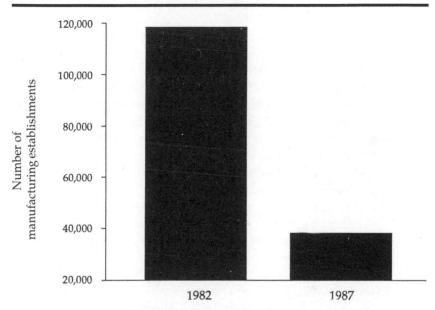

SOURCE: Center for Strategic and International Studies.

industrial firms. Those firms in turn tend to pass less work on to their suppliers—with the result that the smaller companies at the bottom of the food chain starve.

According to a study by the Center for Strategic and International Studies, the number of manufacturing establishments providing manufactured goods to the Defense Department declined from more than 118,000 in 1982 to 38,000 in 1987—all during a period of major defense *buildup* during which the total number of U.S. firms in the sectors from which defense purchases are normally made increased by 25 percent (Figure 38). It has been suggested that these figures may be somewhat overstated because of the difficulty of gathering such statistics, but it is clear that the supplier base is in fact declining precipitously as the onerous terms and conditions of defense procurement and a declining budget take their toll. According to the CSIS study, the Small Business Administration estimates that thirty-five hundred to four thousand small defense contractors will go bankrupt this year alone.

This fourth category comprises the small but truly vital specialty firms whereby, potentially, "for the want of a nail the war was lost." In one recent case, a small manufacturer of rayon yarn went bankrupt—

not an overwhelmingly noteworthy event except that this firm happened to be a *sixth*-tier supplier of the particular rayon needed in rocket motors, and as the only such supplier in America, its closing threatened to shut down much of America's military space program.

Similarly, a few days after the breakout of the October 1973 war in the Middle East means were sought to increase rapidly the production of tanks in the United States in order to replace those that had been provided to our ally Israel. It was found that there was but a single foundry in the United States capable of producing turret and hull castings of the size needed and that this foundry was already building tank components at near capacity. Even with Herculean efforts it took several years merely to double annual production—which even when accomplished was still merely a trickle as compared with loss rates on the modern battlefield or the rate of Soviet production.

In the same vein, a few years earlier when it was learned that the last U.S. supplier of precision jeweled bearings was going out of business, the government stepped in to preserve the basic capability—this time with a Japanese company providing the needed management. And of the ninety-four thousand government-owned metal-cutting machines in the United States today, 62 percent are more than twenty years old. In fact, most of the critical machine tools that power the defense industry come from Germany, just as most of the equipment manufacturers that underpin the semiconductor industry are now in Japan.

In contrast to the relative apathy in the United States toward our industrial base (not just defense base), recognition by the Soviet Union of the importance of industrial strength makes an interesting saga dating as far back as 1921. In that year Lenin intriguingly pointed out, "The only possible economic foundation of socialism is a large-scale machine industry. Whoever forgets this is no Communist." In China, Mao Tsetung pointed out (in a book with the fascinating title *On the Correct Handling of Contradictions among the People*), "Heavy industry is the core of China's economic construction." Soviet infatuation with industrialization was captured well by John Gunther a number of years ago writing on contemporary Russian literature:

> A really big dramatic scene in a novel will have to do with the faulty operation of a valve in a factory, and dialogue seems to consist mostly of talk about nuts and bolts. . . . the last three novels I picked up were all about factories. Industrialization has replaced the great patriotic war as the favorite theme. One critic suggested perfectly seriously a few months ago that a love story should be written about the Lenin metallurgical works.

But as the Soviets have learned, writing about industrialization is a great deal simpler than implementing it, and implementing it is a great deal simpler than perpetuating it, particularly in an overcontrolled, highly bureaucratic society with very little profit motivation or other personal incentives.

America can no longer take its own defense industrial base for granted. To be sure, a slimming down and belt tightening are much in order—even overdue—but so, too, are some long-range thinking and planning about where we wish to head. Although the need for a substantial defense industrial base certainly does not at this moment seem to have great priority, history would suggest that it is difficult to predict when reconstitution of such a capability will be needed. In fact, the very absence of such a capability increases the likelihood that the capability *will* be needed.

The most critical thing to ensure that our defense industrial base can be reconsituted in times of urgency is *not* the preservation of top management nor even the factories themselves: it is those few highly experienced *design* teams owned by each major defense manufacturer. A crucial element of our strategy to downsize our defense industrial base should be to preserve these experienced teams of perhaps twenty to two hundred individuals each, which represent an asset taking decades to constitute.

And here, for once, the law of the belligerency of economics does not seem to apply: the highest priorities for a peacetime industrial base are those that cost the least. First priority should go to research, where major, war-winning breakthroughs most often are to be found; this happens to be the very least costly phase of the acquisition process. Fortuitously, the next least costly is also the next highest priority: building prototype hardware. It is this phase that ensures that our R&D does not become lost in ivory-tower laboratories, and at the same time preserves our critically important design teams. The subsequent phase, full-scale engineering development, is much more costly—and actual production still more so, but of less importance in times of dwindling forces..

Further, the time needed to achieve a surge in production even in an emergency—such as a major conflict in the Middle East—is very long regardless of whether an item is beginning full-scale development or is in a state of "warm base" (in other words, costly) production. In these two cases, some six and three years, respectively, would be required to add a *significant* number of items to our combat inventory. This is because for most items (the atomic bomb being the most notable exception), merely pushing a *few* additional articles off the assembly line has little impact in a military context. This is also why *most* (not all) military outbreaks can be expected to be come-as-you-are wars. An effective peacetime strategy therefore needs to shift the decision to go ahead with a new acquisition project to the beginning of engineering development rather than the beginning of production, as has sometimes been the case in the past. Approval for engineering development should be made today only with the clear intention of proceeding into production with a system offering *major* new capabilities. On the other hand, an alternative "by-pass" is needed to circumvent the existing ritualistic development system and encourage high-risk/high-payoff prototyping of important new capabilities—a few of which will ultimately warrant entry into full development (and production).

At the other end of the equipment cycle there is the challenge of keeping geriatric hardware up-to-date with new technology. Given the realities of today's defense budget, much of our defense equipment will have to last some forty or more years, even though it will become technologically obsolescent in perhaps only ten years. The solution to this dilemma is technology insertion: slipping new components (electronics and missiles, for example) into old "platforms" (ships, airplanes, tanks) and thereby further stretching their useful lifespan. Foraging off the commercial industrial base is a key element of planning for any emergency reconstitution: this minimizes the risk inherent in a weakened defense industrial base.

Defense industrial planning could probably best be *overseen* outside of the Pentagon and the defense industry, because of the breadth of issues and organizations involved. Establishment of an office on the defense industrial base within the National Security Council would seem to be in order, as would the establishment of a joint or select committee of Congress to provide legislative focus on these same matters.

Myth 6: *There is no need to worry about the pay and image of the people who run our government; lots of folks are around who would like to have those jobs.*

The quality of our nation's security efforts depend directly and heavily upon the quality of people who serve in government.

Without a doubt there exists an abundance of people who would be willing to take key positions in government for $40,000 to $80,000 per year—just as there are probably people who would be willing to pilot the airplanes in which we fly or to take out our appendix or gall bladder for far less than respected physicians currently charge. But the basic fact is that America's government must compete with the private sector for the people who serve in Congress, who fill key management positions in the executive branch, or who carry out the myriad other high-responsibility tasks expected of our public employees. The reason for serving the public should never simply be one of economics—but neither should the reason for *not* serving.

Inadequate pay *is* in fact a major reason that some of the most capable people in government have recently been abandoning careers as civil servants, especially those members of that highly productive and experienced age group that has children entering college and therefore faces imminent major personal financial demands. And it is not just the actual numbers on the paycheck that are a problem; even more important at times can be the negative message that may leap forth *from* those numbers—a message that tells our civil servants that their employer really doesn't care very much about them as individuals. And when one's employer happens to be the American people, that message can presumably be profoundly discouraging.

That disheartening message is reinforced by the low opinion so many people in positions of high visibility in our country seem unable to avoid publicly voicing about federal employees.

In assuring national security, as in most other undertakings, the starting point is people. But the stopping point, as it happens, is also people. Key decision makers and workers at every level of the procurement structure must be thoroughly qualified—particularly when making multibillion-dollar decisions. Programs must be headed by competent, motivated, dedicated, experienced individuals who receive the support necessary to get the job done, who remain in place long enough to bring their capabilities fully to bear, and who are still around when the time comes to add up results and responsibilities. Quality people instill trust and honor in an organization. They combat wrongdoing and will not tolerate abuse at any level or from any source. They will not be swayed by unreasonable claims made by overly zealous members of industry or by demands of tyrannical members of government.

But major deterrents to government service exist today. As a consequence, some of the finest people are leaving government employment, and many of the nation's most promising young college graduates steer away from public service as a career. These deterrents include inappropriately low pay, inexplicably low prestige, and unreasonably vague conflict-of-interest laws. These laws, although altogether well meaning, discouraged capable people from serving in positions in which they can apply their knowledge and have produced a hemorrhaging of the government's finest people to the private sector. An expert in defense matters from the private sector can safely serve in the Department of Housing and Urban Development but probably not in the Pentagon.

Similarly, an expert in public housing can join the nuclear-planning staff of the Department of Defense but probably not the Department of Housing and Urban Development. The exception might be an individual who is prepared to retire upon completing a period of potentially personally damaging government service, but such a criterion would at the very best still eliminate tremendous numbers of capable people from the pool of talent available to oversee our government's critical affairs. In a recent speech, Deputy Secretary of Defense Don Atwood remarked that "a number of high-ranking officials left the government to avoid the uncertain impact ['revolving door'] restrictions would have on their future career opportunities. Moreover, we often found it difficult to find qualified people willing to take their places."

Government's growing inability to attract talent or to use it optimally applies not only to senior appointed officials but also, and in fact probably *more so*, to career public servants. Unless steps are taken to stanch the depletion of the ranks of our nation's most able civil servants, we risk a very serious decline in the quality of federal service. A survey of more than a thousand top managers in government reports that 61 percent would not suggest a similar career for young people. And, as noted in *U.S. News and World Report*, "Young people are clearly getting the message. At Harvard, a survey of the 1986 graduating class found only 4 percent heading for public service." According to Paul Light, dean of the University of Minnesota's Institute of Public Affairs, "The problem is that young people are no longer interested in government careers."

The nation must continue to find very large numbers of individuals to fill the multitude of responsible positions that constitute our public management system. As Ross Perot has noted, "Eagles don't flock—you have to find them one at a time." Don Atwood, himself a very successful industry executive with General Motors before joining the federal government upon retirement, is quoted in *Aerospace Daily* as having observed that government policy making is becoming "the purview of the young looking for experience" who can tolerate low pay and of "those who have completed their careers in business and are already financially secure. We are losing the skill and expertise of the vast pool of people in between."

Atwood himself, upon agreeing to serve the government (at a nontrivial reduction in pay), was—curiously enough—forced by ethics laws to purchase at his own expense several insurance policies on the survival of his former employer, the General Motors Corporation. The reason was that a perception might exist that, in the event General Motors should ever appear to be going broke during Atwood's term at the

Pentagon, he might try to save that firm—and the pension to which he was entitled—by awarding General Motors defense contracts. Such is the measure of confidence we now place in our nation's highest and most dedicated public servants.

Even when persuaded to become presidential appointees, most individuals don't stay around long. The Center for Business and Government at Harvard found that top-level appointees during the Reagan administration averaged only two years in office. One-third lasted not even eighteen months—including the learning and leaving phases, which constitutes a hefty portion of this period. This decline in tenure continued uninterrupted through the Johnson, Nixon, Carter, and Reagan years. It seems that Washington, D.C., has become a nice place to visit.

For some reason, the public has not concerned itself greatly with the quality of those individuals who will in the future carry out critically important roles in government, particularly in the civil service. In selecting a surgeon, a person generally devotes a good deal of time to choosing a highly competent, experienced professional. It would seem only prudent to go to the same trouble to guarantee the capability of those who help determine whether we are prepared to go to war and, if we do, how well we will fight. As a former vice president of the United States once asked, "Is 'okay' enough for those who direct the next Shuttle mission? After Three Mile Island and Chernobyl, what level of competence do we want inspecting our nuclear plants? The next time you take an air flight, do you tell your family not to worry—the controllers aren't the best, but they are okay?"

Both of us look back on our years as public servants as among the most exciting, challenging, and thoroughly demanding of our lives. Both of us worked alongside some of the finest, most competent, and most committed people we have ever known. And the stakes involved in government decision making demand no less.

SIX

DEFENSE PROCUREMENT:
The Tunnel at the End of the Light?

To challenge the cornucopia of myths that exist about the defense procurement process, as was done in Chapter Five, is not to deny that the process is beset with serious problems. It is in fact burdened with problems of extraordinary magnitude. Further, these problems are not altogether of recent vintage. According to the U.S. Congressional Research Service, the U.S. Navy in 1794 sought to procure six frigates. (The needed broad political backing—to prove nothing much has changed here, either—had been ensured by awarding the contracts to shipbuilders in Portsmouth, Boston, Philadelphia, New York, Baltimore, and Norfolk.) Delivery was to take place in about a year, but construction eventually dragged on for four years even though half the ships were canceled. Cost grew by nearly 200 percent. In too many ways the picture is agonizingly similar to that today, nearly two hundred years later.

What seems to be needed is a heavy dose of *Pentastroika*.

Where to Begin?

As the old farmer giving complicated instructions on how to find one's way to Chicago is said to have finally concluded, "If I were goin' to Chicago I wouldn't start from here." Yet, we are where we are. And although the opportunity for increased efficiency is enormous, if one is to propose changes, one must first decide whether the goal is to produce shocking headlines or to achieve real and lasting improvements. The following is a compendium of realities that must be addressed if we are to achieve real enhancements to the country's defense procurement process.

Reality 1: *The defense procurement process needs to follow Plato's dictum that justice consists of everyone doing one's own job—and that regulations are no substitute.*

David Packard, the highly regarded cofounder of the Hewlett-Packard Company and a former deputy secretary of defense, once stated to a congressional committee, "Frankly, gentlemen, in defense procurement we have a real mess on our hands, and the question you and I have to face up to is what are we going to do to clean it up." He has also observed, "Defense procurement has been 'micromanaged' to death."

Some, of course, would say that micromanagement, like deterrence, is in the eye of the beholder; on at least one occasion it has not entirely facetiously been described as "all that takes place above one's own level on the organization chart." But the fundamental and inescapable fact is that the defense acquisition process is simply too large and too complex to manage without relying upon some delegation of both responsibility and authority to large numbers of people. That is, a degree of earned trust is needed—not to mention capable people. It has been pointed out by management consultant Mort Feinberg that this need for delegation was recognized in biblical times by Jethro, who advised his son-in-law, Moses, "What you are doing is not good. You and the people with you will wear yourselves out, for the thing is too heavy for you; you are not able to perform it alone." The question boils down to the amount of "micromanagement" that is most efficient.

But along with delegation must come the clear assignment of responsibilities. Probably the most succinct assessment of the problem of vague and shared responsibilities in defense management was made some twenty years ago in the report of the Blue Ribbon Defense Committee chaired by Gilbert Fitzhugh, a former CEO of a major life insurance company. This assessment concluded, in so many words, that the problem with defense procurement is that *everybody is responsible for everything and nobody is responsible for anything.*

Unarguably, the management of defense procurement involves huge numbers of people not only in the military services themselves but also in the upper levels of the Department of Defense, the various committees in the Congress and their staffs, and the Office of Management and Budget—almost any of whom can stop or divert almost any defense procurement undertaking. The *Washington Post* once referred to some among these as "The Abominable No Men." The program manager for the Joint Surveillance, Targeting and Reconnaissance System had to give fifty-seven briefings before gaining approval to initiate the highly promising project. Approval of a new air-to-air missile recently slipped through with only fifty-two briefings. The average defense R&D program is voted on by Congress alone an average of 18 times a year in its 8-year life—a total of 144 opportunities to change something.

One result of such a process, aside from the decision-making constipation it implies, is that there is no one individual who feels accountable for results—and when things go wrong there is no one to stand and accept responsibility; there are always lots of persons who can be pointed at as having had their fingers in the pie. The problem is a management structure that permits no single individual to be truly responsible for anything, even at the highest organizational levels—up to and including the president of the United States.

In stark contrast, the practice used to manage business-related functions in the private sector is to place a single individual in charge and to give that individual the resources and responsibility to carry out that undertaking. The individual is also held accountable for measurable goals. This practice of course greatly increases the risk felt by that individual, but it also demonstrably increases the probability of getting the job done.

Lyndon Johnson, responding to the question why he did not fire the individual who had undermined one of the president's favorite programs, is said to have replied, "*Fire* him? . . . I can't even *find* him!"

Consider, the situation that results when a person even of such rank as the secretary of defense tries to close an obsolete military base or to cancel a program viewed by the military itself as unneeded (fairly strong indications in their own right!). Without question, one of the most *difficult* tasks ever undertaken by one of us in a third of a century of government and industrial management was to attempt to close a group of unneeded military installations. After four years of effort and the accumulation of abundant scar tissue, one single installation was finally shut down. (This was, revealingly, considered a momentous victory by veterans of the base-closing wars!) Another eleven years passed before the next base closed.

The Congress, increasingly and understandably frustrated with the performance of both the defense industry and the Pentagon, has over the years elected to interpose itself to an ever greater extent in the day-to-day management of defense acquisition affairs, not even excluding the oversight of highly detailed technical matters. In a generally well-meaning attempt to prevent problems, the legislative branch typically resorts to its principal tool: the passage of a law.

But when the only tool in your tool kit is a hammer, every problem starts to look like a nail. Congress, for example, recently directed that a particular helicopter program could not proceed beyond a certain point until the secretary of the military department involved submitted *to the Congress* the engineering results from the dynamic tests of a new rotor system. In another case the Congress specified the computer language to be used in a particular command and control system, thereby causing a major redesign. The weight of the small intercontinental ballistic missile and the weight margin to be designed into space launch vehicles are also mandated by law. Even the price of a military toilet seat is established by Senate bill S-1958. But in effect, the practice of having the Congress manage the diverse day-to-day activities of the defense industry can properly be equated to trying to herd chickens from horseback.

The extent of congressional oversight is nothing short of amazing. In 1977, the budget-supporting data required of the Pentagon by Congress totaled a "mere" 12,350 pages. By 1988 the total had grown to 30,114 pages. The *Wall Street Journal* cited this practice as Congress's attempt "to sacrifice entire forests in the cause of micromanaging U.S. defense." One defense contractor reported more than eighty thousand visits and inspections at its plants in a single year by government personnel. Another reported that more than four hundred government personnel are located in its plant full time to monitor production of jet engines for the military. At the same plant, where some of the finest commercial jet engines in the world are manufactured, the commercial customers do not have a single full-time quality inspector. The integrity of the commercial product is assured by the manufacturer's reputation—and, most importantly, by the manufacturer's desire to *keep* that reputation. The management lesson to be learned is that it is not possible to audit quality into a product. Quality can only be designed into a product and then built into that product at each step in its creation.

According to a study by the Center for Strategic and International Studies, one U.S. company whose business is principally in the commercial sector provides a key component of a telecommunications system to the government entirely free, simply because it can't afford to comply on its commercial line with all the oversight requirements the government imposes. The chairman of Gulfstream Aerospace is quoted as saying about one new aircraft:

I personally believe that the C-20 program procurement could have been completed in a two- to three-week period instead of the eight or nine months spent in proposal preparation and source selection activity. The C-20 proposal and source selection cost Gulfstream over 1.3 million dollars, and we delivered over four thousand pounds of written material and data.

The contract Gulfstream uses with its commercial customers for the same airplane is thirty pages long, and the specifications sixty-five pages.

As has already been noted, government management practices cannot always simply be carbon copies of industrial practices. Nonetheless, certain analogies can provide insight with regard to the business-oriented task of managing the defense procurement process.

Congress, for example, would be more effective were it to function, insofar as managing the procurement process is concerned, more as a corporate board of directors—setting policies, strategic goals, allocating overall resources, and monitoring results. The entanglement of any corporate board in detailed day-to-day operations to the extent currently practiced by the Congress would almost certainly assure the failure of the business enterprise being supervised.

The staff of the secretary of defense, in this business model, would perform a function more closely paralleling that of a corporate staff—making first-level suballocations of resources, overseeing progress on specific projects, coordinating the activities of subsidiary organizational elements, and taking high-level corrective actions whenever necessary. Instead, during most of the recent three decades, the staff of the secretary of defense has been heavily involved in the detailed execution of programs. Ironically, critically important national security questions go largely unaddressed by the same key people because of the lack of time to examine the forest rather than the trees—other than as a by-product of the traditional bottom-up budget preparation process. Top-down questions might hypothetically include such uplifting matters as the following: Should we have more carrier battle groups and fewer mechanized divisions? Should we have fewer strategic nuclear submarines and more research and development? Should we have less command and control for tactical forces and more civil defense? All are extremely difficult questions—but also extremely consequential. Over the years we have become increasingly like the drunk who looks for his keys not in the alley where they were lost but rather under the lamp post down the block—because it's easier to see there.

If the suggested realignment of responsibilities were to be made, the military services themselves could then assume a role in the acquisition process paralleling the role of the operating companies in a large corporation—that is, the military services would be responsible for executing the day-to-day affairs of the enterprise, and they would also be held accountable for such undertakings.

The principle of assigning clear responsibilities is superbly illustrated by the practices of the maintenance shop of a successful Texas Cadillac dealership where the shop manager has adopted an interesting manner of encouraging quality repair work. When a car is brought into the shop, the car owner is given a one-page biography of the mechanic who will be responsible for the work to be performed. The biography tells of the technical training the mechanic has received, the years of experience accrued, any specialties the mechanic has mastered, and any professional awards he or she may have received. But the punch line is the last sentence in the biography—which, in case of problems, provides the car owner with the mechanic's *home* telephone number.

In contrast, if the Department of Defense procurement system does not perform to satisfaction, the GI whose life depends on the item produced can only call (202) 545-6700, the Pentagon "main switch"—as it is aptly called—which is more than likely to result in a referral to the Senate, the House of Representatives, the National Security Council, the GAO, the OMB, the GSA, the FBI, or most any other permutation of the twenty-six letters of the alphabet taken three at a time.

Some senior government officials may ask, "Won't the increased delegation of responsibility simply lead to errors by individuals less experienced than those who have worked their way to the top?" The answer is yes. But *not* to delegate is to introduce the even greater danger that errors will be made by decision makers both unfamiliar with the details and having insufficient time for careful consideration of the implications of detailed decisions.

Our present policy seems to be aimed primarily at not letting anything go wrong—but is often having the unintended consequence of precluding us from letting anything go right. Lamennais's apothegm applies: "Centralization breeds apoplexy at the middle and anemia at the extremities." The key to effective management of the defense acquisition process is really very simple: employ capable people, establish clear goals, monitor results, and get out of the way.

Reality 2: *The notion that programs can be managed by audit needs to be discarded.*

The bad news is that twenty-six thousand auditors are now monitoring the Department of Defense and its toilet seat purchases. The good news is that a Soviet delegation recently visited the United States to learn how we audit.

The audit function *is*, as it turns out, absolutely essential and, constructively performed, can make a critically important contribution. All substantial commercial enterprises have both internal and external audit staffs to ensure that the organization's policies are being effectively implemented. If it were not for the existence of these auditors, few corporate or government executives would be able to sleep at night—if indeed they do anyway. One cannot, however, use audits as a surrogate for management—which is the situation now on the horizon in the defense acquisition process. And the purpose of auditing cannot be simply to scour the battlefield and shoot the wounded.

Many of the standards that Pentagon auditors seek to enforce were not designed as part of an integrated management policy. Rather, these standards evolved in much the same way as common law; each time a problem occurred, a regulation was established to ensure that that particular problem would never happen again. Patches were plastered on top of patches until a huge mass of overlapping and sometimes even self-contradictory regulations was constructed.

This phenomenon is not unique to defense management. In one eastern city an ordinance required hospitals to keep the temperature of hot water in patients' rooms at more than 110 degrees to promote sanitation; a federal statute at the same time demanded that water in patients' rooms be maintained at less than 110 degrees to avoid accidental burns. A meat-packing plant is reported to have been told by one federal agency to wash its floors several times a day to ensure cleanliness; a different federal agency instructed the plant to keep its floors dry at all times to promote safety.

For large numbers of public servants as well as many in the defense industry, the rewards of success have become less significant than the hazards of being caught in violation of a regulation. This coincides with the push by many social engineers and theorists toward a risk-free society. Consequently, the tendency is to do it "by the book"—even when the book makes absolutely no common sense. Great care is taken to be certain that files are stuffed to show that unsound regulations are being followed to the letter. Many government and industry employees, no longer willing to take the risk of exercising prudent, professional judgment within a set of overall guidelines, seek refuge in rulebook answers to any problem that might arise. This ultimately stifles the very creativity that is so badly needed if America is to build the finest military equipment practicable with a reduced budget and a downsized industry.

The Defense Authorization Act, for example, requires that the Department of Defense submit proposed programs for multiyear procurement (funding approval granted in advance for more than one year) *only* when "the proposed multiyear contract . . . achieves a 10 percent savings as compared with the cost of current negotiated contracts." But isn't it possible that taxpayers might appreciate a saving of, say, a mere 1 percent of a $1 billion program—$10 million? The goal becomes one of complying with the regulations, not one of solving the problem.

This lack of management latitude in defense acquisition decisions contrasts with the more practical approach of commercial executives to unforeseen technical problems in nondefense matters. If, midway in the development of a product in the private sector, a noncritical goal is found to be generating inordinate cost and difficulty, the solution is often to abandon or redefine that goal. But in today's defense procurement environment, companies avoid making such changes for fear of being accused of fraud; government contracting officials likewise resist such commonsense changes for fear of being accused of going easy on contractors. Hence, everyone simply continues to spend money to meet dubious goals.

In the case of a helicopter program a number of years ago, both the government and the contractor knew what changes were needed to fix a serious problem that had caused the prototype to crash. But the contractor refused to initiate the modification because this action would be construed as noncompliance with the original specifications and acceptance of responsibility for the change. Similarly, the government declined to *direct* the change for fear of creating the perception of itself having accepted responsibility for the new design. Mercifully, Congress put both parties out of their misery; it canceled the whole effort.

In short, our managers have been left with very little latitude to manage. We have confused regulation with management. In our eagerness to ensure that there will be no failures, we have reduced the possibility of successes. In our eagerness to ensure that the rare individual who would take improper advantage of the system will be deterred, we have demotivated the many dedicated, honest, talented participants who would otherwise do their creative utmost to make the system work.

The notion of taking *considered* risks is anathema to most auditors and to much of the media—particularly if things do not work as hoped. But prudent risk-taking is critical to virtually any pursuit, be it business, sports, or life itself—and this is especially true of high-tech endeavors. In a time of declining defense budgets, R&D managers especially must be *encouraged* to take reasonable risks. The alternative is often to forgo the possibility of seizing upon significant breakthroughs of the type that have been described in Chapter Three.

Ironically, one of the management innovations most needed is a small group of auditors to audit the auditors, for the timeless question endures: *Quis custodist ipsos custodes?* Who will watch the watchdogs? Although this suggestion may at first blush appear to be a facetious one, it is offered altogether seriously. Probably no other group of twenty-six thousand people in government or elsewhere has the power of today's defense acquisition auditors, yet so little oversight imposed on their own activity. Those performing the audit function bear significant responsibilities and enormous power and therefore should have their own professional standards to meet, knowing that they, too, are being monitored for excellence. It is ironic that resistance to such a notion should exist within, of all places, parts of the auditing community itself.

In the end, we have no choice but to place a considerable degree of trust in those who actually labor in the trenches of the defense procurement process, both in government and in industry, believing that they will perform in a responsible manner. As previously observed, if individuals knowingly and willfully violate this trust, they should be ferreted out and punished according to the law. But it makes no sense that in effect the *taxpayers* should be punished or our national security compromised through the perpetuation of a process so narrowly focused on preventing errors that no energy is left over for generating new successes. No grocery store could operate if it hired hordes of extra employees to ensure that a can of soup were never stolen. That is not to say that stealing soup is in any way acceptable; rather it is to recognize pragmatically that in some cases the cure can be worse than the disease. We should continue to keep an eye out for those who would steal a can of soup, but we should devote even greater attention to helping those who are trying to make the soup in the first place—and to squelching those few who might be scheming to make off with a whole shipment.

Auditing is thus important and necessary, but it is best undertaken with the underlying objective of finding legitimate problems and thereby helping the system work more effectively. When undertaken simply to spotlight differences in judgment or to justify its own continued existence, the auditing function can be extremely counterproductive. What is needed, in short, is "a few good auditors."

But the best thing we can do is to place our trust in a cadre of highly qualified program managers who are left in their jobs long enough to feel the burden of accountability and to get the job done. The task of acquiring multibillion-dollar systems upon which people's lives will depend is simply too important to be left to amateurs. Each service needs a professional acquisition corps composed of people blending military operational experience with program management experience. This notion has for some reason been surprisingly elusive. No military leader would believe for a moment that corporate officials could be placed in command of an air wing, an infantry division, or a battle group—yet, for years we sought to do the converse.

When David Packard was deputy secretary of defense he strove valiantly to increase the acquisition-related experience level of military program managers, often with the opposition of the military services. He therefore was particularly heartened when his staff showed him a *Washington Post* clipping regarding the filling of a key assignment with a professional manager that quoted senior navy officers as saying: "By constantly changing our director every two or three years, we have destroyed continuity. . . . If you had a million-and-a-half-dollar business, would you want to change bosses every three years for someone who didn't have any experience? Most directors come right from sea duty to this job, and it can take a full year to get to know the ropes. . . . How many people in the Navy do you think know things like scheduling problems?"

Secretary Packard was visibly disappointed, however, when his staff subsequently advised him that the article referred not to the manager of the navy's newest fighter aircraft or submarine, but rather was taken from the *sports page* and concerned the position of athletic director at the Naval Academy.

Reality 3: *Turbulence in the defense acquisition management process must be eliminated.*

Turbulence is the financial black hole of the defense acquisition system. Huge sums of money are lost to turbulence each year—although one seldom sees that in the newspaper because the practices that lead to turbulence make much less colorful and understandable copy than do toilet seats and coffee pots. Projects are started, stopped, accelerated, or slowed; budgets are increased or decreased; schedules, objectives, designs, and even people are continually changed. All of this drives the price of weapons dramatically upward, slows their development, and demoralizes individuals who are seeking to perform their day-to-day work in an efficient manner. This, it turns out, is the mother lode of waste in the defense management process. The average development program today takes over eight years. It takes fourteen years, on average, to go from the beginning of the concept formulation stage to operational development (Figure 39). The two newest radar-directed air

Figure 39   **Length of U.S. War and Peace Compared with Average Time to Deploy New Defense Systems Today**

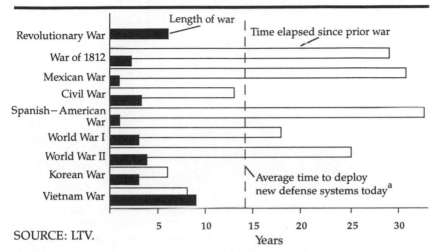

SOURCE: LTV.

NOTE: [a]Time from concept to initial operating capability.

defense systems to enter the inventory each took eighteen years. Even the great pyramid of Khufu was built in twenty years.

It has been difficult for our country to sustain even a consistent top-level budgetary policy toward defense, as reflected in the fact that national defense spending reversed direction (from increasing to decreasing or vice versa) thirteen times over the past forty years. U.S. policy toward security assistance funds (for our allies) reversed nineteen times since 1955. In contrast, Soviet defense spending—as measured by the U.S. government in U.S. purchasing power—shows only three such reversals in the last quarter century, with the overall trend being steadily upward.

The budgeting process is one of the main culprits in promoting instability (Figure 40). For instance, there is the seemingly chronic difficulty encountered by the Congress in producing a budget by the beginning of the fiscal year. At one point a decade or so ago, it became commonplace for the fiscal year to be nearly half over before a budget was finally established—including a budget for projects already under way. In such instances, disagreements that occurred among congressional committees over the level of funding for ongoing efforts sometimes left program managers with the dilemma of whether to spend at the lower limit of the rates being debated, thereby having a budget reduction become a *fait accompli*, or to spend at the higher limit, thereby

Figure 40   **Defense Budgets Compared with Amount Actually Appropriated**

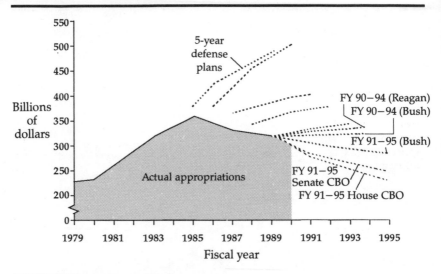

SOURCE: Department of Defense.

NOTE: Constant FY91 dollars.

running the risk of violating the law by not being able to cover costs in the event funds were ultimately denied.

Fortunately, Congress found the ultimate solution to this schedule problem; it passed a law delaying the start of the fiscal year for all future years by three months! Soon, however, even the new deadline began to slip, with the result that in many years no appropriations act whatsoever for national defense was passed (Figure 41). Instead, a succession of stopgap continuing resolutions was adopted. This whole scenario brings to mind a suggestion once made by John Lowenstein of the Baltimore Orioles, who, when asked what could be done to improve the game of baseball, suggested that first base be moved back a step to eliminate the close plays.

In one recent defense budget debate, the Senate changed seven hundred line items from the president's request, and the House changed twelve hundred. In the military construction subelement of the budget, four hundred of the fifteen hundred line items were revised. The current result is for the Congress to change 60 percent of the individual line items in the president's defense budget request.

Figure 41   **Congressional Delays in Passing Appropriation Acts, 1965–1990**

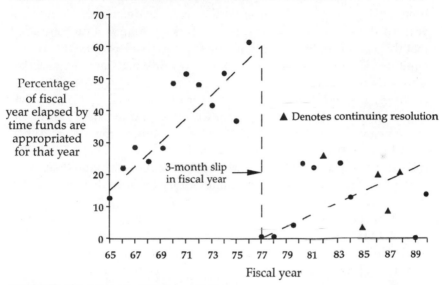

SOURCE: Department of Defense budgets.

Just ten years ago in the Senate there were sixteen floor amendments to the defense authorization bill. More recently there were eighty-three. The House and the Senate not long ago generated more than sixteen hundred funding differences and four hundred policy differences between themselves on the defense budget. That same year there were also thirty add-on issues in the national defense bill that were altogether unrelated to defense, ranging from child nutrition and the school lunch program to the use of petroleum products from Angola. When the House and Senate reached an impasse in their efforts to resolve the myriad issues dividing them, they took decisive action; they set up a committee. The House, for starters, appointed seventy-seven members to the committee.

Frank Carlucci, former defense secretary, calculated that from 1970 through 1988, had the Defense Department each year simply been given the same number of real dollars that it received in 1970—well before the Reagan buildup and the subsequent draw-down—approximately the same amount of money would have been available to defense without all the congressional wrangling and could undoubtedly have been spent far more efficiently.

There is also the turbulence-producing practice of budgetary "chicken" that results as Congress and the administration seek to establish future defense-spending levels. The final Reagan budget, as has been noted, called for a 2 percent real increase in defense spending each year for the succeeding five years. The Bush administration concluded that this spending level would not be supportable—presumably in recognition of what appeared to be a strong consensus in Congress that zero real growth was more acceptable. But when the administration accordingly revised its budget estimate for the initial budget year downward to zero real growth, many in Congress immediately concluded that a negative 2 percent would actually be a more proper level. When the administration ultimately submitted a budget, on the heels of the collapse of communism in Eastern Europe, containing a minus 2.6 percent real "growth," Congress immediately instituted plans for still deeper cuts.

Unfortunately, *two* can play this game, and typically the executive branch's budget for future years calls for growth far above the level of growth likely to be accepted by Congress. The administration doesn't dare reduce the budget forecast to a more realistic figure because as soon as it does, the Congress will very probably reduce the budget even further—the Congress having cut $275 billion in constant 1990 dollars from defense spending since 1970. Thus, the nation's defense-planning process lurches forward toward an uncertain objective, governed by a plan that everyone knows is wrong. All this creates doubt and confusion among the workers in the trenches who have the unenviable task of establishing contracts that have relatively little tolerance for vagaries. It is all like barreling down a curving road at seventy miles per hour trying to drive by looking out the rear-view mirror.

Another version of this same phenomenon took place in regard to inflation rate forecasts during the Carter administration. The Office of Management and Budget habitually issued what appeared to be intentionally low inflation rate forecasts, because an officially sanctioned increase in projected inflation rate would almost certainly turn into a self-fulfilling prophecy. Unfortunately, the program manager at the other end of the budget pipe, seeking to determine how large a factory to build, how many machines to procure, and how many employees to hire, was faced with the virtual impossibility of performing realistic long-range planning. Very few medals were given to defense program managers in those days for not having cost overruns!

Turbulence takes its toll not only on fiscal efficiency but also on human incentive and morale. For example, a manufacturing plant had been assigned the task of increasing production of a relatively complex

Figure 42   **Impact of Program Stretchouts on Production Cost**

Item	1987 quantity	1988 quantity	Percent quantity decrease	Percent budget increase per item
M1 Tank	806	600	25	13
Blackhawk	82	61	26	25
AV8B Harrier	42	32	24	25
EA6B EW A/C	12	6	50	64
E2C Hawkeye	10	6	40	50
Sidewinder	627	288	54	163

SOURCE: *Washington Post*

NOTE: Includes fixed costs and all other costs—some not necessarily a consequence of stretchout.

item of military hardware from about fifty per month all the way up to three hundred per month in a short period. Finding it extremely difficult to accelerate production as quickly as desired, three of the company's senior executives flew to the plant some one thousand miles away from the firm's headquarters each Saturday for the better part of a year and devoted the entire day to reviews with local managers, in an effort to ensure that all needed resources and focus were available to expedite production. Finally, after a year of Herculean effort by the literally thousands of people involved in the project at the contractor's own plant and the several tiers of suppliers supporting the project, a production rate of three hundred per month was finally achieved. Only a few weeks later, notice was received that a change in funding had occurred and that the production rate should promptly be cut in half.

Unfortunately, it is highly inefficient to tool a production line and train workers for one rate and then build at another (Figure 42). Furthermore, and often overlooked, the next time these same workers are asked to devote extra effort to meet an objective that is said to be of considerable importance, the management will probably have very little credibility in motivating them. Many years ago, working in his first supervisory job, one of us had the wrenching experience, after a major program cancellation, of shifting from preparing overtime lists to layoff lists in the span of just two hours.

Because of the tendency to overestimate the amount of future funding that will be available for national defense, more programs are initiated than can ultimately be supported. Cancellations and inefficient stretch-outs are the result. Consider the history of one missile development program with which one of the authors had first-hand experience.

The program began in July 1977, innocuously enough, with the award of an engineering development contract after several years of preliminary work by the contractor and the government. All was proceeding satisfactorily until December 1987 when Congress cut the program's budget in half. The reduced funding resulted in a stretched-out program, which further increased costs and caused the program to be terminated in April 1982. Reconsideration of the Soviet military threat led the administration to request funds to reinstate the program. In December 1982 Congress increased the president's request by a factor of sixteen. By March 1983 the administrative steps had been accomplished to permit the program to restart, and the same month, after a test in which nine firings produced eight direct hits, a limited number of R&D items were deployed with the operational forces on an urgent basis. A preproduction contract was awarded in December 1983, but by 1984 it was realized that the missile technology was so obsolete that a new design would be needed. Work on an updated design began under a new contract in February 1984. But in December 1984 a 20 percent budget cut by Congress necessitated a program restructuring. By January 1986 the program was again ready to begin manufacturing, and a letter contract was signed to expedite production. But in December of the same year another 30 percent congressional reduction was imposed, and in January 1987 the military department concluded that the program could not be sustained and issued a stop-work order to which the contractor responded by beginning to shut down the project. In May 1987, however, a decade after the original contract, the program was reinstated, and in September of that year a new preproduction contract was awarded. In December 1987, responding to increasing budget pressures, the Defense Department stopped all future funding for the project, and two months later the military service canceled all ongoing work. This time, the program died dead.

Compounding this problem, the costs of individual programs have commonly been underestimated by contractors participating in them, thereby increasing the difficulty of achieving realistic budgeting. Industry has traditionally been guilty of creating these extremely optimistic estimates—sometimes to the point of irresponsibility—because of its desire to win competitions for new contracts. Compounding the problem, the military services, seeking congressional approval of new systems perceived by them to be sorely needed to carry out their assigned roles, have likewise tended to be unduly optimistic in cost estimating. Finally, Congress itself possesses an inherent desire to defer budget demands at least until the next election, so it in turn tends to be at best tolerant and at worst receptive to optimistic estimates.

None of this necessarily implies any dishonesty—merely a lack of prudence and an unjustified optimism. Enormous uncertainties legitimately exist in estimating the cost of tasks being undertaken for the first time—as, in the case of research and development, is implicit even in the definition of the undertaking. Depending on how conservative or optimistic one wishes to be, cost estimates can and do vary widely. Yet a definite incongruity is built into the system, as just described. Instituting programs based on overly optimistic cost estimates made by the various would-be recipients of the funds—who will inevitably require more funds than originally budgeted—is like trying to deliver lettuce by rabbit.

In the prolonged period of declining defense budgets that is now under way, it is of even greater importance that realistic budgetary plans be generated. Only two choices exist with regard to estimating the costs of new systems: either deal with the bad news at the outset of the undertaking, or face it later—on the installment plan. The former, and far superior, of these choices could be made the standard practice, first by making it extremely difficult to initiate new programs and second by insisting that any new programs that are initiated be conservatively funded from the outset. More will be said of this later.

Still another way to eliminate turbulence is to make it more difficult to interfere with programs once they are started. It should be policy that after a decision has been made to initiate a project, that decision cannot be reopened, except at the most senior level, and then only because of significant changes in the fundamental factors underlying the initial approval. Today, uncountable numbers of individuals have within their purview the ability to make arbitrary reductions in a program's budget and changes to its schedule. When technical problems are encountered, which they almost *always* will in any state-of-the-art undertaking, it is generally best to "tough it out" and complete the basic programs, albeit sometimes with revisions. The habit of terminating existing programs with known problems in order to initiate new programs—with unknown problems—is an exercise in self-delusion and one that has far too often been followed.

Some budget cuts take a particularly ironic twist. One year a congressional committee reduced a program's funding with the justification being that it was frustrated that the program had fallen behind schedule. Needless to say, when a program's budget is cut, it only places that program *further* behind schedule.

But what is most needed to reduce turbulence is a longer-term budget agreement between the Congress and the administration. If a more rational baseline could be established, one that both entities could support under all *normal* circumstances with only minor subsequent tuning, enormous efficiencies could be derived. This practice, coupled with more discipline in the execution of programs, could have a profound positive impact on the efficiency of the entire acquisition effort. A first step in this direction would be to adopt a true two-year appropriation process, rather than allocating funds for multiyear tasks on a one-year basis. This step could be buttressed by granting approval and funding to programs from major milestone to major milestone—as is done in almost every other nation—rather than from year to year.

Finally, turbulence in the form of continually reassigning managers needs to be curtailed. This long-standing practice dilutes accountability and guarantees inexperience. Congressman Nicholas Mavroules is quoted in *Aerospace Daily* as saying, "We ordered longer tours. In 1984 they (program managers) averaged only twenty-five months on the job. Today they average only twenty-one months. Some improvement!"

Reality 4: *Realistic contingency planning must be introduced into the management of defense acquisition.*

When planning the fuel load for a commercial airline flight, the captain calculates the impact of such influencing factors as anomalous winds en route, weather in the landing area, the distance to alternative airports, and the passenger load; the captain then adds a fuel reserve to assure that a safe landing can be achieved even given the advent of a combination of contingencies. To a budgeteer this fuel reserve may seem wasteful; it represents an additional and usually unnecessary load that must be carried, which in turn consumes still more fuel and money. But to the passengers, it may occasionally mean the difference between landing on the runway and on a highway.

In planning defense programs, "fuel reserves" are generally not permitted. Allowing contingency funds somehow implies that either something is expected to go wrong or, worse yet, that one doesn't know precisely what is needed in the first place. Further, if funds are budgeted without an explicit *a priori* rationale for each dollar sought, these particular funds will almost invariably be deleted during budget review process and directed toward other, "more clearly defined" needs. Programs thus proceed on a "green light" basis, assuming that everything will work as hoped and that nothing will occur as feared.

But the truth is that *any* complex undertaking, whether in the military or the commercial world, will generally encounter unforeseen difficulties at some point in its evolution. It is common commercial practice that when problems are encountered in a high priority development pursuit, additional funds are quickly made available so that the problems can be resolved promptly and the schedule maintained. In a very real sense, time is money: there are "standing armies" in the factories and management offices who must await the resolution of whatever problem has arisen.

In contrast, when technical problems are encountered in government projects, the only manner in which new funding can be obtained involves winding one's way through the labyrinthine and time-consuming budgeting and appropriations processes—typically a one- to three-year undertaking. As a consequence, defense program managers seek to manage their way out of unexpected near-term difficulties by sliding the schedule of their programs and reallocating to the troubled areas whatever funds can thereby be scraped up from the untroubled tasks. Such changes have a way of cascading down through a prime contractor, a handful of subcontractors, and literally thousands of third- and fourth-tier vendors, wreaking contractual havoc every step of the way.

Stated differently, in the commercial world, near-term money is used to maintain schedule and *save* larger sums of money in the longer term. In the defense procurement world, schedule delays are used to offset the unavailability of additional short-term money, thereby *increasing* costs in the longer term. The application of near-term money is most often the control variable in the commercial world; schedule is nearly always the control variable in defense management.

Some will argue that if funding is earmarked in advance for contingencies, a sort of Parkinson's Law will set in and the funds will always be spent. This legitimate danger can, however, be avoided if the contingency funds are held at a high enough organizational level and allocated only when their need has been thoroughly justified.

To make contingency funding feasible, development and initial production cost estimates need to take into account the degree of uncertainty that exists in each element of a project. Cost estimating for such work is of necessity a probabilistic matter, much in the same manner as the preparation of actuarial estimates by insurance companies or prediction of the weather. In the latter case, despite the existence of sophisticated earth satellites and complex mathematical atmospheric models,

Figure 43   **Accuracy of Defense Program Cost Estimates (development and production)**

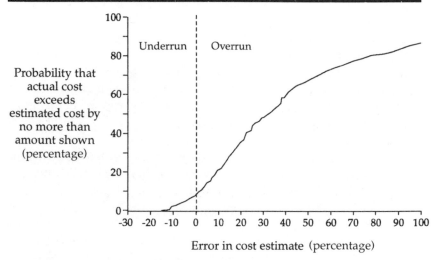

SOURCE: Norman R. Augustine, using Department of Defense statements.

NOTE: Cost estimate at approval of development, corrected for inflation and quantity changes. Includes cost of changed objectives. Based on 81 major programs.

weather forecasts are still presented in probabilistic terms: "There is a 20 percent chance of rain tomorrow." (For many programs in today's defense budget environment, it might be more realistic simply to state there is a 20 percent chance of tomorrow!) Cost estimators for research and development programs would be well advised to emulate this probabilistic approach when establishing initial program estimates.

Historical cost estimates for defense development projects have typically been found to have been generated at the 10 percent confidence level; that is, there is only a 10 percent chance they will prove adequate (Figure 43). It is necessary to increase the confidence in these costs projections to a 50–50 level if overall budgets are ever to be balanced in a responsible fashion. One way to accomplish this objective is with a process called TRACE (total risk-assessing cost estimate), initially applied by one of us to a test sample of procurement projects in the 1970s.

TRACE takes the customary scope and schedule breakdowns for particular tasks and assigns a risk factor to each element based on the statistical likelihood and consequences of problems that might occur.

Using this risk factor, funding and schedule reserves are established. The process is very analogous to planning a fuel reserve for an airline flight and is but one method among several for achieving the more realistic programmatic planning so badly needed.

The increased cost estimates that result may of course make it more difficult to obtain approval for new programs. But would it not be better to be judged by how many programs are finished rather than by how many are begun?

The important aspect—that contingencies be identified and fully disclosed at the outset of a new undertaking—not only helps assure adequate resources to work one's way out of problems as they occur but also heightens focus on areas that may require special attention— thereby frequently enabling potential problems to be avoided altogether.

Finally, given their natural role as advocates for new systems, contractors and service program offices should not bear the ultimate burden of cost estimation. A truly professional, fully independent cost-estimating staff should be (and now has been) placed within the office of the secretary of defense. Most importantly, however, its advice should be heeded. Only this group, after weighing all available evidence including that offered by contractors and government program offices, should be permitted to provide the formal estimates against which defense acquisition programs will be judged for initial approval and subsequent budgeting.

Reality 5: *New incentives must be added to the procurement process.*

Both within the government and the defense industry the lack of a true free-market buyer-seller relationship erodes the incentives normally present in the marketplace. Some needed changes are in fact now being implemented to varying degrees, but the reality that the underlying issues concerning incentives are neither black nor white complicates finding solutions.

Consider the matter of competition, long a mixed blessing in the world of military procurement. "Technical development of aircraft was proceeding at very unsatisfactory rates," notes the report of a House committee, largely as a result of "the destructive system of competitive bidding." The committee, chaired by Florian Lampert, issued its report in 1925.

Competition for development contracts sought by the defense industry is, contrary to popular opinion, very intense—probably more so than in most commercial markets. A new fighter airplane development

Figure 44   **Studies of Cost Savings Attributed to Competition**

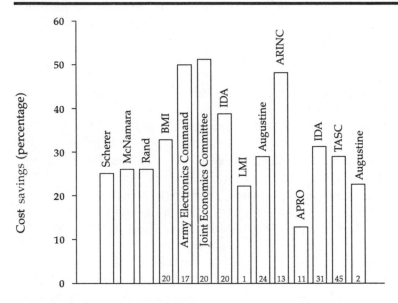

SOURCE: Norman R. Augustine.

NOTE: Number in each column indicates the number of systems.

contract, for example, comes along only once every ten years or so and may produce tens of thousands of jobs. A firm in the fighter business simply cannot afford to lose. But once the aircraft is in production, as was seen earlier, very little opportunity may exist for further competition other than at the subsystem and component levels.

In selected cases, attempts have been made to introduce competition into defense *production* (which at best makes sense only when start-up costs are not prohibitive) with the result that savings on the order of 25 percent have not been uncommon (Figure 44). In this case the original development contractor may be dropped or its participation reduced in favor of some other, less costly producer. This form of competition undeniably focuses a contractor's attention on cost reduction—but sometimes at the expense of other important matters, including investment in future research and quality. Thus, competition has often produced a significant payoff for the taxpayers, but when carried to an extreme, it has also had some very undesirable secondary effects.

How does the practice of seeking continual competition as pursued in defense procurement compare with the business strategy—now enjoying growing popularity among U.S. commercial firms and demonstrated to be effective in Japan—wherein long-term, lasting partnerships are formed between purchasers and suppliers? No less a luminary than W. Edward Deming, the renowned American expert on productivity for whom, interestingly enough, Japan's most prestigious industrial award is named, recently told the U.S. Department of Defense after a review of its procurement practices, "settle on one supplier and build a long-term relationship."

The argument used to justify this alternative to competition-at-any-cost is that teamwork between buyer and seller, the free and open exchange of ideas, the candid addressing of concerns and problems, and the building of institutional loyalties and pride far exceed the benefits of hiring and dumping the supplier of the week via sustained competition. This team-building practice has in fact been effectively applied for many years in a few of the highest-priority defense programs, including the Polaris/Poseidon/Trident series of missiles, the military space program, and to a degree in the land-based ICBM programs.

The fundamental task becomes one of balancing these seemingly conflicting benefits of cost savings resulting on one hand from the establishment of frequent competition and on the other from the promotion of long-standing partnership relationships. The answer lies in the exercise of painstaking case-by-case judgment.

There are, fortunately, some useful guidelines that can be adopted, each tailored to a particular phase of the acquisition process: research, prototyping, full-scale development, and production.

First among these guidelines is to create an intensely competitive environment among several candidate firms to conduct the *research and prototyping* phases of a project. This should be primarily a competition for *ideas*, not simply for low cost. The view widely held among defense suppliers—and equally widely disputed among government officials—is that *anyone* can win a contract competition, as long as they are the low bidder. True or not, most contractors *behave* as if they believe this to be true.

In one recent major competition for a *fixed-price* contract, bids ranged from about $200 million to $700 million—a rather amazing range for such large sums of money, and, sadly, probably only reflect the relative confidence the firms' managements placed in their lawyers' abilities to later escape the price commitments (the low bidder won). In another case, nearly $3 *billion* separated two bidders for an electronic device (again, the low bidder won). Government procurement officials strenuously deny that price—not product quality or contractor competence—is usually the decisive factor in the source selection process. This position makes an interesting backdrop to the report on procurement recently contained in the government publication *Inside the Army*, which stated that, "contract awards will *no longer* be predicated first and foremost upon which candidate offers the lowest bid" (emphasis added). Apparently this was the kind of situation that former Dallas Cowboy quarterback–turned television announcer, Don Meredith, was referring to when he observed, "Pro football isn't what it used to be, and it never was!" Actually, a much-debated section of procurement law (the Competition in Contracting Act) states that "The head of an agency may award a contract . . . [which] would result in the lowest overall cost to the United States." Efforts to change the words "lowest overall cost" to "best value" have thus far met with little success.

In addition, many defense companies in recent years have been cutting back their basic research and other innovative activities because new ideas have too often been accepted by the government with a "thank you" and the promise of a copy of the competitive procurement document that ultimately stems from the firm's idea. The acquisition process, to be effective, must generously reward innovation.

The next phase of the acquisition cycle, *full-scale development*, is where traditional competition is not only appropriate but essential. It is here that truly significant costs begin to be incurred, and it is here that competition constitutes the government's very best lever to assure responsible contractor performance.

But here another type of complexity arises concerning incentivization—in this case centering around the appropriate type of contract to be utilized for development work. There are two basic categories of contract: *fixed-price*, where a specific price is set prior to commencing work; and *cost-reimbursable*, where the seller collects whatever reasonable and actual costs it incurs. Many of the problems now plaguing the government and threatening the financial solvency of major defense firms relate to this single and seemingly arcane issue—which has survived for at least thirty years without satisfactory resolution.

General Eisenhower, in a 1946 policy statement, urged considerable latitude for defense contractors to innovate, with "detailed directives held to a minimum." Defense Secretary Robert McNamara, on the other hand, stated that development projects should not even begin until work is defined with enough specificity to permit a "firm fixed-price or fully structured incentive contract." Six years later Deputy Secretary of Defense David Packard reversed the McNamara policy, saying, "It is not possible to determine the precise production cost of a new complex defense system before it is developed. . . . Cost type prime and subcontracts are preferred where substantial development effort is involved."

But the policy under the Reagan administration reverted once again to that of its Democratic predecessor of the 1960s and was perhaps most clearly enunciated by its strongest advocate, Navy Secretary John Lehman: "A Systems Commander will not proceed [to Engineering Development] until he is satisfied that advanced development has reduced risks sufficiently to enable the contractors to commit to a fixed-price type contract that includes not-to-exceed prices or priced production options." But later in the same administration the policy was reversed once again. This time Deputy Secretary of Defense William Taft directed, "Fixed-price contracts are normally not appropriate for research and development phases. For such efforts, a cost-reimbursable contract is preferable."

The two classes of contract instrument—fixed price and cost reimbursable—are indeed quite different. Under a fixed-price contract where the buyer and seller agree in advance upon precisely the item or service to be delivered and upon a specific price to be paid, the principal risks are borne by the seller. This format is entirely appropriate when the work to be performed is fully understood by both parties and the uncertainties are bounded, such as is generally the case for follow-on serial production of a manufactured item.

But almost by definition, fixed-price contracts are inappropriate for research and development activity, the very nature of which is to perform something that has never before been done. The government's practice in the 1980s of using its monopsonistic clout to force such contracts upon would-be suppliers has had a major adverse effect on America's defense industrial base in the 1990s. With the imposition of fixed-price contracts on companies' R&D activities, the government, abetted by industry managers, planted the time bombs that are now detonating in many firms' earnings statements and are resulting in lawyers rather than managers running defense procurement projects.

The message is getting out. Edmund Woollen, government marketing director for the Raytheon Co., is quoted in *Aerospace Daily* as saying his company "declined the opportunity to invest" in the air force's huge Advanced Tactical Fighter program: "My thinking is, take that $100 million, bank it in T-bills at 10 percent, and ten years later, when ATF is still struggling, go buy the guys that lost their shirt on it." Fixed-price contracting for research and development is a little like surgery for which, by prior agreement, the surgeon, hospital, and staff are to be paid only a fixed amount no matter what medical surprise or need might arise.

The alternative, a cost-reimbursable contract whereby the producer is paid *whatever* its costs may be, unfortunately removes nearly all financial incentives for efficient performance and dumps all the risk on the buyer. This, too, is unacceptable. What then is the answer?

The answer is to introduce still another form of incentive, one borrowed from everyday commercial business practice—namely, tie the opportunity to conduct future business with the purchaser to how well the particular supplier performs its existing business. A private citizen does not return to an auto mechanic or a grocery store that has previously provided poor service or inferior goods. Conversely, one *does* return when treated in a satisfactory or exceptional manner. Too often, the procurement process has suffered from a form of amnesia, whereby experience of the past seems to have no relevance to the decisions of today (Figure 45). By making "past performance" a major (not the *only*, but a major) factor in awarding future contracts, vastly increased pressure to perform effectively can be placed upon the defense industry. Firms would then have to make a long-overdue adjustment: a shift of focus away from making promises concerning future performance toward tending the store here and now. This refocus would result in a win-win situation; the government would receive better products and good contractors would receive more business. There are of course innumerable complexities involved in the implementation of such a practice, but none is insurmountable. Indeed, an initial effort in this direction has recently begun, with the air force taking a leading role.

Turning to the production phase of a major system (as distinguished from a commodity item), the incentive embodied in the Japanese approach of a long-term producer-client relationship should be adopted as a goal, emphasizing teamwork and personal responsibility. The company's reward for good performance becomes one of being permitted to stay on the team, and the penalty for failure is that of being competed against some other source or being summarily dropped from the team. The practice of recent years, whereby the incumbent is routinely dumped in favor of the low bidder of the moment, has often lowered quality, discouraged firms from making long-term capital investments in productivity, and driven leading research and development firms to cut back or eliminate their laboratories so as to be the low-cost producer capable of picking off second-source competitions. Lee Iacocca described an analogous situation that existed in the automotive industry a few years ago, saying, "The average American motorist wants economy so badly they will pay anything to get it." Responsible firms simply will not make major investments in factories if they know they may lose a competition that is to occur every twelve months that would make those factories relatively useless.

Figure 45   **Past Record as Basis of Contractor Selection**

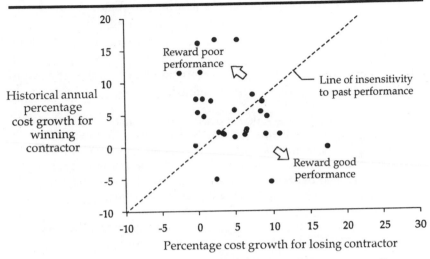

SOURCE: Department of Defense selected acquisition reports, five-year average.

NOTE: 9 Army programs, 8 Air Force programs, 4 Navy programs. Based on business base (major programs) at time of award. Corrected for inflation and quantity changes.

In summary, incentives need to be tailored to the particular phase of the undertaking and to the particular situation involved. No blanket solution suffices. For instance, even if the concept just described were to be adopted for the production phase, a problem still remains in those cases wherein true competition is altogether impracticable as a result of the unassailable sole-source position of a single supplier. This is particularly likely to be the case for major systems such as aircraft and tanks. In these instances, it can be beneficial to apply a technique whereby the contractor's fee is awarded judgmentally by the government within certain upper and lower bounds, according to the decision of a formal (and, under exceptional circumstances, independently appealable) review process. This concept of periodic formal review is already being utilized in one form or another in a growing number of procurement contracts and offers significant advantages. It encourages frank communication between buyer and seller, forcing a periodic "taking stock" in which the government must go on record as to the suitability of effort while work is still being conducted and not merely after the fact. It also appeals to the pride of the contractors' employees who, in effect, are periodically given a report card with a specific grade. This is of much greater importance than one might believe at first glance.

The broad concept of incentives is not altogether new. Those charged with the construction of the Crystal Palace in London during the last century, for instance, had very strong incentives to produce an adequate structure, as described in a contemporary newspaper account of the acceptance tests that were conducted:

> The first experiment was that of placing a dead load of about 42,000 pounds, consisting of three hundred of the workmen of the contractors, on the floor and the adjoining approaches. . . . The fourth experiment—and that which may be considered the most severe test—was that of packing closely that same load of men and causing them to jump up and down together for some time.

Although containing unduly severe consequences, the incentive was unarguable. It is still true that the best parachute packers are those who jump.

SEVEN

CONCLUSION:
Memos to Policy Makers

President Lyndon Johnson was fond of kidding, "Those who can, do. Those who can't, teach." This was a bit of mockery of his old and noble profession of teaching.

Much more apt it is to say, "Those who can, do. Those who can't, write books about it." For it is far easier to pontificate about defense and foreign policies than it is to implement them. That we both know from our twin experiences of government service and book writing.

The great pressures on those in government—of time, of politics, of daily problems—make it nearly impossible for them to read many books. Henry Kissinger once observed that government service draws on the intellectual capital an official has coming in, rather than adding to it once the person is in place. It is critical for those outside government to offer their views on long-range issues, to help point the way in a changing world—and to do so in crisp and compact form.

In this chapter we present our most policy-relevant views in a series of government-style memos to the key actors in defense and foreign affairs. We figure we have a better chance of reaching them with two or three pages than with two or three hundred. And the exercise forced us to condense our discussion to those key points that are most important in today's brave new world.

MEMORANDUM
TO: The President of the United States

You know well the Chinese benediction, "May you live in interesting times." In this regard, fate has been kind to you, Mr. President, as you are our leader in *the* most interesting and promising time in recent history. Your presidency coincides with the triumph of American values in many places around the globe, with the onset of the long-anticipated breakdown of the bipolar world, and with the emergence of new international challenges. The world will no longer be controlled by a single, dominant nation or by two opposing dominant nations. It probably is not to be "controlled" at all—as recent events in the Middle East seem to suggest.

Yet America still stands as the first among alleged equals. For it is the sole "full-service superpower"—the one with worldwide cultural and intellectual appeal (unlike the Soviet Union and China), full political unity (unlike Western Europe), considerable economic prowess (unlike the USSR and China), vast natural resources (unlike Japan), and global military might (unlike Japan, China, and Western Europe).

We cannot merely rely, however, on our current assets to ensure that events keep going our way, with our interests protected and our values advanced. We need to make some fundamental adjustments of our own—a veritable American *perestroika*—to keep pace with the fundamental changes we find elsewhere and the new hazards that are almost certain to emerge.

Matching America's actual military capabilities to our national objectives is more vital than ever, and in this age of sophisticated technology it is perhaps more risky than ever to fail to do so. Walter Lippmann wrote nearly half a century ago, "Foreign policy consists of bringing into balance, with a comfortable surplus of power in reserve, the nation's commitments and the nation's power." With the post–Berlin Wall euphoria now engulfing America, grave danger exists that such a balance will *not* be made, let alone with any "comfortable surplus of power in reserve." One of the most troubling hazards we face is that we may assume we have more capability than we actually possess. This assumption could lead to ill-advised ventures, which could prove costly.

Our capacity for major military involvement in the Middle East is seriously stretched whenever we take action there, as in the recent Gulf crisis. Similarly, twenty or so years ago, U.S. planners were supposedly building forces sufficient to wage "two and a half" wars simultaneously around the world, but soon the Vietnam War escalated and we could not wage even that "half war" to the outcome we had intended.

Part of today's needed reconciliation between our commitments and our power may occur through natural shifts in our alliance relationships, particularly within NATO but also elsewhere. These shifts we need not fear. One has to glance back only a few decades to see that shifting alliances are the norm in international relations. As recently as forty-five years ago, for instance, Germany and Japan were our mortal enemies, and the Soviet Union and China were our allies. A little over three decades ago Cuba was our ally. Fewer than two decades ago, Egypt was aligned to the USSR and antagonistic to us. Slightly more than one decade ago, Iran was our closest ally in the Gulf. The one thing that our planning must recognize is that we must be prepared for events that do not fit our plans, that were not foreseen by our planners, or that seemed inconceivable during our planning. Iraq snatching Kuwait is only the latest example.

As important as are your other responsibilities, your foremost obligation is to provide for the nation's defense. We should not permit those who might wish to test us to doubt our will in protecting America's vital interests. The guiding principle must be to match our capabilities to our objectives—and to the *actual* capabilities of our potential adversaries. U.S. forces should not be designed merely to match the currently stated *intentions* of other nations, because such intentions can suddenly change or be deceptive. In particular, U.S. forces should not be based solely on the actions of any single individual; even Mr. Gorbachev is likely to prove mortal. Interestingly, Mr. Gorbachev is the only major Communist leader other than Premier Markovic of Yugoslavia to last out the year around the fall of the Berlin Wall.

Our nation should not cut Pentagon capabilities precipitously simply in response to an outbreak of political euphoria. We have on several occasions mistakenly eased our guard in the past. We seem to make few new mistakes but keep on making the old ones time and again, for which we pay a high price. Our overexuberance has cost us in a currency of far greater value than mere dollars, namely, in the lives of our young men and women who proudly wore the uniform.

At the outset of World War II our soldiers trained with broomsticks for rifles. After reaching Europe or entering the Pacific, some fought with the same type of equipment their fathers used in World War I. Early in World War II our torpedoes failed to fuze when they hit enemy submarines, and early in the Korean conflict U.S. antitank shells literally bounced off the tanks of a third-rate military power.

As encouraging as the events in Eastern Europe and the Soviet Union have been since you assumed office, history offers little to convince us that the world has suddenly and miraculously become free and peaceful. Wars still rage, rebellions erupt, freedom gets stomped (as in China and more recently in Kuwait).

History moves in zigs and zags. Will and Ariel Durant, writing in *Lessons of History,* tell us that "War is one of the constants of history, and has not diminished with civilization or democracy. In the last 3,421 years of recorded history only 268 have seen no war!"

However new the landscape, however promising the outlook, it seems premature to declare that "peace in our time" has finally and permanently arrived. Political scientist Norman Ornstein reminds us that "the demise of communism in this world does not mean the demise of evil in this world." We somehow seem to continue producing Hitlers, Khomeinis, Qaddafis, Arafats, Saddams, Amins, Noriegas, and their like.

Mikhail Gorbachev indisputably deserves our support for having opened the Soviet Union's traditionally closed society and for having decreased some of the armament of the traditionally highly armed Soviet military. Surely the changes he has brought, and allowed, in Eastern Europe drastically alter the concept of what we have long considered our main line of defense. Europe's security seems much more assured now that the entire region's freedom has become a reality. We can take great delight in the fundamental, and (to our minds) irreversible, nature of change across Europe.

Within the Soviet Union, the death of communist totalitarianism is likewise irreversible. No successor to Gorbachev could restore the legitimacy of the Marxist ideology or of the basic Leninist system, now that *glasnost* has shattered respect for both.

These changes do not necessarily mean, however, that the Soviet Union itself has ceased being a threat to us or even to its own people and neighbors. This caveat to the "irreversibility argument" seems to have been forgotten in the joy of change. Prime Minister Margaret Thatcher warns, "When the ice breaks up, it can be very dangerous."

Although the flight from communism is clearly under way, other undesirable forms of government nevertheless remain a high possibility in the Soviet Union, as has already been demonstrated to some degree in China. Furthermore, the superpower climate, now peaceful, could change for any of a wide variety of reasons—Moscow's potential suppression of a Baltic republic being just one among the many. Yet further failure in the Soviet economy could afford yet another reason for repression.

Additional threats will also appear on the world scene that will be even less predictable and less rational in some ways than the old Soviet threat. Our military, like our entire foreign affairs establishment, will therefore need to develop greater flexibility and maneuverability than it has thus far possessed. That was made clear by the massive lift to the Gulf beginning in August 1990. A whole new landscape will appear with the uniting of the two Germanys and growing strains between the United States and Japan, which has quietly developed the world's seventh-largest military budget. Korea, the critical Middle East, India, Pakistan, China, and Central America—to name but a few potential trouble spots—continue to boil.

The United States remains heavily dependent upon foreign sources for half of the oil that fuels our economy (we quickly and conveniently forgot the gas lines of the mid-1970s), and nuclear proliferation is a growing concern. One can even imagine, in this topsy-turvy world, U.S. forces fighting *alongside* Soviet forces to secure nuclear storage sites in the event of a Soviet civil war or to secure the world's oil supplies. As preposterous as this may seem, we do live in a time when keeping the U.S. Army in Germany is more popular among Soviet citizens than among many American citizens; when there is a Communist party in America but not in Czechoslovakia; when Soviet politicians run for re-election unopposed and lose (as one such politician sadly reported to one of us); and when there is more turnover in membership in the Supreme Soviet than in the U.S. Congress.

Besides changes in defense—which are discussed in more detail in our memos to members of your administration, Congress, and defense contractors—changes must also occur in our intelligence community. As a former director of the Central Intelligence Agency, you may realize the needed reorientation away from weapon "bean counting" (especially of the arms of the Soviets and whatever allies they have left) and toward more global military economic and political perspectives. The intelligence community's decade-long overestimation of the Soviet economy—now confirmed by Soviet economists—and the resulting underestimation of the Soviets' relative defense effort have been rather appalling. The community needs to detect and identify threatening situations earlier and more accurately, which calls for better human means of collection and evaluation. They should not be condemned for failing to anticipate the Gulf crisis ignited by Iraq—but neither should surprise become routine for them. We are still paying the price for dismantling our own intelligence apparatus in the late 1970s.

Your responsibilities as economist in chief approach those you bear as commander in chief. The two are related. The health of our economy is of utmost importance because it helps determine not only our quality of life but also our military capabilities, which in turn help preserve that very quality of life.

The free enterprise system, along with freedom itself, is what has made America great. Free enterprise, however, is seriously endangered in America today, given both the onslaught of competitors backed by foreign governments and the Lilliputian manner in which we bind our own economy's capabilities. International marketplace boundaries no longer coincide with geopolitical boundaries. Traditional rules of competition are routinely being rewritten. Coalitions formed between substantial foreign governments and their respective industries can target and destroy virtually any single U.S. corporation or set of corporations. U.S. industry needs some help from its government, too. Until now, that help has often been passive at best, and downright harmful on other occasions.

A nationally directed industrial policy has been tried elsewhere and clearly does not work. But a strategy to draw together the nation's resources to compete in the modern global marketplace would work! Japan has demonstrated that to be the case. We need a government-business partnership that accomplishes at least the following:

- pushes the management horizon out beyond the next quarterly report

- boosts education generally, with an emphasis on technical education

- amends our traditional antitrust laws so as to recognize that the market extends beyond the United States and that it includes Japan, Western Europe, and other areas

- furnishes new and greater incentives for research and development

- stimulates high productivity

- reduces capital gains taxes to encourage investment

- discourages fast-buck seeking corporate raiders

- removes bureaucratic constraints stifling American industry

- helps hone our technology's cutting edge

In conclusion, Mr. President, your administration has come to power in a time of both great opportunity and lingering peril. Certainly we must continue to seek the lessening of international tensions and the reduction of armament spending, but we should nonetheless proceed toward these goals with circumspection and caution. George Washington, speaking to Congress exactly 200 years ago, left us some sound advice: "To be prepared for war is one of the most effectual means of preserving the peace." As we seek to preserve that peace and reap the peace dividend our strategy has so dramatically produced, we must also maintain a sense of balance that will assure our continued enjoyment of what is perhaps the greatest victory ever achieved without a shot having been fired.

MEMORANDUM (Please Forward!)
TO: Soviet President Mikhail Gorbachev

We're on your side, Mr. Gorbachev.

Or, to put it more precisely, we've *been* on your side. And there we hope to remain, as long as your policies are consistent with what you aptly call "common human values."

By your efforts to further freedom (whether intentional or not), you have surprised and impressed us—and we are not readily impressed by a Soviet leader. Your unleashing the forces of freedom—first in your country, then across Eastern Europe, now rebounding in your country—has transformed the world. Somehow the forces of freedom follow in your wake; as you visited China in May 1989, the democracy movement came alive in Tiananmen Square, even though it ended tragically on June 4 with the massacre. You visited East Germany, and shortly thereafter the democracy movement came alive there too, to culminate happily on November 9 with the shattering of the Berlin Wall.

Named by *Time* magazine in 1989 as "Man of the Decade," you strongly evoke *Time*'s 1977 "Man of the Year," Anwar Sadat. You both were surprises; having long served your governments, neither of you seemed especially remarkable. Nor had either of you done anything special before reaching the top. Once there, however, you both did something very special indeed, something of enduring international effect. Even so, you both received more raves abroad than at home because of your inability to improve materially the lives of your citizens, as they had hoped.

Great historical figures can readily be rejected by their people, if the people come to believe that these figures' historical contribution has already been made. The British swiftly cast Winston Churchill aside after he had saved the nation, and more. The Egyptians did not long mourn for Sadat. And the Soviet people are evidently losing patience with your present combination of more promises and less products.

How much time you have left to round out your mission, therefore, is not at all clear, Mr. Gorbachev. But you have already done several earth-shattering things.

Much of what you have done may have been generated by "the people," but you are the one who furnished the vital spark and created the environment for the people to be heard. Your main historic accomplishment, bar none, has been the removal of fear that permeated the onetime "Soviet bloc," including your own country. Now you must institutionalize your changes so that they outlast your presidency and improve the lives of your people for decades to come.

How? We will start with politics.

Within the Soviet Union, you have taken the bold measure of allowing other political groups to form, eventually to compete with Communist party candidates. There will of course be bumps along the road, but you may well find (as most East Europeans are finding) that democracy may just not be all *that* tough to originate or operate. Contrary to what we Americans believed—that only Western, prosperous societies raised on John Locke could become democratic—many nations have launched and are maintaining democracies, even though these nations lack any so-called democratic tradition. Among them are Argentina, Brazil, Pakistan, the Philippines, South Korea, and Taiwan. Despite the lack of any democratic tradition, your country, too, could find its way toward freedom.

Why? In part because people demand it. But primarily because there's simply no alternative today.

Governments must depend on their people for the one essential element your (and other) regimes have lacked, namely legitimacy. In the 1990s, there is no form of legitimacy aside from popular will. Small wonder, then, that nearly half the world's countries have become democratic, up steadily from a few decades back when there were a mere handful of democracies. The time is passing when tyrants, in the words of Bertolt Brecht,

> Had leaflets distributed [. . .]
> Which said that the people
> Had forfeited the Government's confidence
> And could only win it back
> By redoubled labor. Wouldn't it
> Be simpler in that case if the Government
> Dissolved the people and
> Elected another?*

Granted, your country may have a tougher time instituting a stable democracy than did Greece, Portugal, Spain, and others. For one thing, you have further to go, starting from a totalitarian system, in which nearly every aspect of life is controlled, rather than from simply an authoritarian mode, within which primarily the government itself is controlled. Also, your country lacks a functioning free-market economy, which the other states had enjoyed even under their dictators.

---

*"Die Lösung" ("The Solution").

Yet in the final analysis, the best way to reach democracy is simply to practice it. A man once asked French philosopher Blaise Pascal how to act, now that the man was beginning to lose his faith. "Act as if you're still believing," Pascal counseled, "and then you may still believe." Likewise, Soviet leaders, following your example, should begin by trying to *act* like true democrats—showing tolerance, mustering a consensus, being willing to negotiate, listening to the people—and then they will *become* true democrats. This applies both to your government's dealings in Moscow and to its dealings with sundry Soviet republics that wish to walk their own way.

Behaving like a democrat entails acknowledging responsibility to popular will and relegating authority to governments closer to the people. If the Soviet Union is to live up to its definition in your national anthem as an "unbreakable union of free republics joined together by a Great Union," then it must first move toward allowing space for those same "free republics." No longer can Russia be, in the words of Karl Marx, "the prison of nations."

Charles de Gaulle once pondered the difficulties of governing a country that had over a hundred kinds of cheese. We can only imagine the difficulties of governing one with a hundred kinds of people—to be more precise, with at least eighty-three ethnolinguistic groups.

Your only long-term remedy for your country's long-festering disintegration would seem to be to move toward a confederation. With many of the republics edging toward independence—including the keystone of the Ukraine—and with the prospect of others to follow, you in fact are almost *obliged* to concoct a confederation. Power can devolve from Moscow to the republics informally, by your just letting it happen, or formally, by your calling a national constitutional convention. Eventually, the political structure of the Soviet Union could resemble that of Switzerland, with a weak core and strong cantons, or perhaps that of Canada, a confederation thus far acceptable even to ethnically distinct Quebec. As a first step toward granting independence to the Baltic republics, Lithuania, Estonia, and Latvia—which were incorporated by what your own authorities now acknowledge to have been a sordid Hitler–Stalin Pact—you could for starters grant each its own *independent* seat in the United Nations.

Turning now to economics, it would be easy for you at this point to throw up your hands. Even you, an impressive impresario of surprises, seem to have been genuinely surprised by the true dimension of your country's economic problems. No wonder, since your economy has somehow found a way to begin with stagnation (under Brezhnev) and then grow worse. Consumers face higher inflation, longer lines, and barer shelves.

Although acknowledging this wretched state of economic affairs, you have thus far wandered from one half-formed proposal to another—one day advocating more free enterprise, another day assaulting capitalism and those who would succeed in the embryonic conclaves of a free-market economy. You have even lambasted the new cooperatives, although they were formed at your own initiative and far out-performed your state-run establishments.

Admittedly, you are bound by political constraints, but you can no longer afford to tinker thus at the margins of the problem. You must go ahead and create a real premarket price structure—without which nobody, not even you, can tell what anything costs—and begin to break up the monstrous state-owned monopolies. You must establish personal incentives, and ultimately adopt a convertible ruble.

Somehow you must reestablish a national "work ethic," something seventy years of oppression has managed to destroy (to the extent it existed before). On our recent visits to your country, we were told that "In America people try to keep up with the Joneses. In the Soviet Union, people try to keep the Joneses down with them." Or, as one of your citizens wrote about a hard-working colleague, "I don't want to live like her. I want her to live like me."

Your plight here does not resemble so much that of Dostoevski's Raskolnikov, who did not know the right thing to do, as it resembles that of Hamlet, who knew the right thing to do but was somehow unable to bring himself to do it.

Policies are indeed paramount to progress, but tangible resources matter too. They are sorely needed to build up your country's dilapidated infrastructure. The necessary expenditure cutbacks are possible in several areas.

Which brings us to matters military. The Soviet Union cannot hope to develop economically while keeping on a wartime footing, as you and your predecessors since Khrushchev have attempted. To still devote some 15 to 25 percent of your gross national product to defense (even *you* may not know the correct figure) is to be on a wartime footing. We, in America, allocated up to 14 percent at the height of the Korean War, less than 8 percent at the height of the war in Southeast Asia, and under 6 percent today.

Admittedly, you are in the process of cutting defense resources by some 14 percent—from what total remains a mystery to us all—but this cutback effort is, again, mere tinkering. For you are still spending around

20 percent *more* than was ever allocated during what you have dubbed the "stagnation years" of Leonid Brezhnev.

Why there has been such a lag in tackling this major budget item, only you and your colleagues can explain. But until it is tackled, the economic recovery you need is not likely to take place. When visiting your country, one strangely hears little mention of a "peace dividend" of funds newly available for nonmilitary use. When China embarked on its economic reforms in the late 1970s, its leaders swiftly sliced military spending in half, from around 12 percent of GNP to some 5 percent. One million soldiers were released from service, and military procurement was cut by around one-fifth. You have done nothing like this. It needs doing.

Another of your major economic commitments, aid to communist outposts beyond Eastern Europe, also continues apace. This, too, is bewildering. As an old military adage has it, "Never reinforce failure."

Why not save some $10 billion a year by ceasing the Brezhnev-begun bailouts of Afghanistan, Cuba, and Vietnam? Why spend such considerable sums, much in scarce hard currency, to keep these Marxists in power, mostly distant from Soviet territory, when you have acquiesced to the demission or outright overthrow of Marxists in several neighboring states of East Europe? Surely you don't care more about retaining Fidel Castro in office than you did about retaining Erich Honecker, especially since Castro mocks and defiles everything you personally have come to represent (and Castro may even cost more than Honecker, at $5 billion to $7 billion each year). Nothing in Russian history or the Russian psyche propels you to keep afloat these small, mostly distant despots. Massive aid to them is a relic of the "Brezhnev stagnation" period, which you criticize on every other score.

Speaking of needed cutbacks in expenditures, we return to your historic accomplishment of allowing the people to determine more of their own destiny. Your admirable reform efforts at home have really only just begun, but your reform efforts in Eastern Europe are already close to completion. To finish this chore, you need to remove *all* Soviet troops from Eastern Europe. They now serve no purpose there and are, as you know, not really welcome.

A few final items, Mr. Gorbachev, while we have you (so to speak) on the line. First, if we are to help you in your titanic struggles for Soviet reform, there can of course be no return to Third World adventurism by the Soviet Union. You would seem to have enough to do at home.

So, too, must internal repression within the Soviet Union itself be out of the question. Although the move to a confederation will surely temper some of the rising nationalistic sentiment, it will not eliminate such sentiment altogether. The last thing you or we need is large-scale internal repression in your country (against Lithuania or another republic, for instance).

Worse yet would be an outright civil war, with your twenty thousand nuclear weapons distributed throughout the faltering empire. You and we and the whole world have a huge stake in ensuring that your control over nuclear and chemical weapons stays unwaveringly tight, especially in the potentially more tumultuous times to come. We can share with you our techniques and procedures used effectively here to keep nuclear weapons firmly under presidential control. And we can also share with you our devices that physically prevent an unauthorized individual from firing a protected nuclear weapon.

We can—and, indeed hope to—work on this problem with you, Mr. Gorbachev, just as the Soviets and the United States can work together on an ever-growing number of other problems as well, based on "common human values."

One final thought: Good luck!

MEMORANDUM
TO: Members of the U.S. Congress

As members of Congress, you hold the constitutional responsibility of providing the means for America's defense. The single most important measure you can take to fulfill this responsibility, and many others you bear, is to ensure that only the very highest quality civilian and military people serve in government.

People matter. To attract and retain talent, you will need to furnish real incentives through enhanced prestige and appropriate compensation, and you will have to show a greater willingness to delegate some of your own authority so that motivated, competent individuals realize they can contribute important things to our society through government service.

As members of Congress, you also should, if we might say so, change your procedures on defense matters. Today's process for managing defense is simply unsatisfactory. You have strived to perform functions that properly should be left to the Pentagon, and have fallen short on performing functions that reside only within the constitutional purview of the Congress.

The failure to approve the defense budget each year (as opposed to a mere continuing resolution) is but one such sign of untidiness. In a word, Congress should perform its defense management duties in the style of an active and contributing board of directors of a successful corporation. This includes setting goals, establishing priorities, providing long-term budgets by major categories, and carrying out a generalized oversight function to ensure that the goals, priorities, and budgets are followed. But you must avoid the natural temptation to micromanage or conduct day-to-day operations yourself—as when you review results of helicopter dynamic tests rather than define a strategic deterrent.

Our Founding Fathers' fear that Congress might do too much has been transformed into the problem that Congress now often prevents those in the executive branch from doing much of anything, besides testifying or providing documentation. James Madison wrote in *The Federalist* of "the tendency to aggrandizement of the legislative at the expense of other departments." Madison was speaking of aggrandizement in terms of usurping power; he could never have imagined the relative aggrandizement of Congress through its absorbing so much of the executive's time and energy.

This has in fact happened. On an ordinary day with Congress in session, more than 60 hearings are held by the 250 congressional committees and subcommittees. The toll on the executive branch is crushing. One of us recently participated in a hearing involving a panel of five former senior government officials; the witnesses outnumbered the members present by more than two to one.

The toll on the Pentagon is even worse. Defense Department witnesses average some fourteen hours of testimony each congressional day, with an average appearance consuming approximately one workweek of top level personnel in preparation. Those on Capitol Hill, *each day*, send some four hundred fifty written letters and make an incredible twenty-five hundred telephone calls to the Pentagon. Moreover, they mandate an average of three reports from the Defense Department *every day*, each of which consumes a thousand hours of work and costs some $50,000 on average to prepare, including indirect costs. President Ford once said, "We cannot take the time to have 535 secretaries of state or secretaries of defense."

And the burden on yourselves created by this process is almost draconian. No elected representative can possibly absorb more than a tiny fraction of the information avalanche to which you are subjected. In fact, a recent study shows that the average member of Congress, in a typical eleven-hour workday, reads for only a total of approximately eleven minutes. This paper barrage is generated and consumed primarily by the twenty-eight thousand professional congressional staffers—well over three times the number as recently as the mid-1970s. Overall, the total congressional staff has grown six times faster than the American population since 1970, while the number of elected members has of course stayed the same.

The staff proliferation results in such incongruous situations as the holding of hearings primarily (if not entirely) for the benefit of staff. One of us testified before the Senate Intelligence Committee, a responsible committee, on the hot, volatile topic of arms control verification. During most of the hearing there were only two senators sitting at the table, while seventeen staff members lined the wall. The other of us, serving as a presidential appointee at the time, once testified before a subcommittee hearing conducted entirely by the staff counsel, with *no* members present! Although disappointing for the witness, this situation is understandable when the members' predicament is considered, since each may have three or four committee or subcommittee hearings scheduled *at precisely the same time*.

Elements of a solution are clear. First, while working cooperatively with Congress, it would seem reasonable that an executive witness should be asked to testify before a congressional body *only* as long as that committee or subcommittee maintains a quorum. If the group cannot gather and hold a majority of its members, no executive witness should be asked to testify. This modest step would inevitably reduce the number of hearings, while making each one of them more important and effective. Over time, it would clarify the lines of accountability and eliminate such incongruities as having the Defense Department (or parts thereof) obliged to report to an incredible 107 different committees or subcommittees—and would correspondingly ease the incredible burden now placed upon your institution.

Second, Congress should set an example of great sensitivity in spending taxpayer dollars. Although rightfully criticizing any defense excesses, Congress has largely been mute about its own operating costs, now more than $2 billion a year, which have grown some six times faster than the cost of living in the post–World War II era.

Third, a three- to five-year "core" defense plan should be worked out between Congress and the administration. Subsequent changes should be held to a bare minimum, barring sea changes in the security environment. The savings would be enormous.

Fourth, the age-old dichotomy between authorization and appropriation legislation should end. A great deal of the crushing time demands placed on members could be relieved in this fashion.

Fifth, the attempt by Congress to manage defense by increasing the number of auditors and inspectors should also end. Such practices merely tend to diffuse responsibility when responsibility should actually be more focused. With everyone responsible for everything, nobody is responsible for much of anything. Holding people responsible for improper actions is needed, but watching their every move is not. *Clear rules* should be promulgated as to what constitutes acceptable practice by government and industry personnel and what does not. The vagueness of many of today's rules, compounded by the large numbers of auditors and severe penalties, merely bloats the costs of conducting day-to-day affairs and fuels distrust within the defense management process.

And the spreading "criminalization" of the procurement process heavily reinforces these trends. What is deemed negotiable in normal commercial dealings has been deemed potentially criminal in dealings with the government. So far, more than three hundred thousand federal regulations have been criminalized. This too should be enough.

Sixth, funding of defense programs should be made more rational and efficient. For starters, the adoption of two-year Pentagon budgets would be helpful. Program funding should be approved at least in principle from milestone to milestone, rather than from year to year. Ideally, a defense program's entire development phase, for example, would be given funding approval at a given point; the same program's initial production phase would be given funding at another point, and full production at yet another point. Virtually all other nations utilize such an approach. It is, after all, the logical and prudent way to proceed.

You hold an enviable position from which to direct the changes your constituency seems to be demanding.

MEMORANDUM
TO: The U.S. Secretary of State

By discrediting Marxism as an ideology, Mikhail Gorbachev has simultaneously blunted America's ideological thrust abroad. Gone with messianic communism is messianic democracy. Before Gorbachev, the cosmic battle of ideas provided direction for American diplomacy: communism versus capitalism; despotism versus democracy. Now that freedom and free enterprise have won, the war of ideas is winding down in this, the post–post-war era. But the task of preserving our victory demands no less effort than what went into winning it.

The new era will place unprecedented demands on U.S. foreign policy. As a nation, we are relatively inexperienced in "traditional diplomacy," primarily because the United States has never been a major power in a nonideological world. Now that our national interests have narrowed, managing our economic, political, cultural, and military power abroad involves a more subtly conceived and crafted foreign policy. This was evident during the early days of the Gulf imbroglio, as you and the president nicely crafted a coalition against Saddam Hussein, piece by piece.

The temptation for both you and the president is, perhaps, to emphasize bipartisanship. Although it is beneficial for America to be united, since this strengthens your hand when dealing with foreign powers, it is even more beneficial for America to be right. Where everyone thinks alike, no one thinks very much. In the past the United States has followed the path of bipartisanship into some difficult entanglements. The last major bipartisan military effort was our entry into Vietnam. The uproar over that noble but painful endeavor came late, as bipartisanship was too strong and prevailed too long for our own good. In short, bipartisanship does not prevent us from making errors; it merely ensures that when we do, we make doozies.

We caution against looking for near-unanimity on major foreign policy issues. The search for consensus dampens the normal democratic process and works to quash honest debate—and often leads merely to the lowest common denominator. Those who caution us against a particular course of action, for example, are sometimes called un-American by those seeking unanimity. We need a vigorous and open debate, not one in which criticism is regarded as seditious.

The president and you should guide U.S. foreign policy with a firm hand, consulting Congress constantly yet not being overly concerned about fashioning a universally applauded approach. History will judge you primarily on the basis of results, not process.

We realize the frustration of proceeding with a chorus of different voices—many coming from Capitol Hill, but some even from your own executive branch—on foreign policy. It undoubtedly makes your arduous task even tougher. Yet democracy, particularly our free-wheeling one, is inherently untidy. As Sir John Slessor said in 1941, it is fascinating "to watch the way even the most capable Americans shy off any attempt to formalize or regularize the governmental system."

Fears of neo-isolationism are as excessive today as are searches for bipartisanship. Despite these fears, isolationism is *not* our prime problem today, since it is virtually impossible for a major power to be isolationist in the modern era. The world economy has been globalized to an extent unimaginable but a brief time ago. Economic ownership now knows no national boundaries; German defense companies own portions of British defense companies, which in turn own portions of the same German companies. What happens in the New York Stock Exchange affects the Tokyo Exchange moments later. Citizens of one country have a major and direct interest in the welfare of other nations. This in itself may do more for the stability of the world than anything that governments can contrive.

As an overall diplomatic approach, we suggest that you clearly identify a few specific goals for America to improve relations with each major country. In essence, we should learn from techniques the Chinese perfected when dealing with the Soviets over the past decade: Beijing focused on results rather than process, formulating a clear, concise, and consistent set of standards. China made it clear it would improve relations with Moscow only if the Soviets met China's conditions concerning Afghanistan, Vietnam, and Soviet forces along the Sino-Soviet border. Establishing these "three obstacles" was shrewd *private* diplomacy, since the Soviets then knew what was expected of them, and shrewd *public* diplomacy, since it provided clear performance standards.

China's approach could be adapted for *our* dealings with the Soviet Union, Japan, and other countries today. Such an approach demands clearer formulation of U.S. national interests and more persistence than has been our custom—but we need both anyway.

With the Soviets, for instance, we could request they lower their military spending to beneath a war-time level—say, to below 10 percent of their GNP—and to slow, if not stop, their massive aid to states in our neighborhood such as Cuba. For Japan, an ally of increasing importance, we can persuade Tokyo to purchase more of our agricultural and high-technology products, where we have a comparative advantage, and thereby work together to reduce the trade imbalance. Should these standards not be met, we may have to impose an across-the-board tariff on Japanese goods. We could also seek greater foreign assistance from Japan to key countries such as the Philippines, Pakistan, Turkey, Egypt, and the newly free nations of Central Europe, not to mention the Middle East, given Japan's near-total dependency on foreign oil.

On a larger scale, we should maintain close relations with traditional friends and allies, and welcome newcomers into the world of free states. Working with all these countries and increasingly with the Soviet Union, we can push harder to prevent the proliferation of nuclear and chemical weapons, and of ballistic missiles. These policies, along with more international cooperation to counter terrorism and drug traffic, will help control the looming danger of a resurgence of old rivalries with new weaponry.

We should promote the continued vitality of NATO, including a united Germany. This new NATO would have a far greater political role, but a declining military role—possibly even enticing greater French participation. The old NATO agenda embraced by some, "keep America in, Russia out, and Germany down,"is looking increasingly anachronistic

Finally, the United States has been much slower than most other industrialized democracies to realize that job creation is a major national goal requiring strong government support. American industry should not be relegated to the periphery of our foreign policy. Nor should it be viewed merely as a pawn in international politics.

With the continued strong support of the U.S. trade representative, we should seek to strengthen American industrial competitiveness wherever possible, particularly where quality jobs can result. At the same time, we should be increasingly cautious about selling miltary equipment to dubious allies. This means, at a minimum, that our embassies should be staffed with competent consular officers who push hard the sale of American products abroad, including defense products *where it serves our nation's interests*. During the Carter administration, embassy officers were actively discouraged from helping promote U.S. defense products through directives like the one that came to be known throughout the defense industry as the "leprosy letter." This particular directive proved to be a windfall to West European firms, exporting thousands of jobs from Los Angeles and Detroit to Paris and Stuttgart, just as actions in the 1980s did with regard to Saudi Arabia. It is no sin to help the American economy and worker, just as we have for decades helped build other nations' economies and benefited their workers. It is time for a Marshall Plan here at home.

MEMORANDUM
TO: The U.S. Secretary of Defense

Yours is certainly one of the two toughest jobs in America today. The challenges you face in downsizing defense in the early 1990s while holding emerging threats at bay, Mr. Secretary, are even tougher than those facing your predecessor in boosting defense in the early 1980s. And *that* was tough enough.

With congressional cooperation—itself a difficult and on-again, off-again thing—you need, ironically, to achieve even more continuity than before in U.S. defense efforts. Our national security cannot be efficiently or effectively ensured by a succession of one-year budgets, two-year people, five-year plans, eight-year development programs, and perpetual audits—especially when these programs are hampered (as they are) by an array of last-minute, budget-wrenching legislation.

For sure, the new international environment, although cause for optimism, is still laden with unpredictability. Defense needs certainly have not vanished, as we learned so jarringly in the Persian Gulf recently. No one should now embark upon a race to determine who can disarm the quickest and become weakest soonest. "The moment we knew the armistice was to have been signed, we took the harness off," President Woodrow Wilson explained in his annual message to Congress in 1918. That, we subsequently learned, was a huge mistake.

A rerun of massive defense cuts today would also be a mistake. Clearly, we should reduce defense spending gradually over the years ahead, depending primarily on how much the threats *throughout the world* decline beforehand. But the public should also appreciate how defense costs have *already* dropped substantially. Over the past five years, real U.S. defense spending has fallen by nearly 14 percent. It promises to slide even faster now—perhaps half that amount this year alone, excluding add-ons for increased operational costs.

Admittedly, European security has undergone a sea change; the forty-year threat we faced there has vanished in the form we knew it. This is a major development, which portends the dawn of a new day in European security, and beyond. World security has also changed dramatically. The Noriegas and Saddams in other regions continue to threaten our people, interests, and security. Besides, we must keep in mind that Soviet defense efforts still remain mighty. Despite Gorbachev's reforms, the USSR is still the sole power capable of inflicting irreparable damage on us. And despite Gorbachev's reforms, the

Soviets keep building forces on a wartime footing. Indeed, his defense budget is still of staggering proportions, still unprecedented, still producing an impressive modern military capability.

That having been said, worries over the ability of our economy to handle gradual but substantial military cuts are in many cases groundless. Our economy created 2 million jobs per year throughout the 1980s. After World War II, the economy handled a huge readjustment with relative ease; American defense spending plunged from nearly 40 percent of our gross national product in 1944 to less than 4 percent in 1948. Ten million people left the military, and 12.5 million left defense industries during those years, out of a population only two-thirds the size of today's. Granted, there was at that time a pent-up demand for goods and services; but the current defense restructuring has already cut 150,000 jobs in industry with relatively little impact on the overall economy.

But the impact on the defense industrial base itself—its efficiency, ability to attract quality people, and capability to be reconstituted should that one day be needed, are matters of considerable import and deserve your attention just as does the number of infantry divisions.

On the other hand, some public expectations of the economic benefits allegedly to accrue from a "peace dividend" also are inflated. Many supposed "cuts" are actually cuts in previous projections of future spending, not in actual current outlays. Moreover, as we stress technology or capability more and weapons arsenals or quantity less, we invariably move to higher unit costs. There will be a peace dividend for sure—but it will be lost in the scale of today's overall governmental spending.

Your guidelines for downsizing defense, Mr. Secretary, should start from a strategic perspective that encompasses the objectives and commitments we retain, the threats we face, and the forces we need to do the job. A five-year defense program should *implement* your strategy, but the five-year defense plan cannot in itself *constitute* a strategy, even though that presumption has usually been taken as the centerpiece of national security discussions.

Today's debate over a 3 percent real reduction in defense spending versus a 10 percent real reduction does not a strategy make. As you yourself have made clear, this debate should be the *result* of a strategy, not the essence of one.

We must avoid the mistakes of the late 1970s, when defense cuts led into the hollowing out of American forces. We then had a large number of troops, units, and bases, too often deprived of essential training, sophisticated equipment, and adequate maintenance. This was particularly true of the reserve and National Guard forces—an error we cannot afford to repeat today.

The president and you could choose to take the politically easy way out, thereby minimizing opposition. This route would involve retaining all our foreign commitments as they are, maintaining all domestic bases and high manpower levels as they are, skimping on training and operating and maintenance expenses, downplaying reserves and curtailing modernization. This approach, however, would not serve our long-term interests.

You should instead take near-term political flack and adopt a long-term perspective. This route entails planning for a vanishing threat from the Warsaw Pact per se (though still not necessarily discounting a threat from the Soviet Union itself, at least for a time) and for rising threats elsewhere in the world. This approach means realizing that there are fundamentally new strategic situations, notably in Europe, that allow for decreased deployment of U.S. defense forces there. Hence the big message: U.S. armed forces, though still needed, will be different. They must be more mobile, better equipped, more dependent upon reserves, more flexible—and smaller.

The future may actually hold less low-intensity than medium-intensity conflict by the traditional definition of the terms, since most countries' militaries are becoming quite sophisticated and increasingly powerful. The number of armored vehicles within third world nations has already grown fourfold over the past two decades. Iraq by itself has more tanks than Rommel had in his Afrika Korps; more, in fact, than Rommel, Montgomery, and Eisenhower combined in the North Africa campaigns; more than Hitler had when he invaded Poland. Today more than a dozen countries have over a thousand main battle tanks each. Another dozen to fifteen of them may now have or will soon acquire ballistic missiles. Today Iraq has ballistic missiles with a range of nearly one thousand kilometers, and more than a dozen nations hold *both* chemical warfare and ballistic missile capabilities. In addition, many of these countries now have first-line fighter aircraft as well. This poses the challenge to U.S. force designers to build highly deployable, mobile forces that can stand up to well-equipped, heavily armored opponents.

Overall, more or less in order of priority, we would advise the adoption of the following measures:

- Maintain a survivable strategic deterrent capability based on our offensive forces, but reduced in size in keeping with verified Soviet reductions.

- Continue to explore a defense-based strategic umbrella to protect against those who might not be otherwise deterred.

- Increase funding for research aimed at technological break-throughs.

- Retain a well-trained, highly competent officer and senior enlisted corps.

- Support constant readiness through training and maintenance.

- Modernize forces primarily through product improvement, introducing new systems only when significant technological breakthroughs warrant.

- Increase force mobility and deployability—but maintain some heavy-force capability.

- Emphasize force multipliers, such as surveillance, command and control, countermeasures, and precision-guided ordnance.

- Strengthen reserve and National Guard units in size and in capability, through equipment modernization and especially through better training, including the expanded use of simulation.

- Provide the basis in industry for reconstituting larger forces over a period of a few years, should the need arise.

- Reduce the overall size of the force to a level consistent with affordable national objectives and acceptable levels of risk when viewing the world as a whole.

With regard to manpower, the transfer of active forces to reserve status should proceed selectively; active forces specializing in rapid intervention should be augmented, and certain of those staffing our strategic forces must be maintained. Other active duty units can be cut, but in a balanced fashion—including the people, units, bases, equipment support, and overhead that accompany the resulting structure—especially the latter.

Whatever level of force is retained should be superbly equipped, mobile, highly motivated, and well trained. British recruits now train for thirty weeks or more, and Israelis for twenty-two weeks; U.S. Army and Marine troops, in contrast, train for ten weeks or fewer. With less, we need a more dynamic force. A greater part of the U.S. Army should be modeled after an augmented rapid deployment force, and the expanded reserve forces should be better trained and far better equipped than ever.

Regarding equipment, we should improve airlift and sealift capabilities for our lighter, more modern forces. During the 1989 Panamanian operation, for instance, 16-ton Sheridan tanks were used because the nearly 60-ton Abrams tanks were too heavy to be transported quickly—and, importantly, the threat did not demand the better armor of the heavier tanks. This will not always be the case; we need to maintain a strong anti-tank capability in our rapidly, deployable forces—a difficult challenge indeed.

Planning for newer equipment must be done expeditiously, as it takes many years to bring new weapons into the arsenal. Highest priority should go to conducting research on promising new technologies and to developing *totally new* system concepts, as opposed to introducing new systems merely to enhance traditional capabilities in the inventory. At the same time, scarce defense dollars can go farther by infusing new technology into existing equipment to extend its life and by using more commercial off-the-shelf provisions, whenever feasible. Brand new systems most certainly should be implemented *only* when they offer quantum leaps in capability.

In contrast to recommendations from the defense reform movement some years back, which stressed employing greater numbers of relatively lower-technology equipment, the future probably holds an expanded role for high-technology arms. This type of weaponry is needed not only to compensate for reduced force size but also because one of the objectives of future combat will be to limit the number of casualties rather than to inflict massive destruction.

Given the coming shrinkage in our overseas base structure, we will need more "go it alone" weapons. The B-2 Stealth bomber is one such example, if we can afford to acquire these bombers in large enough quantities to make the unit price acceptable. The 1986 U.S. raid on Libya used some twenty ships in two carrier battle groups, along with thirty-five support aircraft and eighty-four combat aircraft operating from eight foreign bases. Mounting that mission took nearly five days; performing it put nearly one hundred fifty crewmen at risk. The same raid could have been performed by two B-2 Stealth bombers with conventional weapons and by two tankers, all taking off with little warning time from U.S. territory. Indeed, B-2 Stealth bombers operating from a network of only four bases, two here and two abroad, could deliver a full conventional payload to any spot on earth with a single midair refueling. But this will demand far more attention to what that payload of conventional ordnance should be than has been given in the past. Nonnuclear, sea-launched cruise missiles can perform similar surgical strikes, and with great accuracy as can carrier task forces. But to be affordable, many high-technology systems such as the B-2 must be procured in reasonably large quantities. Therein lies the crunch.

Highly sophisticated systems—especially the three *S*'s of stealth, SDI, and space systems, all of which rest to one degree or another on the fourth *S*, semiconductors—play into our relative strength of overall technological superiority, not into the Soviets' comparative advantage of brute power. Moreover, such advanced systems help negate the effectiveness of Soviet military spending priorities such as air defense, which has cost them a whopping $350 billion over the past two decades, and a succession of Soviet land-based missiles, such as their SS-18, SS-19, SS-24, and SS-25.

With respect to administration, as you have recognized, Mr. Secretary, the current approach to managing the defense establishment needs vast improvement. This improvement will involve cuts in civilian personnel, in some muscle-bound layers of management, and in "overhead" organizational entities. We've learned over the years that if enough layers of management are superimposed one on top of the other, disaster will no longer be left to chance.

Additional authority should be given the chairman of the Joint Chiefs of Staff to ensure that our military forces are an integrated operating entity, not merely a collection of individual service contributions. This process was helped along by the Goldwater-Nichols Act. It should be advanced still further, even though the 1989 Panamanian operation and 1990 Saudi Arabian deployment showed the considerable progress that has been made since the 1983 Grenada operation.

Although maintenance of our strategic nuclear deterrent remains vital, you should place more emphasis on coping with conventional warfare at the lower levels, down to and even emphasizing counterterrorism, through the increased use of special forces and far better intelligence.

Finally, and most regrettably, it has become evident that our present defense acquisition system is broken. The fact that America has been able to produce the quality of hardware that it has, despite the nature of the acquisition process now in place, is to a large extent a tribute to the military and civilian personnel serving in that system. Repairing the acquisition process—so essential if we are to furnish our forces with the best tools available—demands basic structural changes. More patchwork, piling one expedient measure on another, no longer suffices. How to repair this acquisition system is outlined in the memo to your under secretary for acquisition, but the real difficulty lies in the doing.

MEMOS TO POLICY MAKERS

Yet another big assignment shoved your way! But we know you can handle it.

MEMORANDUM
TO: The U.S. Under Secretary of Defense
for Acquisition

Welcome to another of the tougher jobs in Washington! The performance of your responsibilities—that is, the equipping of America's military in the way our troops deserve—demands radical reform. Because defense acquisition today operates only haltingly, wholesale *perestroika* is urgently needed.

The system's ills are evident to you by now. Equipment almost always takes too long to acquire, often costs too much, and sometimes is unreliable. It is ironic that when a truly important new system comes along, it is invariably pulled from the clutches of the acquisition process and afforded special treatment. Examples range from Vietnam-era gunships to the Trident submarine, from the military space program to SDI and Stealth.

The existing system also places undue human burdens on those who must cope with a process beset by administrative and financial turbulence and stifling micromanagement. And the relationship between the government and the arsenal of democracy—America's defense industry—ranges from deep suspicion to outright hostility. Other than that, the domain you have inherited is in pretty good shape.

With the downsizing of defense must come more, not less, risk taking on revolutionary new weapon concepts. The current defense supply environment, burdened with audit mania and subject to public snickering at any hint of failure, discourages those who might in a less risk-averse climate be willing to take a chance on developing a more promising defense concept. All the incentives now favor covering one's flanks rather than coveting one's creativity.

To make the acquisition process operate optimally will require an increase in the stability of funding and in the length of time that experienced people are assigned to work in the acquisition process. A cadre of career professional acquisition managers, preferably with military operational experience, must be developed. Budget reserves should be established to provide in advance for uncertainty, that is, to overcome the unexpected problems that invariably occur even in the best-managed programs.

You should devote special attention, Mr. Secretary, to the preservation, if not outright enhancement, of our technology base. Much of our military's comparative advantage comes from technology. Qualitative advantage grows more important as quantity shrinks and more difficult as technology becomes more diffused throughout the world. It also becomes more important as light, mobile units may be called on to counter heavy, established forces.

The Defense Department, and your office in particular, should ensure the maintenance of a robust, if smaller, industrial base for defense needs. Such an industrial base once was taken for granted; now it must be actively cultivated.

Diversified companies are today seeking to leave the defense business in droves, and many companies wholly within the defense industry are contracting and weakening. The all-important second and third tier of suppliers is vanishing. By encouraging the designing of military equipment to make greater use of commercially available components and systems, you can greatly reduce dependence on the unique defense industry. In short, the Department of Defense must learn to live off the land.

To enhance our industrial base and produce the weapons we need, risks and rewards must be equitably allocated between buyer and seller. This takes, among other things, the right kind of contracts. Fixed-price contracts are most appropriate when the risks are well understood and clearly bounded, such as continued production of a manufactured item. This type of contract is, however, altogether inappropriate for research and development efforts, which are by nature chancy—a lesson we have learned twice in the last twenty-five years, at a cost of some $10 billion, mostly, but not entirely, borne by the defense industry.

Finally, although this view may not serve bureaucratic interests, it needs to be expressed anyway: the acquisition process is too large to be managed on a daily basis from the office of the secretary of defense. Your own office should set goals, establish policies and priorities, allocate funds, monitor performance, and, when necessary, take corrective actions. But the principal responsibility for the day-to-day acquisition of equipment should be lodged in the military services and, through them, in America's industry.

In short, as under secretary, you should set goals, delegate clearly defined responsibilities, keep people in place longer, and hold them strictly accountable. That formula may not sound startling to you as the experienced manager you are, but it would be startling to see it applied in the organization you now head.

You also face the difficult but all-important challenge of establishing a defense research and development strategy. The problem, of course, is that to develop new systems and then simply put the drawings "on the shelf" is expensive, does not improve our present forces, and still leaves us three to five years from any significant new deployed military capability, even in times of urgency. To build a factory and then put it in "moth balls" is very expensive and still leaves us at least two years from significant inventory increases. The plant mostly just gathers moths.

On the other hand, to put an item in production but only in very low quantities results in high unit costs—*à la* the B-2. And once in production, the effort to keep a line open ("hot" in the vernacular) by stretching output over a prolonged period of time, *à la* the M-1 tank, can also result in increased costs due to volume ("critical mass") inefficiency. But the alternative of stopping all new technology after the prototyping phase leaves the nation five or so years from any significant new operational capability based on that design, even under surge conditions, and a dozen years under what have come to be "normal" conditions.

So, what to do?

Unfortunately, there *is* no truly satisfactory answer—as you undoubtedly have already discovered. On the other hand, our warning time is increasing—if we will be smart enough to heed any disquieting signals. We nonetheless respectfully offer the following policy as a starting point:

- Assign first priority to research and early exploratory development that promise major breakthroughs in capability or lead to entirely new conceptual approaches for performing important missions.

- Place greater emphasis on university and industrial basic research, reducing the government's in-house overhead structure that has grown over the years.

- Draw as heavily as possible on the country's commercial (non-defense) production base by standardizing commercial components wherever practicable and designing to use our commercial manufacturing base, especially in time of emergency.

- Make it extremely demanding to initiate new full-scale development programs, insisting on truly significant potential military benefit from all programs that are approved.

- Increase substantially the effort to build R&D prototypes of new systems and components (as opposed to production prototypes). R&D prototypes cost much less and have greater flexibility, all while preserving critically important design teams.

- Carry no system beyond R&D prototyping (that is, into engineering development) unless there is a firm intent to manufacture and deploy it.

- Pursue "breakthrough systems" based on new concepts and on new technology into engineering development and production —but insist on fly-before-buy demonstrations.

- Produce those systems that do in fact receive production go-ahead at the most efficient rate and then shut down the lines, preserving tooling, and in selected critical cases stockpiling limited numbers of components that have particularly long lead times.

- Prolong the life of "platforms" (aircraft, ships, tanks) as long as possible by introducing new technology from time to time as subsystem upgrades. This appears to be the only way to keep platforms that must last forty or more years moderately current with technology that has a half life of ten or fewer years.

- Seek cooperative programs to buy and sell hardware from and to allied nations to stretch defense dollars and help keep production lines warm where practicable. Be prepared to add our own countermeasure provisioning to some of these systems. On the other hand, avoid joint research and development projects— such programs are hard enough with a *single* customer.

- Seek to apply new technology not only in the traditional manner—to increase operational capability—but also to reduce cost.

- Employ only the amount of concurrency (overlap between consecutive phases of a program) that is needed to maintain an efficient program plan, since time is less critical in the new geo-strategic environment.

- Insist on joint programs among the services to a much greater degree than in the past in order to stretch available procurement dollars as far as possible—even if compromises are required.

- Establish an office to address and eliminate impediments to potential wartime reconstitution of a large-scale defense industrial base, should that again be required.

- Avoid the temptation to take over from the military departments all research, development, and production activities and absorb them into your own organization.

- Once programs have passed the new, exceedingly stringent go-ahead gate, fire the first person or organization that begins to meddle with the funding, schedule, or requirement. Tough out the problems and finish things once started.

- And above all else you must guard against procurement's four horsemen of the apocalypse: turbulence, adversarialism, inadequate personnel, and insufficient margins (overpromising).

Many of these recommended policies will not be particularly popular with the defense industry, the services, or both. The proof of the pudding is in the execution. As Shakespeare's Hotspur told Glendower when the latter had bragged "I can call spirits from the vasty deep"— "Why, so can I, or so can any man; but will they *come* when you do call for them?"

Your job is to make it happen. Soon.

MEMORANDUM
TO: The U.S. Defense Industry

You, the U.S. defense industry, have the misfortune, deserved or otherwise, of having one of the worst public reputations in American enterprise—which makes you a standout among nonstandouts.

It is important to our national security—to say nothing of your self-esteem—that this loss of confidence be reversed and that you, once again, become deservedly known as the arsenal of American democracy.

Such a turnabout is long overdue but can come only from solid performance and impeccable ethical standards—not from massive public relations campaigns, better lobbying, or mere promises to improve. The race to provide America's security is not a sprint but rather a marathon.

Bracing for the long haul and lifting your industry's current image will require, first off, more self-policing. You should spot and make known any violations of rules and regulations within your dominion even *before* those violations are uncovered by outside inspectors or auditors. Granted, this advice probably runs counter to that of your legal counsel, which stems from concern over possible self-incrimination of your firm or employees. Nonetheless, self-policing and disclosure is the *right* thing to do.

Second, you must strive for greater efficiency, which will inevitably involve the outright elimination of unneeded layers of management. Lopping off these layers will both improve efficiency and significantly reduce costs. (Perhaps the most imaginative example of this to date is to be found in a *USA Today* news article on Northrop's strategy for dealing with defense cuts. The article reported that Northrop's CEO "also said Northrop would continue to sell nonproductive assets. Last year it sold its headquarters." Now *that* is provocative!)

Third, you must establish the manufacturing of top-quality products as your top priority. Striving for excellence does not clash with the desire to make profits. If you routinely produce only top-quality products, the system, despite its myriad problems, still remains fair enough in most cases to assure that your corporate profitability will take care of itself.

Fourth, you must recognize your *special* responsibility as a key creator and curator of American technology. Nearly everyone understands the vital role of technology in assuring our national defense and a healthy American economy. Less widely recognized, however, is the need for defense companies to continue both investing substantial sums of money and using their most talented people in the creation of advanced defense-related technology, especially now that defense funds are shrinking. To meet this special responsibility, your industry needs to resist the fierce pressures currently pervading America's economic system to adopt a short-term strategy and, simply stated, cut and run from defense research and development. The short-term approach may boost the coming quarter's profits, but only at the expense of our nation's long-term health.

Shifting from a sprint to a marathon perspective entails continuing patiently to stress investments both in research and development and in productivity-enhancing factories. Applying this long-term perspective also means avoiding the chase after "get rich quick" hostile takeovers. Such *hostile* attempts to make fast returns by bottom fishing for crippled defense contractors can place these companies heavily in debt, forcing them to reduce their research and development budgets still further, decrease their productivity, risk their people's pension security, and jeopardize other future-oriented investments. The short-term approach clearly runs counter to the defense industry's and the nation's best interests—not to mention the well-being of its employees. In short, we need fewer business leaders chasing fast deals and more running fast factories.

Many of your sector's great companies, both those widely commercialized as well as those narrowly centered on furnishing defense equipment, now face a critical decision: whether or not to remain defense suppliers. Many have already made that decision—and left.

Certainly, the restructuring of your industry is appropriate and necessary, but supplying the country's defense needs is also necessary and is too important to entrust to any but America's finest firms. During prosperous times you were quite content, even eager, to serve the cause of national defense. You should be willing to serve the nation's defense in tough times as well, for yours is an industry with responsibilities that include but also transcend the financial goals of less critical firms. In short, and perhaps going against the grain, with regard to defense you should make every effort to stay the course as long as a need and market remain. Your contributions to the nation's defense and to its technological development in the past have been substantial.

You will undoubtedly be called upon in the future. It is important that you be ready. Plato's words, sadly, seem altogether likely to remain true: "Only the dead have seen the end of war."

What we have written to Presidents Bush and Gorbachev, to the secretaries of state and defense, and to all the others is far more easily said than done. Despite the frightful difficulties of moving from here to there, it's essential to know where "there" is beforehand. We tried our best to act as interpreters in the body of this book, and then as guides in the memos at the end.

That much of what we have written has gone from improbable to familiar in the time we took to write this book merely reinforces our confidence in the overall views we have espoused. While some dangers posed to American life, values, and interests have fundamentally changed, others have not. Saddam Hussein, for all his sins, retaught Americans that lesson during the summer and fall of 1990. He furnished a needed "wake-up call": we have yet to arrive in the Promised Land, no matter how many people claim they've seen it.

While acknowledging the awesome problems of moving into a new international environment, we remain confident. America's bipartisan path has proved stunningly successful over the past forty years. We've gained so much for so many people—for Americans, Europeans, friends and allies everywhere—that we have a right to be proud. But we also have an obligation to beware, for the truth of history is that no author, president, Congress, or any other being can precisely predict the future. Who among us in, say, 1988 foresaw a NATO nation with large numbers of Soviet troops on its soil, or that this could happen without a shot being fired, or that this would be viewed as a great victory for the West, or that the NATO nations would voluntarily agree to pay some $8 billion in part to help with the maintenance of those Soviet troops?

By exercising prudent caution in projecting and preparing for the future, Americans can ensure that we will furnish material for future authors to write books describing how we managed the problems we face now, and in the years immediately ahead, with the same wisdom and determination our leaders managed in the post–World War II world. Nothing could be finer.

INDEX